FAMILY MEALS FOR A FIVER!

Good Housekeeping

FAMILY MEALS FOR A FIVER!

Over 250 tried and tested recipes
and ideas for budget meals and
cooking with leftovers

COLLINS & BROWN

First published in Great Britain in 2009
by Collins & Brown
10 Southcombe Street
London W14 0RA

An imprint of Anova Books Company Ltd

The Good Housekeeping website is
www.allaboutyou.com/goodhousekeeping

Reasonable care has been taken to ensure the accuracy of
the information contained in this book however prices of
ingredients will vary from store to store. The Publishers
make no representations or warranties as to the costs of
meals and any liability for inaccuracies or errors relating to
the material contained in the book is expressly excluded to
the fullest extent of the law.

10 9 8 7 6 5 4 3 2

ISBN 978-1-84340-537-5

A catalogue record for this book is available from the British
Library.

Repro by Dot Gradations UK, Ltd
Printed by Times Offset, Malaysia

This book can be ordered direct from the publisher at
www.anovabooks.com.

NOTES

- Both metric and imperial measures are given for the recipes. Follow either set of measures, not a mixture of both, as they are not interchangeable.
- All spoon measures are level.
  1 tsp = 5ml spoon; 1 tbsp = 15ml spoon.
- Ovens and grills must be preheated to the specified temperature.
- Use sea salt and freshly ground black pepper unless otherwise suggested.
- Fresh herbs should be used unless dried herbs are specified in a recipe.
- Medium eggs should be used except where otherwise specified. Free-range eggs are recommended.
- Note that certain recipes, including mayonnaise, lemon curd and some cold desserts, contain raw or lightly cooked eggs. The young, elderly, pregnant women and anyone with an immune-deficiency disease should avoid these, because of the slight risk of salmonella.
- Calorie, fat and carbohydrate counts per serving are provided for the recipes.
- If you are following a gluten- or dairy-free diet, check the labels on all pre-packaged food goods.
- Recipe serving suggestions do not take gluten- or dairy-free diets into account.

GF = Gluten Free | DF = Dairy Free | V = Vegetarian

Picture credits

Nicki Dowey (pages 48, 51, 54, 55, 56, 57, 58, 63, 64, 65, 66, 67, 68, 70, 71, 72, 73, 74, 75, 76, 77, 80, 81, 90, 94, 98, 99, 100, 101, 109, 111, 115, 120, 128. 130, 133, 140, 144, 145, 146, 147, 150, 151, 152, 155, 156, 158, 159, 160, 164, 165, 166, 169, 171, 181, 184, 185, 186, 189, 194, 197, 200, 203, 204, 206, 207, 208, 210, 211, 212, 213, 217, 222, 226, 228 [bottom], 229, 231, 232, 233, 235, 240, 241, 242, 246, 249, 250, 251); Craig Robertson (pages 29, 31, 32, 33, 34, 35, 36, 37, 38, 39, 40, 41, 43, 45, 50, 59, 61, 62, 69, 83, 84, 85, 87, 88, 92, 96, 107, 106, 110, 118, 122, 124, 131, 142, 168, 174, 180, 182, 192, 193, 196, 201, 205, 209, 216, 218, 219, 221, 223, 225, 234, 237); Lucinda Symons (pages 19, 52, 60, 82, 89, 113, 114, 116, 135, 139, 161, 187, 227, 236, 243, 244); Neil Barclay (pages 91, 93, 102, 112, 138, 147, 162, 177, 198, 220, 228 [top], 247); Martin Brigdale (pages 95, 103, 175. 176, 224, 230, 245, 248); Will Heap (pages 86, 134, 136, 143, 167, 172, 173, 190)

CONTENTS

Foreword

Here at Good Housekeeping, we always say the test of a good cookbook is how often you turn to it for inspiration – and how messy the pages are. We know this book, packed with information for the busy woman, will be used many times and, of course, is timely. Thrift is the order of the day now and *Family Meals for a Fiver!* is packed with clever ways to save you time and money, and help you budget for family meals.

From the hundreds of reader letters and queries we receive every month, it's clear that cooking supper from scratch every night can be a challenge. To help you, we've come up with the ultimate store cupboard stocked with basic ingredients so you'll always have the makings of a meal. We've also highlighted some extra items that are really good to keep in. These products might cost slightly more – extra virgin olive oil, for instance, or a small tub of dried porcini mushrooms – but the returns in flavour will be worth it. Plus there are handy habits to adopt while shopping and key notes on avoiding waste – something we should all take note of.

Flick to the recipe collection and you'll see we've gathered together a handful of classics and thrown in some new favourites too. All of the recipes have been triple-tested in the Good Housekeeping Institute cookery kitchens to make sure they're foolproof and work every time for you. Enjoy,

Emma

Emma Marsden
Cookery Editor
Good Housekeeping

THE BASICS

Get thrifty

Old-fashioned thrift is back on the menu and we see it as a great reason to go back to home cooking. *Family Meals for a Fiver* shows you how to eat well and healthily on a budget. There are lots of ways to save money on your weekly food bill without compromising on quality or making your family go without. Not every meal has to be a complicated recipe. Some of the tastiest, most popular family suppers are the most simple and straightforward – and the cheapest. That's why Cottage Pie and Bread and Butter Pudding are still culinary classics. Planning ahead, clever shopping, managing your store cupboard and knowing how to take advantage of a bargain, combined with the great recipes in this book, are all simple steps that will transform mealtimes and make cooking from scratch a pleasure.

Five ways to get thrifty

1. GET ORGANISED Check what's in your store cupboard and make a list of what you need – once you've got the basics, you'll cut down on cost each time you go shopping. Check out what's in the fridge and freezer. Rotate foods regularly to avoid waste. See pages 12–15.

2. PLAN AHEAD Decide on your menus for the week and make shopping lists. Don't waste fuel – if you're cooking a meal, it sometimes make sense to double the quantity and freeze half, especially when it's a time-consuming recipe, such as lasagne or beef casserole. Use the oven's capacity to cook a meal for today and a casserole for tomorrow. Sauces are also particularly useful as you can make a big batch and create speedy midweek meals that are all different. A simple tomato or Bolognese sauce tossed with pasta is always a great stand-by for a quick supper. See page 27.

3. SHOP SENSIBLY Plan your shopping carefully – make a shopping list and stick to it – and keep it seasonal. See page 16.

4. STRETCH YOUR MEALS Cook now, eat later. Make the oven and the freezer work for you. See page 28.

5. USE UP YOUR LEFTOVERS Whether they're planned or you've got food to use up before its 'use-by' date, you'll find lots of ideas on pages 24–25.

Eating a balanced diet

Eating thriftily doesn't mean eating unhealthily – in fact, far from it! Cooking from scratch is not only cheaper and creates less waste and packaging, it also means you can control exactly what you put in your family's food – and that can only be a good thing. Processed food is more expensive to buy than fresh ingredients and often includes more salt, sugar and fat than the homemade version, which isn't good for our health.

When you're planning your weekly menus, try to keep in mind the Food Standards Agency's Eatwell Plate (www.eatwell.gov.uk). It shows how much you should eat from each food group every day, including snacks. Also look at the portion sizes on page 17. Remember, variety is also the key to good health so don't be tempted to stick to the same meals each week.

- Fill the plate with plenty of vegetables and fruit – choose the cheaper, filling varieties, such as carrots, dark leafy cabbage or parsnips. Save the more expensive varieties for their proper seasons when they will be cheaper and tastier (see pages 20–21).
- Accompany each meal with filling bread, rice, potatoes, pasta or other starchy foods – choose wholegrain varieties whenever you can.
- Include some milk and dairy foods, as they are an important source of calcium for healthy bones. This could be milk in a cheese sauce or yogurt in a curry.
- Always include a small amount of meat, fish, eggs, beans and other non-dairy sources of protein.
- Allow just a small amount of foods and drinks high in fat and/or sugar – and if they're homemade you'll be sure of the amounts.

Make your own...

Whether it's a packed lunch for work or school, a Friday night takeaway or sweet treats for the family, it's cheaper and better to make your own. It's also a great way of using up the leftovers in the fridge.

Packed lunches

Yes, there's lots of choice for lunch on the high street but you don't get much change from a fiver nowadays. Add that up day by day and there's a substantial saving to be made if you make your own. If you have access to a microwave at work, make an extra portion of your supper the night before and take in the rest for tomorrow's lunch. Otherwise, use up leftovers, like Sunday's roast chicken, in salads and sandwiches. Here are a few recipe ideas:
- Cheese Coleslaw with Roast Chicken (page 61)
- Smoked Mackerel Salad (page 62)
- Chicken Falafels (page 93)
- Mushroom and Bean Hotpot (page 212)

Soup

Soups are so cheap to make and perfect for using up leftover vegetables. Freeze them in one-portion batches and pull them out for packed lunches (if you don't have access to a microwave during the day, heat and pour into a vacuum flask) or a filling Saturday lunch with crusty bread. They can even be turned into first courses for special family dinners. Try these recipes:
- Leek and Potato Soup (page 50)
- Carrot and Coriander Soup (page 55)
- Quick Winter Minestrone (page 56)
- Easy Pea Soup (page 59)

Bread

There's nothing quite like the smell of homemade bread, is there? It doesn't take long to make and the rising times can be fitted around your daily routine. Even better, it costs pennies and can contain less salt than some processed versions. A homemade loaf won't last as long as a shop-bought version because it doesn't contain artificial additives, but any leftovers can be turned into breadcrumbs or a scrumptious Bread and Butter Pudding (page 221). Try these recipes:
- White Farmhouse Loaf (page 43)
- Brown Loaf (page 43)
- Soda Bread (page 44)

Pizza

Pizza is a favourite takeaway but it's cheaper to make your own. It's a great way of using up leftovers. Have a rummage in the fridge and scatter the pizza base with scraps of ham or salami, slices of mushroom, the odd cherry tomato or two, a few frozen peas... the choice is endless and so adaptable. Get the kids involved too. They'll love kneading the dough (see page 45) and choosing their own toppings. Why not have a go at these recipes to get you started?
- Napolitana Pizza (page 137)
- Fresh Tomato Sauce (page 27)
- Asparagus, Mushroom and Tomato Pizza (page 202)
- Garlic Cheese Pizza (page 203)

Biscuits and cakes

We all love a sweet treat and eaten in moderation they are one of life's pleasures that are even more enjoyable when homemade. Fill up the cake tin with some of these indulgent recipes:
- Blueberry Muffins (page 243)
- Chocolate Victoria Sandwich (page 245)
- Peanut and Raisin Cookies (page 250)

Friday night takeaway

Takeaways are a welcome treat if you're tired after a long week, but they are expensive and often contain lots of unnecessary fat, salt or sugar. Make your own takeaway alternative and it will not only save you money, but also taste fantastic and won't take long to cook either. By the time you've ordered a meal from the local shop and picked it up or had it delivered, you could have whipped up one of these recipes yourself and saved money:
- Chicken Stir-fry with Noodles (page 92)
- Spiced Tikka Kebabs (page 94)
- Chicken Tarragon Burgers (page 99)
- Prawn and Vegetable Stir-fry (page 132)
- Quick Fish and Chips (page 144)

Get organised

A well-stocked store cupboard, fridge and freezer will help you prepare nutritious, budget-friendly meals for the family and avoid expensive waste too. Don't be put off by the size of the charts below. For a relatively small initial cost you'll have a core set of ingredients that will help you cook cheap and nourishing meals for the family. But resist the urge to stock up on interesting ingredients that you 'might use one day'.

YOUR STORE CUPBOARD

Baking powder
Cans of tomatoes, tuna, salmon, anchovies, coconut milk
Chutneys and pickles
Cocoa powder
Curry paste
Dried fruit (apricots, sultanas, raisins)
Dried herbs (oregano, rosemary, thyme, sage, bay leaves)
Dried yeast
Flour (self-raising, plain, strong white and wholemeal, cornflour)
Jam, marmalade and honey
Mayonnaise
Mustard (Dijon, English, wholegrain)
Oils (olive, sunflower)
Pasta and noodles
Pulses (canned or dried)
Rice (long-grain, basmati, pudding)
Sauces (Worcestershire, soy, chilli)
Spices (cayenne, cinnamon, coriander, cumin, curry powder, ginger, paprika, nutmeg, turmeric)
Stock cubes (chicken, beef, vegetable bouillon)
Sugar (granulated, caster, icing)
Tomato ketchup and purée
Vinegar (white and red wine, balsamic)

Stocking your cupboard

Once you've got a well-stocked cupboard, you can avoid the frustration of not having the right basic ingredients when you want to rustle up a meal. First, make a list of what you already have – you might be surprised at what's lurking at the back of the shelves.

The chart (left) lists the basic ingredients that you will need for most recipes.

Worth buying

Some ingredients seem expensive but only need to be used sparingly to get the full impact of their flavour, which makes them a good investment to have in stock.

EXTRA VIRGIN OLIVE OIL An expensive oil that shouldn't be used for cooking; use standard olive oil instead. Use for salad dressings, to sprinkle over pasta or antipasti or as a dipping oil with balsamic vinegar with good bread.

BALSAMIC VINEGAR Buy this expensive rich, sweet vinegar (from Modena in Italy) in small bottles and use a few drops at a time. Add to salad dressings and extra virgin olive oil for dipping or drizzle over pasta, fish and even strawberries.

DRIED PORCINI MUSHROOMS Also known as ceps, fresh porcini mushrooms are only available for a short time so the dried version is usually used. Only a small amount (about 15–25g/½–1oz) is needed for each recipe and they have an intense flavour that adds depth to risottos, stews and pasta dishes. To avoid deterioration, store in an airtight container or jar out of the light.

CHOCOLATE For cooking, check out the baking ingredients aisle in the supermarket for 'chocolate for baking' brands. If your chocolate has developed a white 'bloom' – it won't impair the flavour and can be used in recipes where appearance isn't a factor.

PINE NUTS Not an essential ingredient but worth having if you like to make fresh pesto. Also good toasted and scattered over salads or pasta dishes.

A few rules on storage

- Keep food cupboards cool and dry.
- Line shelves for easy cleaning and clean regularly.
- Organise shelves – put new goods to the back and use up those in front.
- Canned food, once opened, should be transferred to a bowl and kept covered in the fridge.
- Store dried pulses, herbs, beans and spices in sealed containers.
- Check use-by dates regularly.
- Avoid overcrowding storage areas – it'll be easier to do a weekly stock take and quickly find what you need when you're cooking.
- Make ingredients work harder: for example, porridge oats can be used in breads and biscuits as well as for a nutritious breakfast; stir mustard into sauces for extra flavour; use honey in marinades.
- Buy herbs and spices in small amounts – they lose their flavour and aroma within a couple of months.
- Avoid expensive ingredients, such as speciality oils and vinegars, flavoured salts or unusual pasta or rice.
- Nuts can quickly go rancid – buy small packets as and when you need them.

Thrifty Tip

It's cheaper to grow herbs on your windowsill or pots in the garden – some, like rosemary, bay, thyme and sage, are hardy and can be snipped during the winter. Tender herbs, such as parsley, coriander, basil and chives, are happy on a sunny windowsill or grown in pots outside during the summer.

Store cupboard recipes

Here are some ideas for recipes you can produce from a well-stocked store cupboard and just one or two fresh ingredients:

Cream of Chicken Soup (page 49)
Easy Pea Soup (page 59)
Pasta, Salami and Tapenade Salad (page 73)
Couscous and Haddock Salad (page 77)
Lemon Chicken (page 84)
Sticky Chicken Thighs (page 90)
Chicken Rarebit (page 97)
One-pan Chicken with Tomatoes (page 98)
Garlic and Thyme Chicken (page 100)
Tangy Chops (page 105)
Egg and Bacon Tarts (page 108)
Garlic Pork (page 109)
Croque Monsieur (page 112)
Healthy Burgers (page 115)
Trout and Dill Fishcakes (page 136)
Crusted Trout (page 143)
Sardines on Toast (page 146)
Cheesy Tuna Melt (page 146)
Simple Smoked Haddock (page 147)
Quick and Easy Carbonara (page 152)

Ravioli with Red Pepper Sauce (page 157)
Pea, Mint and Ricotta Pasta (page 158)
Spicy Tomato Pasta (page 163)
Risotto Milanese (page 171)
Simple Fried Rice (page 175)
Fast Macaroni Cheese (page 177)
Tomato and Butter Bean Stew (page 180)
Tomato and Herb Quiche (page 183)
Stuffed Peppers (page 186)
Leek and Potato Cold-night Pie (page 191)
Black-eye Bean Chilli (page 192)
Glamorgan Sausages (page 194)
Courgette and Parmesan Frittata (page 196)
Chickpea Patties (page 200)
Creamy Baked Eggs (page 206)
Classic French Omelette (page 207)
Beans on Toast (page 210)
Rösti Potatoes with Fried Eggs (page 211)
Rice Pudding (page 218)
Express Apple Tart (page 220)
Bread and Butter Pudding (page 221)
Cinnamon Pancakes (page 232)
Quick Chocolate Slices (page 247)

Stocking your fridge

The fridge is the main culprit for waste, and the bigger it is the more it becomes a repository for out-of-date condiments and bags of soggy salad leaves. Check the shelves and salad drawer regularly and rotate foods as you buy fresh supplies. Keep the fridge stocked with the ingredients listed in the box above. Pin up a contents list of the fridge with use-by dates and cross off items as you use them.

How to store food
- Cool cooked food to room temperature before putting in the fridge.
- Wrap or cover all food except fruit and vegetables.
- Practise fridge discipline. The coldest shelves are at the bottom so store raw meat, fish and poultry there.
- Always separate cooked meat and poultry from all raw foods.
- Use the salad drawer for leafy and salad vegetables and other vegetables such as leeks and cauliflower.
- Don't store tomatoes, potatoes or bananas in the fridge.

Make sure the fridge works properly
- Don't overfill it.
- Don't put hot foods in it.
- Don't open the door more than necessary.
- Clean it regularly.

Expensive ingredients worth buying for the fridge

PARMESAN An expensive hard cheese, with a strong flavour. Only a little is needed. Use in sauces and pasta dishes. Freeze the rind until needed, then add to minestrone soup while cooking for extra flavour. Remove before serving.

FRIDGE STORAGE TIMES

Vegetables and Fruit

Green vegetables	3–4 days
Salad leaves	2–3 days
Hard and stone fruit	3–7 days
Soft fruit	1–2 days

Dairy Food

Cheese, hard	1 week
Cheese, soft	2–3 days
Eggs	1 week
Milk	4–5 days

Fish

Fish	1 day
Shellfish	1 day

Raw Meat

Bacon	7 days
Game	2 days
Joints	3 days
Minced meat	1 day
Offal	1 day
Poultry	2 days
Raw sliced meat	2 days
Sausages	3 days

Cooked Meat

Joints	3 days
Casseroles/stews	2 days
Pies	2 days
Sliced meat	2 days
Ham	2 days
Ham, vacuum-packed	1–2 weeks

(or according to the instructions on the pack)

MATURE CHEDDAR A little goes a long way and it adds great depth to a dish. With a good brand, you won't need to use as much for sandwiches or in cooking.

BUTTER Choose butter rather than manufactured spreads as it is a natural product free of artificial additives. Adding a little to your frying oil will give extra flavour to recipes and make cakes and biscuits simply taste better.

Stocking your freezer

The freezer is an invaluable storage tool and if you use it properly – particularly with batch-cooking – you can save money and prevent wastage. Invest in lidded plastic containers and freezer bags so you'll be ready to store leftovers in the freezer. Keep the freezer stocked with the ingredients listed in the box above. Pin up a contents list of the freezer and cross off items as you use them.

How to store food
- Freeze food as soon as possible after purchase.
- Label cooked food with the date and name of the dish.
- Freeze food in portions.
- Never put warm foods into the freezer, wait until they have cooled.
- Check the manufacturer's instructions for freezing times.
- Do not refreeze food once it has thawed.

What not to store in the freezer
WHOLE EGGS Freeze whites and yolks separately
FRIED FOODS They lose their crispness and can go soggy
VEGETABLES Cucumber, lettuce and celery have too high a water content
SOME SAUCES Mayonnaise and similar sauces will separate when thawed

Thawing and reheating food
As a rule:
- Some foods, such as vegetables, soups and sauces, can be cooked from frozen – dropped into boiling water, or heated gently in a pan until thawed.
- Ensure other foods are thoroughly thawed before cooking.
- Cook food as soon as possible after thawing.
- Ensure the food is piping hot all the way through after cooking.

Make sure the freezer works properly
- Defrost it regularly.
- Keep the freezer as full as possible.
- If you have the space, a small chest freezer is a good investment. They are surprisingly cheap and start at fridge size. They're especially useful for large families wanting to take advantage of special offers on meat and poultry.

Expensive ingredients worth buying for the freezer
CHICKEN Look in the freezer aisle of the supermarket for packs of frozen chicken breasts and thighs. They're smaller fillets but cheaper and make a good stand-by when you want to use up store cupboard ingredients.
FISH Packs of frozen fillets are another convenient stand-by and can be cooked from frozen. Allow a few minutes extra cooking time and make sure it is piping hot. Frozen fish is excellent for using in fish pies too.

FREEZER STORAGE TIMES

A rough guide to recommended maximum storage times. Ensure frozen food is defrosted in the fridge until completed thawed.

Dairy produce

Cream (use in cooked sauces or soups)	6–8 months
Butter	3–4 months
Cheese, hard	4–6 months
Cheese, soft	3–4 months
Ice cream	3–4 months

Fish

White fish	6–8 months
Oily fish	3–4 months
Fish portions	3–4 months
Shellfish	2–3 months

Meat and poultry

Beef and lamb	4–6 months
Pork and veal	4–6 months
Offal	3–4 months
Bacon	2–3 months
Poultry	4–6 months
Minced meat	3–4 months

Shopping

Good planning will make your life much easier when you're shopping on a budget. Unlike our grandmothers who shopped daily and often only had a pantry for storage, we have the fridge and freezer to work alongside our store cupboard. Clever use of all three makes our lives easier and shopping trips fewer. Nowadays, Sunday's roast doesn't have to be Monday's cottage pie if it's prepared and popped in the freezer for another day.

Change your shopping habits

- Do a big supermarket shop once a month for non-perishables – even better, order your shopping on-line to avoid impulse buys and keep an eye on the running total before you place the order. Some delivery companies offer free delivery at less popular times.
- Top up with daily or weekly shops at supermarkets, independent shops or street markets for fresh ingredients.
- Only buy special offers or BOGOFs (buy one, get one free) if you have time to batch cook or space to freeze the extra.
- Avoid ready-meals and ready-prepared ingredients, such as chopped onions – you are paying more for convenience.

Before you go shopping

- Can you delay your food shop for another day? Check the store cupboard, fridge or freezer for ingredients that can make another meal.
- Check the diary and plan the week's menu according to family activities.
- Do a quick weekly stock take of the store cupboard, fridge and freezer. Can ingredients near their use-by or best-before date be incorporated into the week's menu?
- Don't forget nature's free store cupboard – blackberries in hedgerows, sweet chestnuts and sloes, for example.

The weekly menu

This needn't be a hefty document, simply jot down:

- An idea for every day of the week, including some dishes that you've already made and stored in the fridge or freezer.
- Some recipes that make creative use of leftovers.
- Some recipes that stretch – bolognese tonight, chilli tomorrow.
- Some quick meals that need a trip to the shops for one or two fresh ingredients.
- Include vegetables or other accompaniments in your plan, but remember that you can always change your mind if you find a bargain in the supermarket.
- Rethink your approach to cooking – meat and fish are expensive, so make two nights a week vegetarian.

When you're shopping

- Tuck a notebook in your bag listing ingredients for family favourites and you'll be ready to take advantage of special offers on expensive ingredients such as meat and poultry.
- Make a shopping list and stick to it.
- Keep it seasonal (see pages 20–21).
- Does the product cost less whole or in portions – for example, it's cheaper to:
  - buy a whole chicken and joint it into pieces yourself (see page 29, or ask your butcher to do it). Use the carcass for stock.
  - cut a whole salmon into fillets or steaks then freeze in portions.
- Compare the price per kilo. Loose fruit and vegetables can cost considerably less than pre-packed versions, for example.

Avoiding waste

By checking store cupboards, planning your weekly menu and always shopping with a list, you are well on your way to avoiding waste in the kitchen, as well as saving money. But it's inevitable that there will be some leftovers from time to time; for example, if last-minute plans prevent you eating a supper that has already been planned for the week. A regular check of use-by dates of ingredients in the fridge should prevent this and the leftovers ideas on pages 24–25 will help you to use them up in quick suppers or dishes to freeze for another day.

Expiry dates

These are a major area of debate. Supermarkets are extremely strict on expiry dates and will throw out any food the moment it is 'out of date'. Once you have purchased a product, you are asked to use it within the 'use by' date. After this, you are encouraged to throw it out and start again. However, with the odd exception – and using your judgement on certain danger foods like fish and chicken – you can simply check if it's okay to use by smell, look and feel. Follow your instincts: if it smells bad, bin it.

How can I tell if my eggs are fresh?
Worried about how long you've had your eggs? Before you throw them away, do this check. A fresh egg should feel heavy in your hand and will sink to the bottom of the bowl or sit on its side when put into water. Older eggs will stand up. Do not use eggs that float.

PORTION SIZES (PER PERSON)

As a rough guide, vegetables should half-fill the plate while meat, fish or poultry should take up one quarter, with the remainder filled with carbohydrates, such as rice, pasta or potatoes.

Soup	300ml (½ pint)	
Fish, poultry and meat	175g (6oz)	off the bone
Whole chicken, leg of lamb or pork	1.4kg (3lb)	should serve 4 people with leftovers
Casseroles, stews	225g (8oz)	trimmed meat
Shellfish	125g (4oz)	as main course
Vegetables	50g (2oz)	assuming you are serving three vegetables
	75g (3oz)	assuming you are serving two vegetables
Potatoes	3	small roast
	175g (6oz)	mashed
	125g (4oz)	new
Rice (as an accompaniment)	50g (2oz)	pre-cooked weight
Couscous and bulgur wheat (as an accompaniment)	50g (2oz)	pre-cooked weight
Dried pasta	75–100g (3–3½oz)	
Salads	1 dessert bowl	

How to shop

Only buy perishables that you can cook/eat before the use-by date. Select food wisely and buy it in optimum condition. Check that the packaging is undamaged and that cans are not dented or bulging. Supermarkets now sell all manner of produce all year round – fresh strawberries at Christmas, asparagus way before June – so it's easy to forget where food comes from and when it is in season. Food bought in its true season will taste vastly different from forced produce, and you'll benefit from lower prices (see pages 20–21).

Choosing beef

- A light red meat doesn't necessarily indicate quality. Look for a meat that is dark red.
- Fat should be creamy white.
- A fair amount of fat should be distributed through the meat as fine marbling – this tenderises the meat during cooking.
- Look for neat cuts; there should be no splinters of bone or ragged edges, and the cut should be trimmed of sinew.
- The thickness of the piece of meat should be uniform for even cooking.
- Look for the Quality Standard Mark as an assurance of quality.
- Select the cut of beef as follows: Roasting and braising: rib, top rump, topside, silverside. Stews, casseroles and mince: neck or clod, chuck steak, thin flank, shin. Grilling and frying: rump, fillet, sirloin, entrecôte.

Choosing lamb

- Meat from young English lambs is pale with a small amount of creamy white fat. There should be a light marbling of fat within the flesh.
- Joints and chops are smaller than those of imported lamb.
- Imported lamb tends to be slightly darker and coarser.
- The bones should be cleanly cut, with no splinters.
- Look for the Quality Standard Mark as an assurance of quality.
- Select the cut of lamb as follows: Roasting, grilling and frying: all lamb cuts except middle neck and scrag. Stews and casseroles: middle neck, scrag, shoulder, chump chops. Mince: leg.

Choosing pork

- Look for pale pink, firm, smooth-textured flesh.
- The fat should be white.
- The rind/skin should be smooth and hairless.
- Look for neat cuts; there should be no splinters of bone or ragged edges, and the cut should be trimmed evenly.
- Ask the butcher to score the rind/skin for you – with his large, super-sharp knives he can do it much quicker than you'll be able to at home.
- Select the cut of pork as follows: Roasting: most cuts are good for roasting. Stews, casseroles and mince: diced shoulder, spare ribs, belly, neck. Frying and grilling: tenderloin or fillet, chops, escalopes.

Choosing chicken

- Birds should have a neat shape, an even colour and no blemishes or tears on the skin.
- The body should look meaty and plump.
- Chicken is available as poussins (baby), spring chicken (slightly older), boiling fowl, corn-fed (yellow) and as portions. To save money, buy a whole chicken and joint it yourself (see page 29).

Choosing fish and seafood

- Try to buy fish and seafood on the day you want to eat it, as it spoils very quickly.
- Use your nose and your eyes when buying fish – it must be absolutely fresh and smell of the sea, eyes bright and clear, gills bright pink or red and flesh firm.
- When you press the fish with your finger it should not leave an indentation, and when you pick it up it should not flop.

- The fishmonger will scale, clean, fillet or skin fish if you ask him.
- When choosing molluscs (scallops, mussels, clams, oysters), look for those with tightly closed, undamaged shells.
- Fish stocks need to be protected, so go for line-caught fish and those from sustainable sources – Icelandic or Norwegian cod, for example.
- Types of fish: White fish: large fish such as cod and coley, are usually sold as steaks, fillets or cutlets. Smaller fish, such as whiting and haddock, are sold in fillets. Flat fish: halibut and turbot are sold in fillets or as steaks. Smaller flat fish, such as plaice, lemon and Dover sole are usually sold whole, trimmed and filleted. Oily fish: mackerel, herrings and sardines, are usually sold whole. Salmon are sold whole or in steaks. Shellfish: these are divided into two groups – those with legs (crustaceans) and those without (molluscs). Most are available all year round.

Choosing fruit and vegetables

- Buy from a shop with a high turnover to get the freshest produce. Look out for good deals at farmer's markets.
- Buy in season (see pages 20–21).
- Look for bright, fresh colours and crisp leaves.
- Avoid bruised, discoloured or damaged produce.
- Don't prod fruit and vegetables with your fingers – weigh in the palm of your hand.
- Buy unripe as well as ripe fruit to ensure that you'll have fruit to eat throughout the week.
- Don't buy more than you need for a week.

False economies

When buying fresh food:
- Don't be seduced by low prices for bulk purchasing or by reduced stickers, unless you're sure you can use the food before it deteriorates, or there's room in your freezer.
- The same goes for the BOGOF offers (buy one, get one free) – you may find you're throwing away not just food, but money.

A note on street markets
Supermarkets are fine for doing the big once-a-week shop, but using street markets and farm shops, as well as local butchers, greengrocers and bakers, can often reap rewards in terms of expertise, quality and variety. Take your pick of seasonal fruit and vegetables.

Why is it a good idea to buy from one?
- It cuts down on packaging and removes the middleman, so more of the profits go direct to the supplier.
- It's generally cheaper than buying from supermarkets (their prices usually include costs such as transport).
- There is greater variety. The produce doesn't go through lots of handling stages, where each vegetable has to conform to a set standard.
- Produce often tastes better because it hasn't travelled miles in controlled conditions.
- Sometimes you can pick up bargains with boxes of slightly blemished or misshapen fruit and vegetables.

Keep it seasonal

Why? Because not only will the produce you buy taste fantastic, it will cost less. Look out for good deals at supermarkets, farm shops, markets and greengrocers where you can sometimes buy larger, cheaper quantities for freezing or batch cooking. Pick Your Own farms often charge half the price of the supermarkets. You can pick fruit and vegetables at their ripest and enjoy a fun day out with the family too.

JANUARY

VEGETABLES Beetroot, Brussels sprouts, cauliflower, celeriac, celery, chicory, jerusalem artichoke, kale, leeks, parsnips, potatoes (maincrop), rhubarb, swede, turnips
FRUIT Apples, clementines, kiwi fruit, lemons, oranges, passion fruit, pears, pineapple, pomegranate, satsumas, tangerines, walnuts
FISH Brill, clams, cockles, haddock, halibut, hake, lemon sole, mussels, plaice

FEBRUARY

VEGETABLES Brussels sprouts, cauliflower, celeriac, chicory, kale, leeks, parsnips, potatoes (maincrop), rhubarb, swede
FRUIT Bananas, blood oranges, kiwi fruit, lemons, oranges, passion fruit, pears, pineapple, pomegranate
FISH Brill, cockles, cod, haddock, halibut, hake, lemon sole, mussels, salmon

MARCH

VEGETABLES Cauliflower, chicory, kale, leeks, purple sprouting broccoli, rhubarb, spring onions
FRUIT Bananas, blood oranges, kiwi fruit, lemons, oranges, passion fruit, pineapple, pomegranate
FISH Cockles, cod, hake, lemon sole, mussels, salmon, sea trout

APRIL

VEGETABLES Asparagus, broccoli, Jersey royal potatoes, purple sprouting broccoli, radishes, rhubarb, rocket, spinach, spring onions, watercress
FRUIT Bananas, kiwi fruit
FISH Cockles, cod, salmon, sea trout

MAY

VEGETABLES Asparagus, broccoli, Jersey royal potatoes, new potatoes, radishes, rhubarb, rocket, spinach, spring onions, watercress
FRUIT Cherries, kiwi fruit, strawberries
MEAT Lamb
FISH Cod, crab, halibut, lemon sole, plaice, salmon, sea bass, sea trout

JUNE

VEGETABLES Artichoke, asparagus, aubergine, broad beans, broccoli, carrots, courgettes, fennel, mangetout, Jersey royal potatoes, new potatoes, peas, radishes, rocket, runner beans, spring onions, turnips, watercress
FRUIT Cherries, strawberries
MEAT Lamb
FISH Cod, crab, haddock, halibut, herring, lemon sole, mackerel, plaice, salmon, sardines, sea bass, sea trout

JULY

VEGETABLES Artichoke, aubergine, beetroot, broad beans, broccoli, carrots, courgettes, cucumber, fennel, french beans, garlic, mangetout, new potatoes, onions, peas, potatoes (maincrop), radishes, rocket, runner beans, turnips, watercress

FRUIT Apricots, blackberries, blueberries, cherries, gooseberries, greengages, kiwi fruit, melons, peaches, raspberries, redcurrants, strawberries, tomatoes

MEAT Lamb, rabbit

FISH Cod, crab, haddock, halibut, herring, lemon sole, mackerel, plaice, salmon, sardines, sea bass, sea trout

AUGUST

VEGETABLES Artichoke, aubergine, beetroot, broad beans, broccoli, carrots, courgettes, cucumber, fennel, french beans, garlic, leeks, mangetout, marrow, new potatoes, onions, peas, peppers, potatoes (maincrop), radishes, rocket, runner beans, sweetcorn, watercress

FRUIT Apricots, blackberries, blueberries, damsons, greengages, kiwi fruit, melons, nectarines, peaches, plums, raspberries, redcurrants, tomatoes

MEAT Lamb, rabbit

FISH Cod, crab, grey mullet, haddock, halibut, herring, lemon sole, mackerel, plaice, salmon, sardines, sea bass

SEPTEMBER

VEGETABLES Artichoke, aubergine, beetroot, broccoli, butternut squash, carrots, courgettes, cucumber, fennel, garlic, leeks, mangetout, marrow, onions, parsnips, peas, peppers, potatoes (maincrop), radishes, rocket, runner beans, sweetcorn, watercress, wild mushrooms

FRUIT Apples, blackberries, damsons, figs, grapes, melons, nectarines, peaches, pears, plums, raspberries, redcurrants, tomatoes, walnuts

MEAT Lamb, rabbit, goose

FISH Clams, cod, crab, grey mullet, haddock, halibut, herring, lemon sole, mackerel, plaice, sea bass, squid

OCTOBER

VEGETABLES Artichoke, beetroot, broccoli, butternut squash, carrots, celeriac, celery, fennel, kale, leeks, marrow, onions, parsnips, potatoes (maincrop), pumpkin, swede, turnips, watercress, wild mushrooms

FRUIT Apples, chestnuts, figs, pears, quince, tomatoes, walnuts

MEAT Rabbit, goose

FISH Brill, clams, crb, grey mullet, haddock, halibut, hake, lemon sole, mackerel, mussels, plaice, sea bass, squid

NOVEMBER

VEGETABLES Artichoke, beetroot, Brussels sprouts, celeriac, celery, chicory, kale, leeks, parsnips, potatoes (maincrop), pumpkin, swede, turnips, watercress, wild mushrooms

FRUIT Apples, chestnuts, clementines, cranberries, figs, passion fruit, pears, quince, satsumas, tangerines, walnuts

MEAT Rabbit, goose

FISH Brill, clams, haddock, halibut, hake, lemon sole, mussels, plaice, sea bass, squid

DECEMBER

VEGETABLES Beetroot, Brussels sprouts, cauliflower, celeriac, celery, chicory, kale, leeks, parsnips, potatoes (maincrop), pumpkin, swede, turnips

FRUIT Apples, chestnuts, clementines, cranberries, passion fruit, pears, pineapple, pomegranate, satsumas, tangerines, walnuts

MEAT Rabbit, goose

FISH Brill, clams, haddock, halilbut, hake, lemon sole, mussels, plaice, sea bass

One week's menu and shopping list

Once you get into the habit of planning your weekly shop, you'll soon see the difference in the food bills. If you're planning a Sunday family roast, find a recipe to use up the leftovers and buy the extra ingredients in advance. Then you'll be ready to prepare the meal straight away. Otherwise that tasty leftover roast meat won't look quite so appetising a few days later. Here's a typical week's menu with its shopping list...

SUNDAY

LUNCH Maple, Ginger and Soy-roasted Gammon
(page 110)
- Cook half or all of the recipe depending on numbers

Leftovers
- Sandwiches for Monday lunch
- Monday's supper

TEATIME Chocolate Victoria Sandwich (page 245)
Hazelnut and Chocolate Flapjacks (page 249)

Leftovers
- Add to lunchboxes during the week

MONDAY

DINNER Savoury Pudding (page 111)
- Uses leftover gammon from Sunday lunch

TUESDAY

DINNER Aubergine and Chickpea Pilaf (page 182)
- Stir in leftover cooked vegetables from Sunday lunch into the pilaf a few minutes before the end of cooking (replacing the fresh spinach in the recipe)
- Option: Make extra for tomorrow's packed lunch

WEDNESDAY

Use up something from the freezer, such as:
DINNER Simple Bolognese Sauce (page 27) and serve with a mixed salad with Vinaigrette Dressing (page 26)

THURSDAY

A quick late-night supper using up eggs:
SUPPER Classic French Omelette (page 207) made with chopped smoked salmon trimmings

FRIDAY

Checking the store cupboard and freezer to delay the weekly shop
DINNER Sticky Chicken Thighs (page 90) served with rice and frozen peas

SATURDAY

Pop a soup on to simmer while you go about your weekend chores, such as:
LUNCH Squash and Sweet Potato Soup (page 49)
- And add any leftover vegetables from the fridge that need using up.

Treat yourself to a homemade takeaway:
DINNER Chicken Curry with Rice (page 85)

FROM THE STORE CUPBOARD

Sliced bread
Butter
Dijon mustard
Mature Cheddar
Milk
Eggs
Nutmeg
Oil
Soy sauce
Onions
Butter
Long-grain rice
Stock
Can of chickpeas
Extra virgin olive oil
White wine vinegar
Dried pasta

Parmesan
Frozen peas
Frozen chicken
Garlic
Curry paste
Can of chopped
    tomatoes
Cocoa powder
Caster sugar
Flour
Icing sugar
Plain chocolate
Porridge oats

THE SHOPPING LIST – FROM THE SHOPS

Fresh parsley
Smoked boneless gammon joint
Root ginger
Maple syrup
Aubergine
Cumin seeds
Fresh salad, such as lettuce, cucumber
Tomatoes
Smoked salmon trimmings
Fresh chicken thighs
Baby leaf spinach
Coriander
Sweet potatoes
Vanilla extract
Golden syrup
Hazelnuts
Light muscovado sugar

Using leftovers

We all struggle with portion sizing and often have some extra rice, potatoes or other ingredients left at the end of each meal. There is a difference between leftovers and waste food. Leftovers are the bits and pieces that sit in a clingfilm-covered bowl in your fridge, challenging you to use them creatively. If you ignore them for four or five days they become waste. Why not try making the most of your leftover bits & bobs?

VERSATILE LEFTOVERS

There are many ways of using leftover food and slightly over-ripe fruit and vegetables that are starting to wilt.
- Simply add the ingredients to a stir-fry, pasta bake, soup, risotto... the list is endless.
- 'Stretch' the ingredients – sometimes the amount left over is so small it won't go very far in a family setting. Try adding to it. You can cook a little more of it (for example rice), or try adding lentils and tomatoes to leftover mince to create a whole new take on Bolognese sauce (see page 27).
- Make the most of fruit and vegetables that are starting to wilt – use fruit in a smoothie or crumble, use vegetables in soups and bakes.

Below are some examples of typical fridge leftovers you could use in recipes in this book.

LEFTOVER	RECIPE	RECIPE
Cooked pasta	Quick Winter Minestrone (page 56)	Broccoli Pasta Bake (page 157)
Bacon rashers	Bacon and Egg Salad (page 69)	Egg and Bacon Tarts (page 108)
Mixed vegetables	Cheese and Vegetable Bake (page 198)	Simple Vegetable Soup (page 33)
Savoy cabbage	Quick Winter Minestrone (page 56)	Chicken and Vegetable Hotpot (page 83)
Salad	Smoked Mackerel Citrus Salad (page 63)	Warm Bacon Salad (page 65)
Tomato sauce	Mozzarella, Tomato and Basil Pizza (page 202)	Simple Bolognese Sauce (page 27)
Over-ripe bananas	Chocolate Banana Muffins (page 241)	Banoffee Pie (page 236)
Turning apples	Bran and Apple Muffins (page 240)	Rustic Blackberry and Apple Pie (page 229)
Turning pears	Pear and Blackberry Crumble (page 221)	Easy Pear and Toffee Tarte Tatin (page 226)
Custard	Cheat's Chocolate Pots (page 228)	
Pancake batter	Cinnamon Pancakes (page 232)	
Cooked turkey or potatoes	See recipes opposite	

Turkey and Chestnut Soup
Serves 4

25g (1oz) butter or margarine

1 large onion, chopped

225g (8oz) Brussels sprouts

900ml (1½ pints) turkey stock made from leftover carcass and any leftover turkey meat

400g can whole chestnuts, drained

2 tsp freshly chopped thyme or 1 tsp dried thyme

salt and ground black pepper

stock or milk to finish

thyme sprigs to garnish

1. Melt the fat in a large heavy-based saucepan, add the onion and fry gently for 5 minutes until it has softened.

2. Trim the sprouts and cut a cross in the base of each one. Add to the onion, cover the pan with a lid and cook gently for 5 minutes, shaking the pan frequently.

3. Pour in the stock and bring to the boil, then add the remaining ingredients, with salt and pepper to taste. Reduce the heat, cover the pan and simmer for 30 minutes until the vegetables are tender.

4. Leave to cool a little, then whiz in batches in a blender or food processor until smooth. Return to the rinsed-out pan and reheat gently, then thin down with either stock or milk, according to taste. Taste and adjust the seasoning. To serve, ladle into warmed bowls and garnish with sprigs of thyme.

Bubble and Squeak Cakes
Serves 4

50g (2oz) butter

175g (6oz) leeks, finely shredded

175g (6oz) green cabbage, finely shredded

575g (1¼lb) cooked mashed potato

plain flour to dust

1 tbsp oil

1. Heat 25g (1oz) butter in a large non-stick frying pan. Add the leeks and cabbage and fry for 5 minutes, stirring, until soft and beginning to colour. Combine the leeks and cabbage with the potatoes and season well with salt and pepper. Leave to cool. When cool enough to handle, mould into 12 cakes and dust with flour.

2. Heat the oil and remaining butter in a non-stick frying pan and cook the cakes for 4 minutes on each side or until they are golden, crisp and hot right through.

Bits & Bobs

You may not always feel like transforming your leftovers into meals – or there may not be enough to do so. Another option is to freeze the odd ingredient for later use.

A SMALL AMOUNT OF HERBS Freeze in ice cube trays

ONE OR TWO CHILLIES These freeze well and are easy to chop from frozen

DOUBLE CREAM Lightly whip the cream and then freeze

HARD CHEESES These will become crumbly once thawed, but can be used for grating or in cooking

BREAD Whiz in a food processor to make breadcrumbs – these freeze well in a sealed plastic bag. Use to sprinkle over bakes for a crisp topping, or to coat fish or chicken before frying, grilling or baking – or use for bread sauce to serve with game or turkey. Cube stale bread, toss with olive oil and spread out on to a baking sheet. Bake at 200°C (180°C fan oven) mark 6 for 5–10 minutes until golden. Use as croûtons for salads and soups.

A HALF USED PACK OF OLIVES Use in a salad or heat with an onion and tin of tomatoes and serve with pasta.

Simple butters, dressings and sauces

These are all versatile recipes that liven up meals with little effort, especially if you make extra and freeze the rest. Once you've made a big batch, you can create speedy midweek meals such as tomato sauce with pasta, or perk up steaks and fish with flavoured butters, or make salad even more appetising with a zingy dressing.

Flavoured Butters

These are excellent quick alternatives to sauces for serving with grilled meats, fish and all kinds of vegetables. They need to be prepared several hours in advance to allow time to chill and become firm enough to slice.

- Use unsalted butter at room temperature. Beat in the flavouring(s) by hand or using a food processor. Turn on to clingfilm, shape into a log, wrap tightly and chill in the fridge for at least 1 hour. Allow about 25g (1oz) savoury butter per person.
- Add the following flavourings to 125g (4oz) butter, at room temperature.

Variations
Anchovy butter: Add 6 mashed anchovy fillets.
Blue cheese butter: Add 50g (2oz) blue cheese.
Herb butter: Add 2 tbsp freshly chopped mixed herbs, such as flat-leafed parsley, chervil and tarragon, plus a squeeze of lemon juice.
Garlic butter: Add 1 crushed garlic clove and 2 tsp chopped parsley or chervil.
Watercress butter: Add 50g (2oz) chopped watercress.

TO USE Slice and top grilled steak, chicken, fish or vegetables; make garlic or herb bread.
IN THE FRIDGE Wrap in clingfilm and use within two weeks.
IN THE FREEZER Freeze in logs or individual portions for up to four months; defrost before use.

Vinaigrette Dressing
Makes about 300ml (½ pint)

100ml (3½ fl oz) extra virgin olive oil

100ml (3½ fl oz) grapeseed oil

75ml (2fl oz) white wine vinegar

pinch each sugar and English
    mustard powder

1 garlic clove, crushed (optional)

salt and ground black pepper

1. Put the oils, vinegar, sugar, mustard powder and garlic, if using, into a large screw-topped jar. Shake well, season to taste with salt and pepper and store in a cool place.

TO USE Toss with salads or cooked vegetables.
IN THE FRIDGE Store in a jam jar for up to a week. Shake well before use.
IN THE FREEZER Not suitable.

White Sauce
Makes 600ml (1 pint)

25g (1oz) butter

25g (1oz) plain flour

600ml (1 pint) milk

freshly grated nutmeg

salt and ground black pepper

1. Melt the butter in a pan, then stir in the flour and cook, stirring constantly, for 1 minute.

2. Remove from the heat and gradually pour in the milk, stirring well after each addition.

3. Return to the heat and cook, stirring, until the sauce has thickened and is velvety and smooth. Season with salt, pepper and freshly grated nutmeg.

TO USE Use as a base for lasagne or fish pies; stir in cheese, mustard or herbs and serve as a sauce to accompany fish or chicken.
IN THE FRIDGE Store covered with clingfilm to stop a skin forming and use within 2 days.
IN THE FREEZER Freeze in small portions in freezer bags or boxes for up to a month; defrost before use.

Pesto
Serves 4

50g (2oz) basil leaves

1–2 garlic cloves

25g (1oz) pinenuts

6 tbsp extra virgin olive oil

2 tbsp freshly grated Parmesan

squeeze of lemon juice (optional)

salt and ground black pepper

1. Roughly tear the basil and put into a mortar with the garlic, pinenuts and a little of the oil. Pound with a pestle to a paste. Alternatively, work in a food processor to a fairly smooth paste.

2. Gradually work in the rest of the oil and season to taste with salt and pepper. Transfer to a bowl, stir in the Parmesan, check the seasoning and add a squeeze of lemon juice if you like.

TO USE Stir into cooked pasta; spread over fish or chicken before grilling or baking; swirl into soup.
IN THE FRIDGE Put into a sterilised glass jar, cover with a thin layer of oil and use within a week.
IN THE FREEZER Freeze in small portions in freezer bags or boxes for up to a month; defrost before use.

Variations
Sun-dried tomato pesto:
Replace half the basil with 50g (2oz) sun-dried tomatoes in oil, drained and roughly chopped. Use a blender or food processor to work the ingredients together to a paste.
Coriander pesto: Replace the basil with coriander leaves. Add 1 seeded and chopped chilli with the garlic if you like. Omit the Parmesan.
Rocket pesto: Replace the basil with rocket leaves and add 1 tbsp chopped parsley.

Fresh Tomato Sauce
Serves 4

900g (2lb) vine-ripened tomatoes, roughly chopped

2 tbsp extra virgin olive oil

2 garlic cloves, crushed

grated zest of 1 lemon

1 tsp dried oregano

2 tbsp freshly chopped basil

pinch of sugar, or to taste (optional)

salt and ground black pepper

1. Put the tomatoes into a pan with the oil, garlic, lemon zest and oregano. Bring to the boil, cover and simmer gently for 20 minutes.

2. Add the basil, salt and pepper to taste and a little sugar if required. Simmer, uncovered, for a further 10 minutes or until the sauce is slightly thickened. If a smooth sauce is preferred, pass through a sieve and reheat before serving.

TO USE Stir into cooked pasta; use as a sauce to braise white fish or chicken; stir in cheese or herbs and serve as a sauce with fish or chicken; reduce until thick and use as pizza sauce.
IN THE FRIDGE Store, covered, and use within three days.
IN THE FREEZER Freeze in small portions in freezer bags or boxes for up to a month; defrost before use.

Simple Bolognese Sauce
Serves 6

2 tbsp olive oil

1 large onion, finely chopped

2 garlic cloves, crushed

450g (1lb) minced meat

2 tbsp tomato purée

300ml (½ pint) beef stock

400g can chopped tomatoes

125g (4oz) mushrooms, sliced

2 tbsp Worcestershire sauce

salt and ground black pepper

1. Heat the oil in a large pan, add the onion and fry over a medium heat for 10 minutes until soft. Add the garlic and fry for a further minute.

2. Stir in the meat and cook, stirring, over a high heat until browned. Stir in the tomato purée and stock, cover and bring to the boil. Add the tomatoes, mushrooms and Worcestershire sauce and season well with salt and pepper. Bring back to the boil, lower the heat and simmer for 20 minutes or until the meat is tender. Adjust the seasoning before serving.

TO USE Use as a base for cottage pie, lasagne, chilli con carne.
IN THE FRIDGE Store, covered, and use within two days. Reheat in a pan until piping hot.
IN THE FREEZER Freeze in small portions in freezer bags or boxes for up to a month; defrost before use.

Stretching meals

Meat, poultry and fish are expensive items but if you shop carefully and stretch meals with clever shopping and cooking you can save pounds on the food budget and still provide filling, nutritious dishes for the family. Keeping an eye on portion sizes for ingredients and accompaniments will save on waste too (see page 17).

Ways to stretch a meal

- Buy cheaper cuts of meat, such as silverside, pork belly and middle neck of lamb (see page 18 for more cuts) that suit long, slow cooking. You'll need less meat as it flavours the whole dish and they are often cooked in one pot, saving on fuel; for example, Braised Beef with Mustard and Capers, page 114, Winter Hotpot, page 113.

- Replace half the mince in a Bolognese sauce with 200g (7oz) red lentils. Add them after browning the mince – no need to soak them, just stir them in.

- Use vegetable boiling water for gravy or vegetable stock.

- Top stews with cheap-to-make suet dumplings; add mustard, horseradish and herbs to the mix for a change (see below).

Suet Dumplings
Serves 4

125g (4oz) self-raising white flour

pinch of salt

50g (2oz) shredded suet

2 tbsp freshly chopped parsley

2 tbsp freshly chopped thyme

1. Sift the flour and salt into a bowl. Stir in the suet, herbs and about 5 tbsp water to make a fairly firm dough. Lightly shape the dough into 2.5cm (1in) balls.

2. Add to a chicken or beef stew about 20 minutes before the end of cooking time and cook until the dumplings are light and fluffy.

- Make expensive meat and poultry go further with cheaper accompaniments: for example, roast beef and Yorkshire pudding; roast chicken with sage and onion stuffing (see recipes below).

Yorkshire Puddings
Makes 8–12

125g (4oz) plain flour

½ tsp salt

300ml (½ pint) milk

2 medium eggs

1. Sift the flour and salt into a bowl. Mix in half the milk, then add the eggs and season with pepper. Beat until smooth, then whisk in the rest of the milk.

2. Pour off about 3 tbsp fat from the roasting tin and use to grease 8–12 individual Yorkshire pudding tins. Heat in the oven for 5 minutes or until the fat is almost smoking. Pour the Yorkshire batter into the tins. Bake for 15–20 minutes until well risen, golden and crisp. (Use this recipe for Toad in the Hole.)

Sage and Onion Stuffing
Makes sufficient for a 1.4kg (3lb) oven-ready chicken

1 tbsp oil

75g (3oz) onion, chopped

125g (4oz) pork sausage meat

1 tbsp finely chopped sage

salt and ground black pepper

1. Heat the oil in a pan, add the onion and cook gently for 7–10 minutes until soft and golden. Turn into a bowl and leave to cool.

2. Add the sausage meat and sage to the cooled onion mixture and season to taste with salt and pepper.

- Add beans and pulses to soups, stews and casseroles.

- Serve with plenty of cheaper in season vegetables or a tastily dressed salad (see pages 26 and 27 for dressing ideas).

Jointing a whole chicken

Chicken and other poultry may be bought whole for roasting or in pieces ready for cooking. It is often cheaper to buy a whole bird, then joint it yourself into pieces and keep the carcass for stock.

When jointing a chicken, add the wing tips and bones to the carcass to make stock (see page 30).

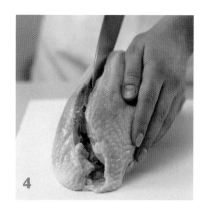

1. Using a sharp meat knife with a curved blade, cut out the wishbone and remove the wings in a single piece. Remove the wing tips.

2. With the tail pointing towards you and breast side up, pull one leg away and cut through the skin between leg and breast. Pull the leg down until you crack the joint between the thigh bone and ribcage.

3. Cut through that joint, then cut through the remaining leg meat. Repeat on the other side.

4. To remove the breast without any bone, make a cut along the length of the breastbone. Gently teasing the flesh away from the ribs with the knife, work the blade down between the flesh and ribs of one breast and cut it off neatly. (Always cut in, towards the bone.) Repeat on the other side.

5. To remove the breast with the bone in, make a cut along the full length of the breastbone.

6. Using poultry shears, cut through the breastbone, then cut through the ribcage following the outline of the breast meat. Repeat on the other side. Trim off any flaps of skin or fat.

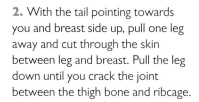

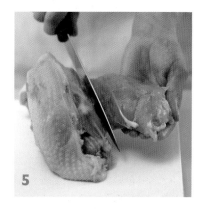

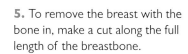

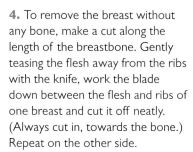

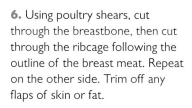

Making stock

Nothing goes to waste in a frugal kitchen, including leftover chicken carcasses, meat bones and vegetables trimmings to make stock. Good stock can make the difference between a good dish and a great one. It gives depth of flavour to many dishes. There are four main type of stock: meat, chicken, fish and vegetable.

Meat Stock
For 1.1 litres (2 pints)

450g (1lb) each meat bones and stewing meat

1 onion

2 celery sticks

1 large carrot, sliced

1 bouquet garni
(2 bay leaves, a few thyme sprigs and 1 small bunch of parsley)

1 tsp black peppercorns

½ tsp salt

1. Preheat the oven to 220°C (200°C fan oven) mark 7. Put the meat and bones into a roasting tin. Roast for 30–40 minutes, turning now and again, until well browned.

2. Put the bones into a large pan with the remaining ingredients. Add 2 litres (3½ pints) cold water. Bring slowly to the boil and skim the surface. Partially cover and simmer for 4–5 hours, skimming away the surface of fat regularly. Adjust the seasoning if necessary.

3. Strain through a muslin-lined sieve into a bowl and cool quickly. Degrease before using (see opposite).

Chicken Stock
For 1.1 litres (2 pints)

1.6kg (3½ lb) chicken bones or a stripped roast chicken carcass

225g (8oz) each onions and celery, sliced

150g (5oz) chopped leeks

1 bouquet garni (2 bay leaves, a few thyme sprigs and 1 small bunch of parsley)

1 tsp black peppercorns

½ tsp salt

1. Put all the ingredients into a large pan with 3 litres (5¼ pints) cold water.

2. Bring slowly to the boil and skim the surface. Partially cover and simmer gently for 2 hours, skimming away the surface of fat regularly. Adjust the seasoning if necessary.

3. Strain through a muslin-lined sieve into a bowl and cool quickly. Degrease before using (see opposite).

Fish Stock
For 900ml (1½ pints)

900g (2lb) fish bones and trimmings, washed

2 carrots, 1 onion and 2 celery sticks, sliced

1 bouquet garni (2 bay leaves, a few thyme sprigs and 1 small bunch of parsley)

6 white peppercorns

½ tsp salt

1. Put all the ingredients into a large pan with 900ml (1½ pints) cold water. Bring slowly to the boil and skim the surface.

2. Partially cover the pan and simmer gently for 30 minutes. Adjust the seasoning if necessary.

3. Strain through a muslin-lined sieve into a bowl and cool quickly. Fish stock does not usually need to be degreased. However, if it does seem to be fatty, you will need to remove this by degreasing it (see opposite).

Vegetable Stock
For 1.1 litres (2 pints)

225g (8oz) each onions, celery, leeks and carrots, chopped
2 bay leaves
a few thyme sprigs
1 small bunch of parsley
10 black peppercorns
½ tsp salt

1. Put all the ingredients into a pan and pour in 1.7 litres (3 pints) cold water. Bring slowly to the boil and skim the surface.

2. Partially cover the pan and simmer for 30 minutes. Adjust the seasoning. Strain the stock through a fine sieve and leave to cool.

Reducing and freezing stock

- Save freezer space by reducing homemade stock and freezing in ice cube trays. Reducing will intensify the flavour and you can use them like stock cubes, popping one or two straight into sauces, stews and casseroles with a little extra water if necessary.
- **To reduce:** strain as directed above, return to the rinsed out pan and boil until reduced to a quarter of its volume.
- **To freeze:** freeze in large batches in freezer-proof boxes or reduce and freeze in ice cube trays. Once frozen, pop out the cubes into freezer bags. Freeze for up to six months.

Degreasing stock

Meat and poultry stock needs to be degreased. (Vegetable stock does not.) You can mop the fat from the surface using kitchen paper, but the following methods are easier and more effective. There are three main methods that you can use: ladling, chilling and pouring.

1. While the stock is warm, place a ladle on the surface. Press down to allow the fat floating on the surface to trickle over the edge until the ladle is full. Discard the fat, then repeat until all the fat has been removed.

2. This technique works best with stock made from meat, whose fat solidifies when cold. Put the stock in the fridge until the fat becomes solid, then remove the pieces of fat using a slotted spoon.

3. For this you need a degreasing jug or a double-pouring gravy boat, which has the spout at the base of the vessel. When you fill the jug or gravy boat with a fatty liquid, the fat rises. When you pour, the stock comes out while the fat stays behind in the jug.

Making soups

Soups are nutritious and full of flavour, and are the perfect way to use up leftover vegetables, meat or poultry. Bulk out with extra pulses and soup pasta.

Thickening soups

You can thicken soup before serving to give it a smoother texture and more richness.

CORNFLOUR Because cornflour is maize flour stripped of everything except the purest starch, it requires little cooking. Measure the cornflour into a bowl – you will need 1–2 tbsp cornflour per 1 litre (1¾ pints) soup. Add about double the volume of cold water and whisk until the cornflour is completely dissolved. Stir into the soup and heat briefly. (Potato starch can be used in the same way as cornflour.)

EGG AND CREAM Cream adds texture and richness, but to thicken a soup, egg yolks and cream work better. Remove the soup from the heat. Using one yolk per 4 tbsp double or whipping cream, whisk them together in a bowl. Add a little of the hot soup – not too much, or the egg will curdle. Whisk well, add more soup, and whisk again. When you have a cupful of liquid, pour it back into the soup. You can turn on the heat again, but don't let the soup simmer or the egg yolk will curdle.

BREADCRUMBS Add fresh or dry breadcrumbs to the soup during cooking, a handful at a time. Cook for 20 minutes or so, then add more if you need to. Purée the soup if you want a smooth texture. (A handful of cooked rice or mashed potato works in the same way, but make sure they cook for a long time until tender.)

BEURRE MANIÉ This butter and flour paste is useful for thickening soups and sauces. Using equal parts of butter and flour – you will need 1–2 tbsp of each for a soup – cream the butter in a bowl with a wooden spoon and then mix in the flour thoroughly to make a smooth paste. Add to the soup gradually in small pieces, stirring well with each addition. Add only as much as you need to get the desired consistency. (You can store any left over beurre manié in a sealed container for up to three days in the refrigerator or freeze for up to six months.)

Chunky soups

1. Cut up the vegetables into bite-size pieces. Heat oil or butter in the soup pan and cook the onions and garlic until soft and lightly coloured.

2. Add the remaining ingredients, putting in the vegetables that need the longest cooking first. Pour in some stock and bring to the boil.

3. Simmer gently until all the ingredients are tender. If too much liquid cooks away, just add more.

4. If any ingredients need brief cooking, add them at the very end. Using something starchy in the soup will thicken the broth, or you can use any of the techniques on this page.

Puréeing soups

USING A JUG BLENDER Allow the soup to cool, then fill the jug about half full, making sure that there is more liquid than solids. Cover the lid with a teatowel and hold it on tightly. Blend until smooth, then add more solids and blend again until all the soup is smooth. (If you have a lot of soup, transfer each batch to a clean pan.)

USING A STICK BLENDER Allow the soup to cool. Stick the blender deep down into the soup, switch it on and keep it moving so that all the soup is puréed.

USING A MOULI The mouli-légumes is a traditional favourite of chefs, who require a perfectly uniform texture in their soups. It makes a fine purée although it takes longer than using a blender. Fit the fine plate to the mouli-légumes and set it over a bowl with a teatowel underneath to keep it from moving on the table. Fill the bowl of the mouli about halfway, putting in more solids than liquid. Work in batches if you have a particualy large quantity of soup. When the solids are puréed, repeat with the liquid.

USING A SIEVE If you don't have a blender or mouli-légumes, you can purée soup by pushing it through a sieve, although this will take a much longer time.

Partially puréed soups

1. For a smooth yet chunky soup, purée one-third to half of it, then stir back into the soup.

2. Alternatively, chop the vegetables, but set aside a few choice pieces. While the soup is cooking, steam or boil these pieces until just tender and refresh in cold water. Just before serving, cut into smaller pieces and add to the soup.

You can use almost any mixture of vegetables to make soup. This simple soup is filling and nourishing.

Simple Vegetable Soup
Serves 4

2 tbsp oil or 1 tbsp oil and 25g (1oz) butter
1 or 2 onions, finely chopped
1 or 2 garlic cloves, crushed (optional)
450g (1lb) chopped mixed vegetables, such as leeks, potatoes, celery, fennel, canned tomatoes and parsnip (these can be chopped finely or cut into larger dice for a chunky soup)
1.1 litres (2 pints) homemade stock
salt and ground black pepper

1. Heat the oil in a large pan and fry the onions until golden, then add the garlic, if using, and fry for a minute or two.

2. Add the vegetables and stock, bring to the boil and simmer for 20–30 minutes until the vegetables are tender. Leave chunky or blend until smooth if you prefer. Season to taste with salt and pepper.

Cooking potatoes, rice, pasta and grains

Wholesome and healthy, rice, grains and potatoes are everyday staples. Easy to prepare and cook, they are not only tasty, but also very economical and bulk out more expensive meat, poultry and fish.

Cooking potatoes

Boiling Potatoes

1. Peel or scrub old potatoes, scrape or scrub new potatoes. Cut large potatoes into even-sized chunks and put them into a pan with plenty of salted cold water.

2. Cover, bring to the boil, then reduce the heat and simmer until cooked – about 10 minutes for new potatoes, 15–20 minutes for old.

Mashed Potatoes
Serves 4

900g (2lb) floury potatoes, such as Maris Piper

125ml (4fl oz) full-fat milk

25g (1oz) butter

salt and ground black pepper

1. Peel the potatoes and cut into even-sized chunks. Boil as above until just tender, 15–20 minutes. Test with a small knife. Drain well.

2. Put the potatoes back in the pan and cover with a clean teatowel for 5 minutes, or warm them over a very low heat until the moisture has evaporated.

3. Pour the milk into a small pan and bring to the boil. Pour on to the potatoes with the butter and season.

4. Mash the potatoes until smooth.

Making risotto

Basic Risotto
Serves 4

1 onion, chopped

50g (2oz) butter

900ml (1½ pints) chicken stock

225g (8oz) risotto rice

50g (2oz) freshly grated Parmesan, plus extra to serve

1. Gently fry the onion in the butter for 10–15 minutes until it is very lightly coloured. Heat the stock in a pan and keep at a simmer. Add the rice to the butter and stir for 1–2 minutes until well coated.

2. Add a ladleful of hot stock and stir constantly until absorbed. Add the remaining stock a ladleful at a time, stirring, until the rice is al dente (tender but still with bite in the centre), about 20–30 minutes. Note: you may not need all the stock.

3. Stir in the grated Parmesan and serve immediately, with extra cheese passed separately.

Perfect risotto
- Use homemade stock, preferably with minimal salt – the stock cooks away, so the salt will be concentrated in the finished dish.
- Make sure the stock is hot while you are ladling it into the rice.

Cooking rice

There are two main types of rice: long-grain and short-grain. Long-grain rice is generally served as an accompaniment; the most commonly used type of long-grain rice in South-east Asian cooking is jasmine rice, also known as Thai fragrant rice. It has a distinctive taste and slightly sticky texture. Long-grain rice needs no special preparation, although it should be washed to remove excess starch. Put the rice into a bowl and cover with cold water. Stir until this becomes cloudy, then drain and repeat until the water is clear.

Long-grain rice

1. Use 50–75g (2–3oz) raw rice per person; measured by volume 50–75ml (2–2½fl oz). Measure the rice by volume and put it into a pan with a pinch of salt and twice the volume of boiling water (or stock).

2. Bring to the boil. Turn the heat down to low and set the timer for the time stated on the pack. The rice should be al dente: tender with a bite at the centre.

3. When the rice is cooked, fluff up the grains with a fork.

Perfect rice
If you cook rice often, you may want to invest in a special rice steamer. They are available in Asian supermarkets and some kitchen shops and give good, consistent results.

Cooking pasta

Use about 1 litre (1¾ pints) of water per 100g (3½oz) of pasta. Filled pasta is the only type of pasta that needs oil in the cooking water – the oil reduces friction, which could tear the wrappers and allow the filling to come out. If the recipe calls for cooking the pasta with a sauce after it has boiled, undercook the pasta slightly when boiling it. Rinse pasta after cooking only if you are going to cool it to use in a salad, then drain well and toss with oil.

Dried pasta

1. Heat the water with about 1 tsp salt per 100g (3½oz) pasta. Bring to a rolling boil, then add all the pasta and stir well for 30 seconds, to keep the pasta from sticking.

2. Once the water is boiling again, set the timer for 2 minutes less than the cooking time on the pack and cook uncovered.

3. Check the pasta when the timer goes off, then every 60 seconds until it is cooked al dente: tender, but with a bite at the centre. Drain in a colander.

Fresh pasta

Fresh pasta is cooked in the same way as dried, but for a shorter time. Bring the water to the boil. Add the pasta to the boiling water all at once and stir well. Set the timer for 2 minutes and keep testing every 30 seconds until the pasta is cooked al dente: tender, but with a bite at the centre. Drain in a colander.

Cooking couscous

Often mistaken for a grain, couscous is actually a type of pasta that originated in North Africa. It is perfect for making into salads or serving with stews and casseroles. It doesn't require cooking and can simply be soaked.

1. Measure the couscous in a jug and add 1½ times the volume of just-boiled water or stock.

2. Cover the bowl and leave to soak for 5 minutes. Fluff up with a fork before serving.

3. If using for a salad, leave the couscous to cool completely before adding the other salad ingredients.

Making omelettes

There are numerous different types of omelette – from the classic folded omelette made from simple beaten eggs to thick omelettes such as Spanish tortilla and Italian frittata.

Classic Omelette

1. To make an omelette for one person, heat a heavy-based 18cm (7in) frying pan or omelette pan. Using a fork, beat 2 eggs and season to taste with salt and pepper.

2. Add 15g (½oz) butter to the pan and let it sizzle for a few moments without browning, then pour in the eggs and stir a few times with a fork.

3. As the omelette begins to stick at the sides, lift it up and allow the uncooked egg to run into the gap.

4. When the omelette is nearly set and the underneath is brown, loosen the edges and give the pan a sharp shake to slide the omelette across.

5. Add a filling (such as grated cheese or fried mushrooms), if you like, and fold the far side of the omelette towards you. Tilt the pan to slide the omelette on to the plate and serve.

Perfect omelettes
- Don't add butter until the pan is already hot, otherwise it will brown too much.
- Beat the eggs lightly.
- Use a high heat.

Potato and Chorizo Tortilla
Serves 4

6 tbsp olive oil
450g (1lb) very thinly sliced potatoes
225g (8oz) thinly sliced onions
2 garlic cloves, chopped
50g (2oz) chorizo, cut into strips
6 large eggs
salt and ground black pepper

1. Heat the oil in an 18cm (7in) non-stick frying pan. Add the potatoes, onion and garlic and stir to coat. Cover and cook gently for 15 minutes, stirring occasionally, until the potato is soft. Season to taste with salt.

2. Preheat the grill. Add the chorizo to the pan. Beat the eggs and season with salt and pepper, then pour into the pan and cook for about 5 minutes until the edges are beginning to brown and the egg looks about three-quarters set.

3. Put the tortilla under the grill and quickly brown the top. Remove from the heat and leave to cool. Loosen the edges of the tortilla and serve cut into wedges.

Making batters

Batters are incredibly cheap to make and can serve a number of purposes. They're remarkably versatile for something so simple. All you need to remember when working with them is to mix quickly and lightly.

Pancakes
Makes 8 pancakes

125g (4oz) plain flour

a pinch of salt

1 medium egg

300ml (½ pint) milk

oil and butter to fry

1. Sift the flour and salt, make a well in the middle and whisk in the egg. Work in the milk, then leave to stand for 20 minutes.

2. Heat a pan and coat lightly with fat. Coat thinly with batter, then cook for 1½ –2 minutes until golden, carefully turning once.

3. Repeat to make 8 pancakes in total.

Thrifty Tip
Use half milk and half water if you don't have enough milk.

Sweet pancake fillings
1. Sprinkle with caster sugar and squeeze over lemon juice.

2. Spread with 1 tbsp chocolate spread and top with sliced banana.

Savoury pancake fillings
Almost any mixture of cooked vegetables, fish or chicken, flavoured with herbs and moistened with a little béchamel sauce, soured cream or cream cheese can be used. Try the following – just spoon on to the pancake, fold over and serve:

1. Chicken and sautéed mushrooms in béchamel sauce.

2. Smoked haddock and chopped hard-boiled egg with soured cream.

3. Ratatouille.

4. Sautéed spinach, pinenuts and feta cheese.

5. Mix 25g (1oz) each grated cheese and chopped ham with 1 tbsp crème fraîche.

Making shortcrust pastry

Shortcrust pastry is the simplest pastry. The homemade version is cheaper and more delicious than shop-bought and can be used for quiches, pies and tarts. When you've got time, make a large batch and freeze in blocks well wrapped in clingfilm.

Shortcrust Pastry
To make 125g (4oz) pastry

125g (4oz) plain flour
a pinch of salt
50g (2oz) unsalted butter, cut into small pieces
1 medium egg yolk

1. Sift the flour and salt into a bowl and add the butter. Using your fingertips or a pastry cutter, rub or cut the butter into the flour until the mixture resembles fine breadcrumbs.

2. Using a fork, mix in the egg yolk and 1½ tsp water until the mixture holds together; add a little more water if necessary.

3. Gather the dough in your hands and knead. Form into a ball, wrap tightly in clingfilm and chill for at least 30 minutes before using. (This 'relaxes' the pastry and prevents shrinkage when it is baked.)

Sweet Shortcrust Pastry
Make as for shortcrust pastry (above), adding 50g (2oz) caster sugar and 2 medium egg yolks at step 2.

Using a food processor

1. You can make shortcrust or sweet shortcrust using a food processor. Put the dry ingredients into the food processor and pulse quickly to mix. Cut the butter into small pieces and add. Process until the mixture resembles breadcrumbs – do not over-process.

2. Add the egg yolk(s) and a little water if necessary and pulse until the mixture just comes together. Continue as step 3 for shortcrust (left).

> ## Quantities
> Tart tins vary in depth, which affects the quantity of pastry needed. Approximate quantities:
>
> | Tart tin size | Quantity of pastry |
> |---|---|
> | 18cm (7in) | 125g (4oz) |
> | 20.5cm (8in) | 175g (6oz) |
> | 23cm (9in) | 200g (7oz) |
> | 25.5cm (10in) | 225g (8oz) |

Lining tart and pie tins

1. Working carefully, roll out the chilled dough on a lightly floured worksurface to make a sheet at least 5cm (2in) larger than the tart tin or pie dish. Roll the dough on to the rolling pin, then unroll it on to the tin, covering it completely with an even overhang all round. Don't stretch the dough.

2. Lift the hanging dough with one hand while you press it gently but firmly into the base and sides of the tin. Don't stretch the dough while you're pressing it down.

3. For a tart case, roll the rolling pin over the tin and remove the excess dough for later use. For a pie dish, ensure the pastry covers the lip of the dish.

4. Push the dough into and up the sides of the tin or dish, so that the dough rises a little over the edge.

Baking blind

Cooking the pastry before filling gives a crisp result.

1. Preheat the oven according to the recipe. Prick the pastry base with a fork. Cover with foil or greaseproof paper 7.5cm (3in) larger than the tin.

2. Spread baking beans on top. Bake for 15–20 minutes. Remove the foil or paper and beans and bake for 5–10 minutes until the pastry is light golden.

3. When cooked and while still hot, brush the base of the pastry with a little beaten egg, to seal the fork pricks or any cracks. This will prevent any filling leaking, which can make it difficult to remove the pie or tart from the tin.

Making cakes

With a few basic ingredients, such as flour, sugar, eggs and butter, you can create magnificent homemade cakes for a fraction of the cost of shop-bought alternatives.

Creamed Sponge

A classic Victoria sponge recipe can be used to make many cakes, including chocolate or fruit.

175g (6oz) softened butter, plus extra to grease

175g (6oz) caster sugar

3 medium eggs

175g (6oz) self-raising flour

150g (5oz) mascarpone

4 tbsp raspberry jam

icing sugar to dust

1. Preheat the oven to 180°C (160°C fan oven) mark 4. Grease two 18cm (7in) sandwich tins and line the base with greaseproof paper.

2. Put the butter and sugar into a bowl and beat with an electric whisk or wooden spoon until pale, soft and creamy.

3. Beat the eggs and gradually add to butter and sugar mixture, beating well until the mixture is thick and of dropping consistency. (If you like, add a spoonful of flour while adding the eggs to prevent curdling.)

4. Gently fold in the flour using a large metal spoon or spatula, then divide the mixture between the two tins and level the surface. Bake for 25–30 minutes until golden and firm to the touch. Cool slightly in the tins, then turn out on to a wire rack to cool completely.

5. When the cakes are cold, spread one with mascarpone and then the conserve. Place the other cake on top and lightly press together. Put on a serving plate and dust lightly with sifted icing sugar.

Cooling cakes

- Sponge cakes should be taken out of their tins soon after baking. Invert on to a wire rack, lined with sugar-dusted baking parchment.
- Leave fruit cakes to cool in the tin for 15 minutes before turning out.
- Allow rich fruit cakes to cool completely before turning out; there is a risk of breaking otherwise.

Testing sponges

1. Gently press the centre of the sponge. It should feel springy. If it's a whisked cake, it should be just shrinking away from the sides of the tin.

2. If you have to put it back into the oven, close the door gently so that the vibrations don't cause the cake to sink in the centre.

Making biscuits

Homemade biscuits are quick and simple to rustle up and most of the ingredients can come from your core store cupboard.

Creamed Choc-oat Cookies

Makes 18 cookies

125g (4oz) unsalted butter, softened, plus extra to grease

125g (4oz) white chocolate

125g (4oz) plain chocolate

125g (4oz) caster sugar

1 medium egg

1 tsp vanilla extract

125g (4oz) porridge oats

150g (5oz) plain flour

½ tsp baking powder

1. Preheat the oven to 180°C (160°C fan oven) mark 4 and lightly grease two baking sheets. Using a sharp knife, chop the white and plain chocolate into small chunks, no larger than 1cm (½in).

2. Cream the butter and sugar together in a bowl until pale. Add the egg, vanilla and oats. Sift in the flour and baking powder and mix until evenly combined. Stir in the chocolate chunks.

3. Place dessertspoonfuls of the mixture on to the baking sheets, spacing them apart to allow room for spreading. Flatten each one slightly with the back of a fork.

4. Bake for 12–15 minutes until risen and turning golden. Leave on the baking sheets for 5 minutes, then transfer to a wire rack to cool completely. Store in an airtight tin for up to one week. Biscuits using this creaming method firm up when cooled.

Bread basics

Baking bread is one of the greatest pleasures of the kitchen and one of the simplest. All you need are a few key store cupboard ingredients to get you started. Simple loaves provide the basis for experimentation, so they are the best place to begin.

Making bread

YEAST Fresh yeast is activated when blended with warm liquid. Dried yeast needs sugar to activate it (no sugar is needed if using milk): blend the yeast with a little of the water plus sugar (or milk) and leave for 15 minutes to froth. Fast-action (easy-blend) dried yeast is sprinkled directly into the flour and the liquid added afterwards. As a rough guide, for 700g (1lb 9oz) flour use 15g (½oz) fresh yeast, 1 tbsp dried yeast or a 7g sachet (2 tsp) fast-action dried yeast.

LIQUID This needs to be slightly warm to the fingertips. Milk gives bread a softer texture than water.

FLOUR Use strong white or wholemeal flour, or Granary flour.

SALT This controls fermentation, strengthens the gluten, which gives the bread its texture, and adds flavour.

FATS Some recipes use fat for flavour and to improve keeping quality.

Shaping loaves

The shape and size of bread can be varied almost endlessly after the first rise. After the second rising, the dough is ready to bake. Understanding the basics will ensure success.

Simple rolls

After knocking back, cut the dough into even pieces, each about 40g (1½oz). Roll each piece with the palm of your hand on a lightly floured work surface to make a ball. Place on a greased baking sheet, seam side down, and press down slightly. Cover with clingfilm and leave to prove for 30 minutes before baking.

Long loaves

After knocking back, cut the dough into pieces, each weighing about 200g (7oz). Roll one piece until it is about 40.5cm (16in) long. Transfer to a baking sheet, seam side down. Repeat with the remaining pieces. Cover with oiled clingfilm and leave to prove (rise) for 30 minutes. Slash 3–4 times before baking.

Cooling

If baked bread is left for too long either in the loaf tin or on the baking sheet, steam will gather and, as a result, the underneath will start to become soggy. To prevent this, always remove the loaf immediately and put it on a wire rack. Then leave it to cool completely before slicing, as you like.

Perfect baking

- Make sure shaped dough has risen sufficiently – usually to double.
- To prevent sticking, always oil or flour the loaf tin or baking sheet.
- Make sure the oven is at the correct temperature before baking.
- Bake on a preheated ceramic baking stone (from good kitchen shops) if possible, even if the bread is in a loaf tin. The heat of the stone will give the bread a crisp base.

Troubleshooting

The loaf hasn't risen enough:
- Not enough liquid was added.
- The yeast was not fresh.
- The dough was left to prove (rise) for too long causing it to collapse during baking.

The loaf is too dense in texture:
- The dough was not allowed to rise.
- Not enough, or too little, liquid.
- Dough not kneaded long enough.

White Farmhouse Loaf
Makes 1 large loaf

550g (1¼lb) strong plain white flour, plus extra to dust

125g (4oz) strong plain wholemeal flour

1 tbsp salt

1 tsp golden caster sugar

1½ tsp fast-action dried yeast (see note)

25g (1oz) butter, diced

vegetable oil

1. Sift the white flour into a large bowl and stir in the wholemeal flour, salt, sugar and yeast. Rub in the butter with your fingertips. Make a well in the middle and add about 450ml (¾ pint) warm water. Work to a smooth soft dough, adding a little extra water if necessary.

2. Knead for 10 minutes until smooth, then shape the dough into a ball and put into an oiled bowl. Cover and leave to rise in a warm place for 1–2 hours until doubled in size.

3. Knock back the dough on a lightly floured surface and shape into a large oval loaf. Transfer the dough to a floured baking sheet, cover loosely and leave to rise for a further 30 minutes.

4. Slash the top of the loaf with a sharp knife, dust with flour and bake at 230°C (210°C fan oven) mark 8 for 15 minutes. Lower the oven setting to 200°C (180°C fan oven) mark 6 and bake for a further 15–20 minutes or until the bread is risen and sounds hollow when tapped underneath. Cool on a wire rack.

NOTE
If available, use 25g (1oz) fresh yeast instead of dried. Crumble into a bowl, add the sugar, 150ml (¼ pint) of the warmed water and 4 tbsp of the white flour. Stir well to dissolve the yeast, then leave in a warm place for 20 minutes until very frothy. Continue as above, adding the frothy yeast to the dry ingredients with the rest of the water.

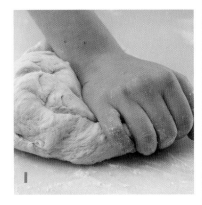

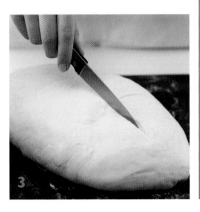

Brown Loaf
Makes 1 large loaf

300g (11oz) strong plain white flour, sifted, plus extra to dust

200g (7oz) strong plain wholemeal flour

15g (½oz) fresh yeast, or 1 tsp ordinary dried yeast

2 tsp salt

vegetable oil

1. Put both flours into a large bowl, make a well in the middle and pour in 325ml (11fl oz) tepid water. Crumble the fresh yeast into the water (if using dried yeast, just sprinkle it over). Draw a little of the flour into the water and yeast and mix to form a batter. Sprinkle the salt over the remaining dry flour, so that it doesn't come into contact with the yeast. Cover with a clean tea-towel and leave to 'sponge' for 20 minutes.

2. Combine the flour and salt with the batter to make a soft dough and knead for at least 10 minutes until the dough feels smooth and elastic. Shape into a ball, put into an oiled bowl, cover with the tea-towel and leave to rise at warm room temperature until doubled in size, about 2–3 hours.

> ### Cook's Tip
> The 'sponging' process in step 1 adds a fermentation stage, which gives a slightly lighter loaf.

3. Knock back the dough, knead briefly and shape into a round on a lightly floured baking sheet. Slash the top with a sharp knife and dust with flour. Cover and leave to rise for 45 minutes–1½ hours or until doubled in size and spongy. Preheat the oven to 200°C (180°C fan oven) mark 6.

4. Bake for 45–50 minutes or until the loaf sounds hollow when tapped underneath. Transfer to a wire rack and leave to cool.

Cornbread
Makes 16 slices

225g (8oz) coarse cornmeal
225g (8oz) strong plain white flour
1½ tsp fast-action dried yeast
1 tsp salt
½ tsp golden caster sugar
400ml (14fl oz) milk
15g (½oz) butter or margarine
vegetable oil

1. Combine all the dry ingredients in a large bowl. Heat the milk and butter in a small pan until the butter is melted, cool until tepid, then work into the dry ingredients to form a soft dough.

2. Knead for 8–10 minutes until smooth, then transfer the dough to an oiled bowl. Cover and leave to rise in a warm place for 1–1½ hours until doubled in size.

3. Oil a 20cm (8in) square cake tin. Knock back the dough and shape into a square a little smaller than the prepared tin. Press into the tin, cover loosely and leave to rise for a further 30 minutes. Preheat the oven to 220°C (200°C fan oven) mark 7.

4. Bake for 25–30 minutes until risen and golden. Leave the cornbread in the tin for 10 minutes, then transfer to a wire rack to cool. Serve cold, cut into fingers.

Soda Bread
Makes 14 slices

350g (12oz) plain wholemeal flour
125g (4oz) coarse oatmeal
2 tsp bicarbonate of soda
1 tsp salt
1 tsp thin honey
300ml (½ pint) buttermilk
2–3 tbsp milk
vegetable oil

1. Preheat the oven to 200°C (180°C fan oven) mark 6. Combine the flour with the other dry ingredients in a large bowl. Make a well in the middle and gradually beat in the honey, buttermilk and enough milk to form a soft dough.

2. Knead for 5 minutes until smooth. Shape the dough into a 20cm (8in) round and put on a lightly oiled baking sheet.

3. Using a sharp knife, cut a deep cross on top of the dough. Brush with a little milk and bake for 30–35 minutes until the bread is slightly risen and sounds hollow when tapped underneath. Cool on a wire rack; eat the same day.

Making pizza

Pizza is a great way to use leftovers – scatter with meat or chicken scraps, cooked vegetables, frozen peas... Just don't overload the base or it will become soggy.

Pizza

225g (8oz) strong white bread flour
7g sachet fast-action (easy-blend) dried yeast
½ tsp salt
4 tbsp extra virgin olive oil
cornmeal or flour to sprinkle

1. Sift the flour into a large bowl, stir in the yeast and salt and make a well in the centre. Pour 150ml (¼ pint) water into the well with 1 tbsp of the oil. Use your fingertips or a large spoon to stir together.

2. Turn on to a lightly floured surface and knead for 5 minutes or until the dough is smooth. It should be quite soft. Lightly oil the mixing bowl, put in the dough and turn it over to coat in the remaining oil. Cover with oiled clingfilm or a clean teatowel. Put in a warm, draught-free place to rise for 45 minutes or until doubled in size.

3. Preheat the oven to 240°C (220°C fan oven) mark 9. Quickly punch the dough to knock it back, then roll it out into a circle or rectangle about 1cm (½in) thick.

4. Sprinkle a baking sheet fairly generously with cornmeal or plain flour. Roll the dough over the rolling pin and lift it on to the baking sheet, then unroll and spread with sauce.

5. Add your choice of toppings (see below) and bake for 20–25 minutes until the rim is crusty and the topping is bubbling.

Toppings
Scatter one or two of the following on top of a basic cheese and tomato pizza:
- Bacon or pancetta bits or slices of prosciutto
- Rocket leaves
- Dried chilli flakes
- Capers
- Sliced sun-dried tomatoes
- Pepperoni slices
- Roasted peppers
- Artichoke hearts, drained and quartered
- Sliced mushrooms

Perfect pizzas
- Pizza should not be a heavy dish so add toppings with a light hand.
- If you can't get good mozzarella, use another cheese instead – Taleggio, Fontina, or even just good Cheddar all work well.
- A ceramic baking stone (from good kitchen shops) is extremely useful for cooking pizza, to help cook the pizza evenly and give crunchiness to the base. (Put the stone into the oven before preheating.) Alternatively, use a metal baking sheet.

2

SOUPS AND SALADS

Autumn Barley Soup

Serves	Preparation Time	Cooking Time	Nutritional Information (Per Serving)
4	10 minutes	1 hour 5 minutes	83 calories | 1g fat (of which trace saturates) 16g carbohydrate | 0.6g salt | **V** | **DF**

25g (1oz) pot barley, washed and drained

1 litre (1¾ pints) vegetable stock

2 large carrots, scrubbed and diced

1 turnip, peeled and diced

2 leeks, washed and sliced

2 celery sticks, trimmed and diced

1 small onion, finely chopped

1 bouquet garni

2tbsp freshly chopped parsley

salt and ground black pepper

1. Put the barley and stock into a saucepan. Simmer for 45 minutes until tender.

2. Add the vegetables to the pan with the bouquet garni and season to taste with salt and pepper. Bring to the boil and simmer for about 20 minutes or until the vegetables are tender.

3. Discard the bouquet garni. Add the parsley, stir well and serve immediately.

Try Something Different
Replace the barley with 75g (3oz) soup pasta and add for the last 10 minutes of cooking.

Squash and Sweet Potato Soup

Serves	Preparation Time	Cooking Time	Nutritional Information (Per Serving)
8	20 minutes	25 minutes	90 calories | 2g fat (of which trace saturates) 17g carbohydrate | 0.1g salt | **V** | **DF**

I tbsp olive oil

I large onion, finely chopped

2 red chillies, seeded and chopped

2 tsp coriander seeds, crushed, or I tsp ground coriander

I butternut squash, around 750g (Ilb 10oz), peeled and roughly chopped

2 medium sweet potatoes, peeled and roughly chopped

2 medium tomatoes, skinned and diced

1.7 litres (3 pints) hot vegetable stock

1. Heat the oil in a large pan and fry the onion until soft – about 10 minutes. Add the chillies and coriander seeds and cook for 1–2 minutes.

2. Add the squash, potatoes and tomatoes and cook for 5 minutes. Add the hot stock, cover and bring to the boil. Simmer gently for 15 minutes or until the vegetables are soft.

3. Cool a little, then whiz the soup in batches in a food processor or blender until smooth. Reheat to serve.

Freezing Tip

- **To freeze:** cool after step 3 and put into a sealable container. Seal and freeze for up to 3 months.
- **To use:** thaw for 4 hours at cool room temperature. Put in a pan and bring to the boil. Simmer for 10 minutes or until hot right through.

Cream of Chicken Soup

Serves	Preparation Time	Cooking Time	Nutritional Information (Per Serving)
4	10 minutes	35 minutes	107 calories | 3g fat (of which 2g saturates) 11g carbohydrate | 0.1g salt

3 tbsp plain flour

150ml (¼ pint) milk

1.1 litres (2 pints) chicken stock

125g (4oz) cooked chicken, diced

I tsp lemon juice

pinch of freshly grated nutmeg

2 tbsp single cream

salt and ground black pepper

croûtons and parsley sprigs to garnish

1. In a large bowl, blend the flour with a little of the milk until it makes a smooth cream.

2. Bring the stock to the boil, then stir it into the blended mixture. Return to the pan and simmer gently for 20 minutes.

3. Stir in the chicken, lemon juice, nutmeg and salt and pepper to taste. Mix the rest of the milk with the cream and stir in. Reheat without boiling.

4. Taste and adjust the seasoning, then pour into four warmed soup bowls. Sprinkle with croûtons and parsley sprigs and serve.

Try Something Different

Swap the chicken for an equal amount of cooked turkey.

Leek and Potato Soup

Serves	Preparation Time	Cooking Time	Nutritional Information (Per Serving)
4	10 minutes	45 minutes	117 calories | 6g fat (of which 4g saturates) 13g carbohydrate | 0.1g salt | V | GF

25g (1oz) butter

1 onion, finely chopped

1 garlic clove, crushed

550g (1¼lb) leeks, chopped

200g (7oz) floury potatoes, peeled and sliced

1.3 litres (2¼ pints) hot vegetable stock

crème fraîche and chopped chives to garnish

1. Melt the butter in a pan over a gentle heat and cook the onion for 10–15 minutes until soft. Add the garlic and cook for a further 1 minute. Add the leeks and cook for 5–10 minutes until softened. Add the potatoes and toss together with the leeks.

2. Pour in the hot stock and bring to the boil. Simmer the soup for 20 minutes until the potatoes are tender. Cool a little, then whiz in a food processor or blender until smooth.

3. Reheat before serving, garnished with crème fraîche and chives.

Try Something Different
Vichyssoise is simply leek and potato soup served well chilled. Pass the soup through a sieve for a finer texture, and serve as an elegant first course.

Cook's Tip
Snip any leftover chives and freeze in an ice cube tray with a little water.

Spinach and Rice Soup

Serves	Preparation Time	Cooking Time	Nutritional Information (Per Serving)
6	10 minutes	25–30 minutes	222 calories | 14g fat (of which 2g saturates) 20g carbohydrate | 0.2g salt | V

4 tbsp extra virgin olive oil

1 onion, finely chopped

2 garlic cloves, crushed

2 tsp freshly chopped thyme or a large pinch of dried thyme

2 tsp freshly chopped rosemary or a large pinch of dried rosemary

grated zest of ½ lemon

2 tsp ground coriander

¼ tsp cayenne pepper

125g (4oz) arborio (risotto) rice

1.1 litres (2 pints) vegetable stock

225g (8oz) fresh or frozen and thawed spinach, shredded

4 tbsp pesto sauce

salt and ground black pepper

extra virgin olive oil and freshly shaved Parmesan to serve

1. Heat half the oil in a pan. Add the onion, garlic, herbs, lemon zest and spices, then fry gently for 5 minutes.

2. Add the remaining oil with the rice and cook, stirring, for 1 minute. Add the stock, bring to the boil and simmer gently for 20 minutes or until the rice is tender.

3. Stir the spinach into the soup with the pesto sauce. Cook for 2 minutes, then season to taste with salt and pepper.

4. Pour into six warmed soup bowls and serve drizzled with a little oil and topped with Parmesan.

Celery Soup

Serves	Preparation Time	Cooking Time	Nutritional Information (Per Serving)
4	10 minutes	30–40 minutes	123 calories | 10g fat (of which 5g saturates) 6g carbohydrate | 0.8g salt | GF

25g (1oz) butter

1 tbsp olive oil

1 medium leek, sliced

6 celery sticks, finely sliced

1 tbsp finely chopped sage

600ml (1 pint) hot chicken stock

300ml (½ pint) milk

salt and ground black pepper

basil sprigs to garnish

1. Melt the butter in a pan and add the oil. Add the leek and fry for 10–15 minutes until soft. Add the celery and sage and cook for 5 minutes to soften.

2. Add the hot stock and milk to the pan, then season to taste with salt and pepper, cover and bring to the boil. Reduce the heat and simmer for 10–15 minutes until the celery is tender.

3. Leave to cool a little, then whiz in a food processor or blender until smooth. Return the soup to the pan, reheat gently and season to taste with salt and pepper. Pour into four warmed soup bowls and garnish with basil and black pepper.

Try Something Different
- Instead of celery, use 500g (1lb 2oz) celeriac, peeled and diced.
- Replace the sage with 2 tsp freshly chopped thyme.

Hearty Chicken Soup with Dumplings

Serves	Preparation Time	Cooking Time	Nutritional Information (Per Serving)
4	20 minutes	40 minutes	319 calories | 15g fat (of which 5g saturates) 29g carbohydrate | 0.3g salt

2 tbsp olive oil

2 celery stalks, roughly chopped

150g (5oz) carrots, roughly chopped

150g (5oz) waxy salad potatoes, thinly sliced

275g (10oz) chicken breast, thinly sliced

2 litres (3½ pints) hot chicken stock

100g (3½oz) plain flour

½ tsp baking powder

1 medium egg, well beaten

25g (1oz) butter, melted

a splash of milk

75g (3oz) frozen peas

salt and ground black pepper

handful of chives, roughly chopped, to garnish

1. Heat the oil in a large pan and add the celery, carrots and potatoes. Cook for 5 minutes or until the vegetables are beginning to caramelise around the edges. Add the chicken and fry for 3 minutes until just starting to turn golden. Pour in the hot stock and simmer for 15 minutes, skimming the surface occasionally to remove any scum.

2. To make the dumplings, sift the flour, baking powder and ½ tsp salt into a bowl. Season with black pepper. Combine the egg, melted butter and milk in a separate bowl, then stir quickly into the flour to make a stiff batter.

3. Drop half-teaspoonfuls of the dumpling mixture into the soup, then cover and simmer for a further 15 minutes. Stir in the peas and heat through. Serve garnished with chives.

Pepper and Lentil Soup

Serves	Preparation Time	Cooking Time	Nutritional Information (Per Serving)
6	15 minutes	45 minutes	109 calories | 4g fat (of which 1g saturates) 16g carbohydrate | 0.1g salt | V | DF

1 tbsp vegetable oil

1 onion, finely chopped

1 celery stick, chopped

1 leek, chopped

1 carrot, chopped

2 red peppers, seeded and diced

225g (8oz) red lentils

400g can chopped tomatoes

1 litre (1¾) pints hot light vegetable stock

25g pack flat-leafed parsley, chopped

salt and ground black pepper

1. Heat the oil in a pan, add the onion, celery, leek and carrot and cook for 10–15 minutes until soft.

2. Add the red peppers and cook for 5 minutes, then stir in the lentils. Add the tomatoes and hot stock and season to taste with salt and pepper.

3. Cover the pan and bring to the boil, then reduce the heat and cook, uncovered, for 25 minutes until the lentils are soft and the vegetables tender.

4. Stir in the parsley, ladle into six warmed soup bowls and serve with toast.

Chicken and Bean Soup

Serves	Preparation Time	Cooking Time	Nutritional Information (Per Serving)
4	10 minutes	30 minutes	351 calories | 6g fat (of which 1g saturates) 48g carbohydrate | 2.7g salt | DF

1 tbsp olive oil

1 onion, finely chopped

4 celery sticks, chopped

1 red chilli, seeded and roughly chopped

2 skinless chicken breasts, about 125g (4oz) each, cut into strips

1 litre (1¾ pints) hot chicken or vegetable stock

100g (3½ oz) bulgur wheat

2 x 400g cans cannellini beans, drained and rinsed

400g can chopped tomatoes

25g (1oz) flat-leafed parsley, roughly chopped

wholegrain bread and hummus to serve

1. Heat the oil in a large heavy-based pan. Add the onion, celery and chilli and cook over a low heat for 10 minutes or until softened. Add the chicken and stir-fry for 3–4 minutes until golden.

2. Add the hot stock to the pan and bring to a simmer. Stir in the bulgur wheat and then simmer for 15 minutes.

3. Stir in the cannellini beans and tomatoes and bring to a simmer. Ladle into four warmed soup bowls and sprinkle with chopped parsley. Serve with wholegrain bread and hummus.

Carrot and Coriander Soup

Serves	Preparation Time	Cooking Time	Nutritional Information (Per Serving)
6	15 minutes	about 30 minutes	140 calories | 11g fat (of which 7g saturates) 10g carbohydrate | 0.2g salt | V

40g (1½ oz) butter

175g (6oz) leeks, sliced

450g (1lb) carrots, sliced

2 tsp ground coriander

1 tsp plain flour

1.2 litres (2 pints) vegetable stock

150ml (¼ pint) single cream

salt and ground black pepper

coriander leaves, roughly torn, to serve

1. Melt the butter in a large pan. Add the leeks and carrots, stir, then cover the pan and cook gently for 7–10 minutes until the vegetables begin to soften but not colour.

2. Stir in the ground coriander and flour and cook, stirring, for 1 minute.

3. Add the stock and bring to the boil, stirring. Season to taste with salt and pepper, then cover and simmer for about 20 minutes, until the vegetables are tender.

4. Allow to cool a little, then whiz in a food processor or blender until quite smooth.

5. Return to the pan and stir in the cream. Adjust the seasoning and reheat gently; do not boil. Serve scattered with torn coriander leaves.

Quick Winter Minestrone

Serves	Preparation Time	Cooking Time	Nutritional Information (Per Serving)
4	10 minutes	45 minutes	334 calories | 11g fat (of which 3g saturates) 47g carbohydrate | 1.5g salt | V

2 tbsp olive oil

1 small onion, finely chopped

1 carrot, chopped

1 celery stick, chopped

1 garlic clove, crushed

2 tbsp chopped fresh thyme

1 litre (1¾ pints) vegetable stock

400g can chopped tomatoes

400g can borlotti beans, drained and rinsed

125g (4oz) small pasta

175g (6oz) Savoy cabbage, shredded

salt and ground black pepper

fresh pesto, toasted ciabatta and extra virgin olive oil to serve

1. Heat the oil in a large pan and add the onion, carrot and celery. Cook for 8–10 minutes until softened, then add the garlic and thyme and fry for another 2–3 minutes.

2. Add the stock, tomatoes and half the borlotti beans. Mash the remaining beans, stir into the soup and simmer for 30 minutes, adding the pasta and cabbage for the last 10 minutes of cooking time.

3. Check the seasoning, then serve the soup in individual bowls with a dollop of fresh pesto on top and slices of toasted ciabatta drizzled with extra virgin olive oil on the side.

French Onion Soup

Serves	Preparation Time	Cooking Time	Nutritional Information *(Per Serving)*
4	30 minutes	about 1 hour	438 calories	21g fat (of which 13g saturates) 45g carbohydrate	1.3g salt	V

75g (3oz) butter

700g (1½lb) small onions, finely chopped

3 garlic cloves, crushed

1 tbsp plain flour

200ml (7fl oz) dry white wine (optional)

1.5 litres (2½ pints) vegetable stock

bouquet garni (see Cook's Tip)

salt and ground black pepper

1 small baguette, cut into slices 1cm (½in) thick, to serve

50g (2oz) Gruyère cheese or Cheddar, grated, to serve

1. Melt the butter in a large heavy-based pan. Add the onions and cook slowly over a very low heat, stirring frequently, until very soft and golden brown; this should take at least 30 minutes. Add the garlic and flour and cook, stirring, for 1 minute.

2. Pour in the wine, if using, and let bubble until reduced by half. Add the stock, bouquet garni and seasoning. Bring to the boil and simmer gently, uncovered, for 20–30 minutes.

3. Discard the bouquet garni and let the soup cool a little. Whiz one-third in a food processor or blender until smooth, then stir this back into the soup in the pan.

4. Preheat the grill. Lightly toast the slices of French bread on both sides. Reheat the soup and adjust the seasoning.

5. Divide the soup among four ovenproof soup bowls. Float two or three slices of toast on each portion and sprinkle thickly with the grated cheese. Stand the bowls under the hot grill until the cheese has melted and turned golden brown. Serve at once.

Cook's Tip
To make a bouquet garni, tie together a sprig each of thyme and parsley with a bay leaf and a piece of celery.

Full-of-goodness Broth

Serves	Preparation Time	Cooking Time	Nutritional Information *(Per Serving)*
4	10 minutes	6–8 minutes	107 calories | 4g fat (of which trace saturates) 9g carbohydrate | 1g salt | **V** | **DF** | **GF**

1–2 tbsp medium curry paste

200ml (7fl oz) reduced-fat coconut milk

600ml (1 pint) hot vegetable stock

200g (7oz) smoked tofu, cubed

2 pak choi, chopped

handful of sugarsnap peas

4 spring onions, chopped

lime wedges to serve

1. Heat the curry paste in a pan for 1–2 minutes. Add the coconut milk and hot stock.

2. Bring to the boil, then add the smoked tofu, pak choi, sugarsnap peas and spring onions. Simmer for 1–2 minutes. Pour into four warmed soup bowls and serve with lime wedges to squeeze in.

Try Something Different
For a non-vegetarian soup, replace the smoked tofu with shredded leftover roast chicken and simmer for 2–3 minutes.

Easy Pea Soup

Serves	Preparation Time	Cooking Time	Nutritional Information (Per Serving)
4	2 minutes, plus thawing	15 minutes	408 calories | 9g fat (of which 2g saturates) 69g carbohydrate | 1.8g salt | V | DF

1 small baguette, thinly sliced

2 tbsp basil-infused olive oil, plus extra to drizzle

450g (1lb) frozen peas, thawed

600ml (1 pint) vegetable stock

salt and ground black pepper

1. Preheat the oven to 220°C (200°C fan oven) mark 7. To make the croûtes, put the bread on a baking sheet, drizzle with 2 tbsp flavoured oil and bake for 10–15 minutes until golden.

2. Meanwhile, put the peas into a food processor, add the stock and season with salt and pepper. Blend for 2–3 minutes.

3. Pour the soup into a pan and bring to the boil, then reduce the heat and simmer for 10 minutes. Ladle into four warmed soup bowls, add the croûtes, drizzle with extra oil and sprinkle with salt and pepper. Serve immediately.

Thrifty Tip
To make your own basil oil, put a large handful of basil into a sterilised jar and cover with extra virgin olive oil. Shake to mix. Store in the fridge for one week and use within two weeks after opening. Strain the oil before using if you prefer.

Tomato Salad Soup with Bruschetta

Serves	Preparation Time	Cooking Time	Nutritional Information *(Per Serving)*
4	15 minutes, plus marinating and chilling	about 30 minutes	469 calories | 23g fat (of which 4g saturates) 52g carbohydrate | 1.5g salt | V

700g (1½ lb) ripe plum tomatoes, thinly sliced

6 spring onions, trimmed and finely chopped

zest of ½ lemon

2 tbsp freshly chopped basil

125ml (4fl oz) extra virgin olive oil, plus extra to drizzle

2 tbsp balsamic vinegar

2–3 garlic cloves

a pinch of sugar

60ml (2fl oz) chilled vodka*

1 tbsp Worcestershire sauce

a few drops of Tabasco

150ml (¼ pint) tomato juice

8 thin slices French bread

fresh basil leaves to garnish

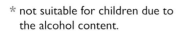

* not suitable for children due to the alcohol content.

1. Put the tomatoes into a large shallow dish and scatter the spring onions, lemon zest and chopped basil on top.

2. Blend together the oil, vinegar, 1 garlic clove, the sugar, vodka, Worcestershire sauce and Tabasco. Season to taste with salt and pepper and pour over the tomatoes. Cover and leave to marinate for 2 hours at room temperature.

3. Whiz the tomato salad and tomato juice in a food processor or blender until very smooth. Transfer to a bowl and leave to chill in the fridge for 1 hour.

4. Just before serving, preheat the grill. Put the bread slices on the grill rack and toast lightly on both sides. Rub each one with the remaining crushed garlic and drizzle with extra virgin olive oil. Spoon the soup into serving bowls and garnish with black pepper and oil. Garnish the bruschetta with fresh basil leaves and serve at once with the soup.

Cook's Tip
If you don't want to use vodka, replace with 60ml (2fl oz) vegetable stock or water.

Cheese Coleslaw with Roast Chicken

Serves	Preparation Time	Nutritional Information (Per Serving)
4	15 minutes	270 calories | 23g fat (of which 7g saturates) | 8g carbohydrate | 0.6g salt | GF

1 baby white cabbage, thinly shredded

4 spring onions, finely chopped

1 large carrot, finely shredded

75g (3oz) mature Cheddar, grated

6 tbsp mayonnaise

ground black pepper

cress to garnish

sliced roast chicken to serve

1. In a large bowl, mix together the cabbage, spring onions, carrot, cheese and mayonnaise. Season with pepper.

2. Divide among four small bowls or plates and snip some cress over. Serve with slices of roast chicken

Try Something Different

- Use Gruyère or Emmenthal instead of Cheddar.
- Add freshly chopped chives or parsley.
- Sprinkle with 1 tbsp mixed seeds just before serving.

Smoked Mackerel Salad

Serves	Preparation Time	Nutritional Information *(Per Serving)*
4	15 minutes	656 calories | 56g fat (of which 10g saturates) | 16g carbohydrate | 2.4g salt | DF | GF

250g (9oz) cooked (vacuum-packed without vinegar) beetroot, diced

1 tbsp olive oil

2 tsp white wine vinegar

350g (12oz) potato salad

1–2 tbsp lemon juice

4 peppered smoked mackerel fillets, skinned and flaked

2 tbsp freshly chopped chives, plus extra to garnish

salt and ground black pepper

1. Put the beetroot into a bowl and sprinkle with the oil and vinegar. Season to taste with salt and pepper and toss together.

2. In a large bowl, mix the potato salad with the lemon juice to taste. Season with salt and pepper. Add the flaked mackerel and chopped chives and toss together.

3. Just before serving, pile the mackerel mixture into four serving bowls. Sprinkle the beetroot over the top of the salad and garnish with chives.

Smoked Mackerel Citrus Salad

Serves	Preparation Time	Cooking Time	Nutritional Information (Per Serving)
6	10 minutes	5 minutes	299 calories | 26g fat (of which 5g saturates) 4g carbohydrate | 1g salt | DF | GF

200g (7oz) green beans

200g (7oz) smoked mackerel fillets

125g (4oz) mixed watercress, spinach and rocket

4 spring onions, sliced

1 avocado, halved, stoned, peeled and sliced

For the dressing

1 tbsp olive oil

1 tbsp freshly chopped coriander

grated zest and juice of 1 orange

1. Blanch the green beans in boiling water for 3 minutes until they are just tender. Drain, rinse under cold running water, drain well, then tip into a bowl.

2. Preheat the grill, then cook the mackerel for 2 minutes until warmed through. Flake into bite-size pieces, discard the skin and add the fish to the bowl with the salad leaves, spring onions and avocado.

3. Whisk all the dressing ingredients together in a small bowl. Pour over the salad, toss well and serve immediately.

Thrifty Tips
This salad is perfect for using up leftover cooked green beans. You can also use frozen green beans as a standby.

Leftover mackerel fillets can be turned into a quick pâté. Whiz in a food processor with the zest of a lemon and enough crème fraîche to make a spreadable consistency.

Warm Tofu, Fennel and Bean Salad

Serves	Preparation Time	Cooking Time	Nutritional Information (Per Serving)
4	10 minutes	15 minutes	150 calories | 6g fat (of which 1g saturates) 15g carbohydrate | 0.8g salt | V | DF | GF

1 tbsp olive oil, plus 1 tsp

1 red onion, finely sliced

1 fennel bulb, finely sliced

1 tbsp cider vinegar

400g can butter beans, drained and rinsed

2 tbsp freshly chopped flat-leafed parsley

200g (7oz) smoked tofu

1. Heat 1 tbsp oil in a large frying pan. Add the onion and fennel and cook over a medium heat for 5–10 minutes. Add the cider vinegar and heat through for 2 minutes. Stir in the butter beans and parsley. Tip into a bowl.

2. Slice the tofu into eight lengthways. Add to the pan with the remaining oil. Cook for 2 minutes on each side or until golden. Divide the bean mixture among four plates and add two slices of tofu to each plate.

Warm Bacon Salad

Serves	Preparation Time	Cooking Time	Nutritional Information *(Per Serving)*
4	10 minutes	10–15 minutes	188 calories | 15g fat (of which 5g saturates) 6g carbohydrate | 0.8g salt

120g bag soft salad leaves

1 medium red onion, thinly sliced

150g (5oz) diced streaky bacon

2 thick slices white bread, diced

4 medium eggs

40g (1½oz) Parmesan, pared into shavings with a vegetable peeler

For the dressing

1 tbsp Dijon mustard

2 tbsp red wine vinegar

2 tbsp fruity olive oil

salt and ground black pepper

1. Put the salad leaves and onion into a large bowl. Fry the bacon in a non-stick frying pan until it begins to release some fat. Add the diced bread and continue to fry until the bacon is golden and crisp.

2. Put all the dressing ingredients into a small bowl, season with salt and pepper and whisk together.

3. Half-fill a small pan with cold water and bring to the boil. Turn the heat right down – there should be just a few bubbles on the base of the pan. Break the eggs into a cup, then tip them gently into the pan and cook for 3–4 minutes, using a metal spoon to baste the tops with a little of the hot water. Lift the eggs out of the water with a slotted spoon and drain on kitchen paper.

4. Tip the bacon, bread and any pan juices over the salad leaves. Add the Parmesan, then pour the dressing over. Toss well, then divide between two plates. Top each with an egg, season to taste with salt and pepper and serve.

Warm Lentil and Egg Salad

Serves	Preparation Time	Cooking Time	Nutritional Information *(Per Serving)*
4	15 minutes	35–40 minutes	317 calories | 10g fat (of which 2g saturates) 37g carbohydrate | 0.7g salt | V | DF | GF

1 tbsp olive oil

1 onion, finely chopped

1 carrot, finely chopped

1 celery stick, finely chopped

2 red peppers, seeded and roughly chopped

200g (7oz) flat mushrooms, sliced

200g (7oz) lentils, rinsed and drained

600ml (1 pint) hot vegetable stock

4 medium eggs

100g (3½ oz) baby leaf spinach

2 tbsp balsamic vinegar

ground black pepper

1. Heat the oil in a large pan. Add the onion, carrot and celery and cook for 5 minutes. Add the peppers and mushrooms, cover and cook for a further 5 minutes. Stir in the lentils and hot stock and bring to the boil, then cover the pan and simmer for 25–30 minutes.

2. Meanwhile, bring a large pan of water to the boil. Break the eggs into the water and cook for 3–4 minutes. Lift them out with a slotted spoon, drain on kitchen paper and keep warm.

3. A couple of minutes before the end of the lentil cooking time, add the spinach and cook until wilted. Stir in the vinegar. Spoon on to four plates or bowls and top each with a poached egg. Season with pepper and serve.

Tomato and Mozzarella Pasta Salad

Serves	Preparation Time	Cooking Time	Nutritional Information *(Per Serving)*
4	20 minutes, plus cooling	10–12 minutes	665 calories | 34g fat (of which 12g saturates) 70g carbohydrate | 0.7g salt | V

2 tsp lemon juice

7 tbsp basil-infused olive oil

2 garlic cloves, crushed

350g (12oz) dried penne pasta

250g (9oz) mozzarella,
cut into chunks

700g (1½lb) vine-ripened tomatoes,
skinned, seeded and cut into chunks

½ large red chilli, seeded and
finely sliced

½ large green chilli, seeded and
finely sliced

salt and ground black pepper

fresh flat-leafed parsley or
basil to garnish

Try Something Different

- To serve this dish hot, put 5 tbsp basil-infused oil in a frying pan, add the garlic and chillies and cook for 1 minute. Add the drained pasta and mix well, then add the tomatoes and mozzarella. Garnish and serve.
- Instead of mozzarella, use Gorgonzola or Brie.
- You can use ½ tsp dried crushed chillies instead of fresh parsley or basil, then serve.

1. Put some salt and pepper into a small bowl, whisk in the lemon juice, followed by the flavoured oil and the garlic, then set aside.

2. Cook the pasta in a large pan of lightly salted boiling water according to the packet instructions. Drain well, then tip into a large bowl and toss with 2 tbsp of the dressing (this will prevent the pasta from sticking together); set aside to cool. Put the mozzarella into a large bowl with the remaining dressing and set aside.

3. When ready to serve (see Try Something Different), add the pasta to the mozzarella with the tomatoes and chillies. Toss together and season well with salt and pepper. Garnish with parsley or basil and serve.

Pasta and Pastrami Salad

Serves	Preparation Time	Cooking Time	Nutritional Information (Per Serving)
4	10 minutes	20 minutes	72 calories	1g fat (of which 0.5g saturates) 12g carbohydrate	0.4g salt	DF

300g (11oz) cooked pasta, cooled

125g (4oz) pastrami, diced

4 tomatoes, chopped

1 cucumber, chopped

3 tbsp freshly chopped parsley

1 medium red onion, finely chopped

For the dressing

wholegrain mustard to taste

6 tbsp vinaigrette dressing (see page 26)

1. Combine all the ingredients for the salad in a salad bowl.

2. Mix the mustard into the vinaigrette, pour on to the salad and toss.

Greek Pasta Salad

Serves	Preparation Time	Cooking Time	Nutritional Information (Per Serving)
4	10 minutes	10–15 minutes	191 calories	14g fat (of which 4g saturates) 13g carbohydrate	1.3g salt	V

5 tbsp extra virgin olive oil

3 tbsp lemon juice

300g (10oz) cooked pasta shapes, cooled

150g (5oz) feta cheese, crumbled

6 tomatoes, roughly chopped

4 tbsp small pitted black olives

1 cucumber, roughly chopped

1 large red onion, finely sliced

salt and ground black pepper

freshly chopped mint and lemon zest to garnish

1. Mix the oil and lemon juice together in a salad bowl, then add the pasta, feta cheese, tomatoes, olives, cucumber and onion.

2. Season to taste with salt and pepper and stir to mix, then garnish with chopped mint and lemon zest and serve.

Bacon and Egg Salad

Serves	Preparation Time	Cooking Time	Nutritional Information *(Per Serving)*
4	10 minutes	10 minutes	360 calories | 27g fat (of which 8g saturates) 9g carbohydrate | 3.1g salt

4 medium eggs

250g (9oz) rindless smoked bacon

150g (5oz) cherry tomatoes

2 slices thick-cut bread

3 tbsp mayonnaise

½ lemon

25g (1oz) freshly grated Parmesan

2 Little Gem lettuces

ground black pepper

1. Heat a pan of water until simmering, add the eggs and boil for 6 minutes. Cool completely under cold water, peel and set aside.

2. Meanwhile, heat a griddle pan, then fry the bacon for 5 minutes until crisp. Remove from the pan and chop into large pieces. Leave to cool.

3. Add the tomatoes and bread to the pan and fry in the bacon juices for 2–3 minutes until the bread is crisp and the tomatoes are starting to char. Remove from the heat, chop the bread into bite-size croûtons and set aside.

4. To make the dressing, put the mayonnaise into a bowl and squeeze in the lemon juice. Add the Parmesan to the bowl and mix. Season with pepper.

5. Separate the Little Gem leaves and put into a large serving bowl. Cut the eggs in half and add to the bowl with the bacon, tomatoes and croûtons. Drizzle the dressing over, toss lightly and serve.

Easy Chicken Salad

Serves	Preparation Time	Nutritional Information (Per Serving)
4	10 minutes	81 calories | 5g fat (of which 1g saturates) | 4g carbohydrate | 0.2g salt | DF | GF

450g (1lb) shredded roast chicken, skin discarded

2 large carrots, chopped

3 celery sticks, chopped

½ cucumber, chopped

200g (7oz) ripe cherry tomatoes, chopped

4 tbsp hummus

1 lemon to serve

1. Put the chicken into a shallow bowl. Add the carrot, celery, cucumber and cherry tomatoes.

2. Top with the hummus and serve with lemon for squeezing over the salad.

Try Something Different

- For an even more nutritious salad, add a few pumpkin seeds or sunflower seeds, or a handful of sprouted seeds such as alfalfa, or chopped watercress.
- For extra bite, add a little finely chopped red chilli; for extra sweetness, add some strips of red pepper.
- For extra flavour, add some chopped coriander or torn basil leaves.

Chicken Caesar Salad

Serves	Preparation Time	Cooking Time	Nutritional Information (Per Serving)
4	15–20 minutes	12 minutes	498 calories | 31g fat (of which 9g saturates) 7g carbohydrate | 1.4g salt

2 tbsp olive oil

1 garlic clove, crushed

2 thick slices country-style bread, cubed

6 tbsp freshly grated Parmesan

1 cos lettuce, chilled and cut into bite-size pieces

700g (1½lb) cooked chicken breast, sliced

For the dressing

4 tbsp mayonnaise

2 tbsp lemon juice

1 tsp Dijon mustard

2 anchovy fillets, very finely chopped

salt and ground black pepper

1. Preheat the oven to 180°C (160°C fan oven) mark 4. Put the oil, garlic and bread cubes into a bowl and toss well. Tip on to a baking sheet and cook in the oven for 10 minutes, turning halfway through.

2. Sprinkle the Parmesan over the croûtons and cook for 2 minutes or until the cheese has melted and the bread is golden.

3. Put all the dressing ingredients into a bowl, season with salt and pepper and mix.

4. Put the lettuce and sliced chicken into a bowl, pour the dressing over and toss. Top with the cheese croûtons.

Orange and Chicken Salad

Serves	Preparation Time	Cooking Time	Nutritional Information *(Per Serving)*
4	15 minutes	10 minutes	252 calories | 8g fat (of which 2g saturates) 20g carbohydrate | 0.5g salt | DF | GF

50g (2oz) cashew nuts (see Cook's Tip)

zest and juice of 2 oranges

2 tbsp marmalade

1 tbsp honey

1 tbsp oyster sauce

400g (14oz) roast chicken, shredded

handful of chopped raw vegetables, such as cucumber, carrot, red and yellow pepper and Chinese leaves

1. Put the cashew nuts into a frying pan and cook for 2–3 minutes until golden. Tip into a large serving bowl.

2. To make the dressing, put the orange zest and juice into the frying pan with the marmalade, honey and oyster sauce. Bring to the boil, stirring, then simmer for 2–3 minutes until slightly thickened.

3. Add the roast chicken to the serving bowl with the chopped raw vegetables. Pour the dressing over the salad, toss everything together and serve immediately.

Cook's Tip
Toasting the cashew nuts in a dry frying pan before adding them to the salad brings out their flavour, giving them an intense, nutty taste and a wonderful golden colour.

Pasta, Salami and Tapenade Salad

Serves	**Preparation Time**	**Nutritional Information** (*Per Serving*)
4	5 minutes	332 calories | 20g fat (of which 6g saturates) | 28g carbohydrate | 2g salt | DF

3 x 225g tubs pasta salad in tomato sauce

75g (3oz) pepper salami, shredded

3 tbsp black olive tapenade paste

3 tbsp freshly chopped chives

salt and ground black pepper

1. Turn the pasta salad into a large bowl and add the salami, tapenade and chives. Toss everything together and season with black pepper. Check for seasoning before adding salt – the tapenade may have made the salad salty enough.

2. Pile the salad into a large serving bowl or four individual bowls. If not being served straight away, this salad is best kept in a cool place (but not chilled) until needed.

Tuna Salad

Serves	Preparation Time	Nutritional Information (Per Serving)
4	10 minutes	157 calories | 4g fat (of which trace saturates) | 9g carbohydrate | 0.5g salt | DF | GF

2 x 400g can mixed beans, drained and rinsed

250g (9oz) flaked tuna

1 cucumber, chopped

1 large red onion, finely sliced

4 ripe tomatoes, chopped

4 celery sticks, chopped

80g bag baby spinach leaves

2 tbsp olive oil

1 tsp red wine vinegar

salt and ground black pepper

1. Put the beans into a bowl and add the tuna, cucumber, red onion, tomatoes, celery and spinach.

2. Mix together the oil and vinegar, season with salt and pepper, then toss through the bean mix and serve.

Cook's Tip
If you prefer tuna in oil, replace the olive oil with the same amount from the tuna tin.

Smoked Mackerel with Potato Salad

Serves	Preparation Time	Cooking Time	Nutritional Information (*Per Serving*)
4	15 minutes	20 minutes	320 calories | 23g fat (of which 5g saturates) 22g carbohydrate | 0.7g salt | DF | GF

- 350g (12oz) new potatoes, scrubbed
- 2 tbsp horseradish sauce
- 2 tbsp crème fraîche
- 1 tbsp lemon juice
- 4 tbsp olive oil
- 2 crisp apples
- 2 smoked mackerel fillets
- 100g (3½ oz) watercress
- ground black pepper

1. Cook the potatoes in a pan of lightly salted boiling water for 15–20 minutes until tender. Drain and set aside.

2. In a bowl, mix together the horseradish sauce, crème fraîche, lemon juice and oil, then season with black pepper.

3. Roughly chop the apples and the warm potatoes, put into a large bowl and toss in the dressing. Skin and flake the mackerel and add to the bowl with the watercress. Toss together and serve.

Try Something Different
- Try baby leaf spinach instead of watercress.
- Use wholegrain Dijon mustard instead of horseradish.

Trout with Apple and Watercress Salad

Serves	Preparation Time	Cooking Time	Nutritional Information *(Per Serving)*
4	15 minutes	15–20 minutes	320 calories | 12g fat (of which 1g saturates) 21g carbohydrate | 0.4g salt | **DF** | **GF**

4 x 150g (5oz) trout fillets

1 tbsp olive oil, plus extra to grease

250g (9oz) cooked baby new potatoes, cut into chunks

2 apples, cored and cut into chunks

4 cooked (vacuum packed without vinegar) beetroot, cut into chunks

150g (5oz) watercress

salt and ground black pepper

For the dressing

1 tbsp extra virgin olive oil

juice of ½ lemon

2 tsp Dijon mustard

1 tbsp freshly chopped dill

1. Preheat the oven to 200°C (180°C fan oven) mark 6. Put each piece of fish on a piece of greased foil, brush the top of the fish with oil and season with salt and pepper. Scrunch the foil around the fish and roast for 15–20 minutes until the fish is cooked.

2. Put the potatoes, apples, beetroot and watercress into a large bowl and mix together lightly.

3. Mix all the dressing ingredients together in a small bowl and season with salt and pepper. Toss through the salad, then serve with the fish.

Couscous and Haddock Salad

Serves	Preparation Time	Cooking Time	Nutritional Information (Per Serving)
4	15 minutes	15 minutes	408 calories | 15g fat (of which 2g saturates) 48g carbohydrate | 1.3g salt | DF

175g (6oz) couscous

125g (4oz) cooked smoked haddock, flaked

50g (2oz) cooked peas

a pinch of curry powder

2 spring onions, sliced

1 tbsp freshly chopped flat-leafed parsley

1 small hard-boiled egg, chopped

2 tbsp olive oil

2 tsp lemon juice

salt and ground black pepper

1. Cook the couscous according to the packet instructions. Drain if necessary.

2. Mix the couscous with the smoked haddock, peas, curry powder, spring onions, parsley and egg.

3. Toss with the oil, lemon juice and plenty of salt and pepper to taste, then serve.

3

MEAT

Mediterranean Chicken

Serves	Preparation Time	Cooking Time	Nutritional Information *(Per Serving)*
4	5 minutes	20 minutes	223 calories | 7g fat (of which 1g saturates) 3g carbohydrate | 0.2g salt | DF | GF

1 red pepper, seeded and chopped

2 tbsp capers

2 tbsp freshly chopped rosemary

2 tbsp olive oil

4 skinless chicken breasts, about 125g (4oz) each

salt and ground black pepper

rice or new potatoes to serve

Try Something Different
Use chopped black olives instead of the capers.

1. Preheat the oven to 200°C (180°C fan oven) mark 6. Put the red pepper into a bowl with the capers, rosemary and oil. Season with salt and pepper and mix well.

2. Put the chicken breasts into an ovenproof dish and spoon the pepper mixture over the top. Roast for 15–20 minutes until the chicken is cooked through and the topping is hot. Serve with rice or new potatoes.

Chicken Tagine with Apricots

Serves	Preparation Time	Cooking Time	Nutritional Information (Per Serving)
4	5 minutes	1 hour	500 calories | 29g fat (of which 5g saturates) 26g carbohydrate | 0.6g salt | DF

2 tbsp olive oil

4 chicken thighs

1 onion, chopped

2 tsp cinnamon

2 tbsp honey

150g (5oz) ready-to-eat dried apricots

75g (3oz) blanched almonds

250ml (9fl oz) hot chicken stock

salt and ground black pepper

freshly chopped flat-leafed parsley to garnish

couscous to serve

Try Something Different
Replace the apricots with ready-to-eat prunes and the almonds with 25g (1oz) toasted pinenuts.

1. Heat 1 tbsp oil in a large flameproof casserole over a medium heat. Add the chicken thighs and fry for 5 minutes or until brown. Remove from the casserole, put to one side and keep warm.

2. Add the onion to the casserole with the remaining oil and fry for 10 minutes until softened.

3. Return the chicken to the pan with the cinnamon, honey, apricots, almonds and hot stock. Season well with salt and pepper, stir once, then cover and bring to the boil. Simmer for 45 minutes or until the chicken is falling off the bone.

4. Garnish with chopped parsley and serve with couscous.

Moroccan Spiced Chicken Kebabs

Serves	Preparation Time	Cooking Time	Nutritional Information (Per Serving)
4	10 minutes, plus marinating	10–12 minutes	190 calories | 7g fat (of which 1g saturates) 1g carbohydrate | 0.2g salt | DF | GF

2 tbsp olive oil

15g (½oz) flat-leafed parsley

1 garlic clove

½ tsp paprika

1 tsp ground cumin

zest and juice of 1 lemon

4 skinless chicken breasts, cut into bite-sized chunks

salt

shredded lettuce, sliced cucumber and tomatoes, and lime wedges to serve

Try Something Different
Instead of chicken, use 700g (1½lb) lean lamb fillet or leg of lamb, cut into chunks.

1. Put the oil into a blender and add the parsley, garlic, paprika, cumin, lemon zest and juice and a pinch of salt. Whiz to make a paste.

2. Put the chicken into a medium-sized shallow dish and rub in the spice paste. Leave to marinate for at least 20 minutes. Meanwhile, soak wooden skewers in water. Preheat the grill to high.

3. Thread the marinated chicken on to the skewers and grill for 10–12 minutes, turning every now and then, until the meat is cooked through. Serve with shredded lettuce, sliced cucumber and tomatoes, and lime wedges.

Chicken and Vegetable Hotpot

Serves	Preparation Time	Cooking Time	Nutritional Information (Per Serving)
4	5 minutes	30 minutes	338 calories | 14g fat (of which 3g saturates) 14g carbohydrate | 1.2g salt | DF

4 chicken breasts, skin on

2 large parsnips, chopped

2 large carrots, chopped

300ml (½ pint) ready-made gravy

125g (4oz) cabbage, shredded

ground black pepper

1. Heat a non-stick frying pan or flameproof casserole until hot. Add the chicken breasts, skin side down, and cook for 5–6 minutes. Turn them over and add the parsnips and carrots. Cook for a further 7–8 minutes.

2. Pour the gravy over the chicken and vegetables, then cover and cook gently for 10 minutes.

3. Season with pepper and stir in the cabbage, then cover and continue to cook for 4–5 minutes until the chicken is cooked through, the cabbage has wilted and the vegetables are tender. Serve hot.

Thrifty Tip

Leftovers can be turned into a hearty soup. Shred any chicken and put into a pan with the vegetables. Add extra hot chicken stock and a drained can of mixed beans. Heat until piping hot.

Lemon Chicken

Serves	Preparation Time	Cooking Time	Nutritional Information (Per Serving)
4	2 minutes	6–8 minutes	231 calories | 7g fat (of which 1g saturates) 13g carbohydrate | 0.2g salt | DF | GF

4 small skinless chicken breasts, about 125g (4oz) each, cut into chunky strips

juice of 2 lemons

2 tbsp olive oil

4–6 tbsp demerara sugar

salt

green salad to serve

1. Put the chicken into a large bowl and season with salt. Add the lemon juice and oil and stir to mix.

2. Preheat the grill to medium. Spread the chicken out on a large baking sheet and sprinkle with 2–3 tbsp demerara sugar. Grill for 3–4 minutes until caramelised, then turn the chicken over, sprinkle with the remaining sugar and grill until the chicken is cooked through and golden.

3. Divide the chicken among four plates and serve with a green salad.

Chicken Curry with Rice

Serves	Preparation Time	Cooking Time	Nutritional Information *(Per Serving)*
4	20 minutes	25 minutes, plus 5 minutes standing	453 calories | 12g fat (of which 2g saturates) 49g carbohydrate | 2.4g salt | **DF** | **GF**

2 tbsp vegetable oil

1 onion, finely sliced

2 garlic cloves, crushed

6 skinless boneless chicken thighs, cut into strips

2 tbsp tikka masala curry paste

200g can chopped tomatoes

450ml (¾ pint) hot vegetable stock

200g (7oz) basmati rice

1 tsp salt

225g (8oz) baby leaf spinach

poppadums and mango chutney to serve

1. Heat the oil in a large pan, add the onion and fry over a medium heat for about 5 minutes until golden. Add the garlic and chicken and stir-fry for about 5 minutes until golden.

2. Add the curry paste, tomatoes and hot stock. Stir and bring to the boil, then cover with a lid and simmer on a low heat for 15 minutes or until the chicken is cooked (cut a piece in half to check that it's white all the way through).

3. Meanwhile, cook the rice. Put 600ml (1 pint) water into a medium pan, cover and bring to the boil. Add the rice and salt and stir. Replace the lid, turn down the heat to its lowest setting and cook for the time stated on the packet. Once cooked, cover with a teatowel and the lid and leave for 10 minutes to absorb the steam.

4. Add the spinach to the curry and cook until just wilted.

5. Spoon the rice into four bowls, add the curry and serve with poppadums and mango chutney.

Chicken and Leek Pie

Serves	Preparation Time	Cooking Time	Nutritional Information (Per Serving)
4	15 minutes	40–45 minutes	591 calories	23g fat (of which 15g saturates) 54g carbohydrate	0.3g salt	**GF**

5 large potatoes, peeled and chopped into chunks

200g (7oz) crème fraîche

3 chicken breasts, with skin, about 125g (4oz) each

3 large leeks, trimmed and chopped into chunks

about 10 fresh tarragon leaves, finely chopped

salt and ground black pepper

1. Preheat the oven to 200°C (180°C fan oven) mark 6. Put the potatoes into a pan of lightly salted cold water. Cover, bring to the boil and simmer for 10–12 minutes until soft. Drain and put back in the pan. Add 1 tbsp crème fraîche, season with salt and pepper and mash well.

2. Meanwhile, heat a frying pan, add the chicken, skin side down, and fry gently for 5 minutes or until the skin is golden. Turn the chicken over and fry for 6–8 minutes. Remove the chicken from the pan and put on to a board. Tip the leeks into the pan and cook in the juices over a low heat for 5 minutes to soften.

3. Discard the chicken skin and cut the flesh into bite-size pieces (don't worry if it is not quite cooked through). Put the chicken back into the pan, stir in the remaining crème fraîche and heat for 2–3 minutes until bubbling. Stir in the tarragon, season with salt and pepper, then spoon into a 1.7 litre (3 pint) ovenproof dish. Spread the mash on top and cook in the oven for 20–25 minutes until golden and heated through. Serve hot.

Try Something Different
- To use leftover chicken or turkey, don't fry the meat at step 2. Add it to the pan with the crème fraîche at step 3. Cook the leeks in 2 tsp olive oil.
- For a different flavour, make the mash with 2 large potatoes and a small celeriac, peeled, cut into chunks and cooked with the potato.

Chicken with Wine and Capers

Serves	Preparation Time	Cooking Time	Nutritional Information *(Per Serving)*
4	5 minutes	25 minutes	234 calories | 10g fat (of which 5g saturates) trace carbohydrate | 0.3g salt | **GF**

1 tbsp olive oil

15g (½oz) butter

4 small skinless chicken breasts

lemon wedges to garnish

boiled rice to serve

For the wine and caper sauce

125ml (4fl oz) white wine (see Cook's Tips)

3 tbsp capers, rinsed and drained

juice of 1 lemon

15g (½ oz) butter

1 tbsp freshly chopped flat-leafed parsley

1. Heat the oil and butter in a frying pan over a medium heat. Add the chicken breasts and fry over a medium heat for 10–12 minutes on each side until cooked through. Transfer to a warm plate, cover and keep warm.

2. To make the sauce, add the wine and capers to the same pan. Bring to the boil, then simmer for 2–3 minutes until the wine is reduced by half. Add the lemon juice and butter and stir in the parsley.

3. Divide the chicken among four warmed plates, pour the sauce over the chicken, garnish each serving with a lemon wedge and serve immediately with boiled rice.

Cook's Tips

Dregs of wine that are a few days past their best can be used in cooking instead.

To avoid the potential risk of food poisoning, particular care must be taken when handling poultry. Bacteria that can cause food poisoning may be present in low levels in raw birds. Provided that poultry is correctly stored – covered in the fridge, with giblets removed (if any) – these bacteria will remain at low levels and, as long as it is then cooked properly within two days, the bacteria will be killed by heat and rendered harmless.

Easy Thai Red Chicken Curry

Serves	Preparation Time	Cooking Time	Nutritional Information *(Per Serving)*
4	5 minutes	20 minutes	248 calories | 8g fat (of which 1g saturates) 16g carbohydrate | 1g salt | DF | GF

1 tbsp vegetable oil

3 tbsp Thai red curry paste

4 skinless chicken breasts, about 600g (1lb 5oz) total weight, sliced

400ml can coconut milk

300ml (½ pint) hot chicken or vegetable stock

juice of 1 lime, plus lime halves to serve

200g pack mixed baby sweetcorn and mangetouts

2 tbsp freshly chopped coriander, plus sprigs to garnish

rice or rice noodles to serve

1. Heat the oil in a wok or large pan over a low heat. Add the curry paste and cook for 2 minutes or until fragrant.

2. Add the sliced chicken and fry gently for about 10 minutes or until browned.

3. Add the coconut milk, hot stock, lime juice and baby sweetcorn to the pan and bring to the boil. Add the mangetouts, reduce the heat and simmer for 4–5 minutes until the chicken is cooked.

4. Stir in the chopped coriander, garnish with coriander sprigs and serve immediately with rice or noodles, and lime halves to squeeze over.

Oven-baked Chicken with Garlic Potatoes

Serves	Preparation Time	Cooking Time	Nutritional Information (Per Serving)
6	10 minutes	1½ hours	376 calories | 16g fat (of which 5g saturates) 32g carbohydrate | 1.2g salt

2 medium baking potatoes, thinly sliced

a little freshly grated nutmeg

600ml (1 pint) white sauce (use a ready-made sauce or make your own, see page 26)

½ x 390g can fried onions

250g (9oz) frozen peas

450g (1lb) cooked chicken, shredded

20g pack garlic butter, sliced

a little butter to grease

salt and ground black pepper

steamed vegetables and Granary bread (optional) to serve

1. Preheat the oven to 180°C (160°C fan oven) mark 4. Layer half the potatoes over the base of a 2.4 litre (4¼ pint) shallow ovenproof dish and season with the nutmeg, salt and pepper. Pour the white sauce over and shake the dish, so that the sauce settles through the gaps in the potatoes.

2. Spread half the onions on top, then scatter over half the peas. Arrange the shredded chicken on top, then add the remaining peas and onions. Finish with the remaining potato, arranged in an even layer and dot with garlic butter. Season to taste with salt and pepper.

3. Cover tightly with buttered foil and cook for 1 hour. Turn the heat up to 200°C (180°C fan oven) mark 6, remove the foil and continue to cook for 20–30 minutes until the potatoes are golden and tender.

4. Serve with steamed vegetables and, if you like, some Granary bread to mop up the juices.

Sticky Chicken Thighs

Serves	Preparation Time	Cooking Time	Nutritional Information *(Per Serving)*
4	5 minutes	20 minutes	218 calories | 12g fat (of which 3g saturates) 5g carbohydrate | 0.4g salt | DF | GF

1 garlic clove, crushed

1 tbsp clear honey

1 tbsp Thai sweet chilli sauce

4 chicken thighs

rice and green salad to serve

Try Something Different

- Instead of chicken, try this recipe with sausages; roast them for 20–30 minutes.
- **Italian Marinade**
  Mix 1 crushed garlic clove with 4 tbsp olive oil, the juice of 1 lemon and 1 tsp dried oregano. If you like, leave to marinate for 1–2 hours before cooking.
- **Oriental Marinade**
  Mix together 2 tbsp soy sauce, 1 tsp demerara sugar, 2 tbsp dry sherry or apple juice, 1 tsp finely chopped fresh root ginger and 1 crushed garlic clove.
- **Honey and Mustard Marinade**
  Mix together 2 tbsp grain mustard, 3 tbsp clear honey and the grated zest and juice of 1 lemon.

1. Preheat the oven to 200°C (180°C fan oven) mark 6. Put the garlic into a bowl with the honey and chilli sauce and mix together. Add the chicken thighs and toss to coat.

2. Put into a roasting tin and roast for 15–20 minutes until the chicken is golden and cooked through. Serve with rice and a crisp green salad.

Lime and Chilli Chicken Goujons

Serves	Preparation Time	Cooking Time	Nutritional Information *(Per Serving)*
4	15 minutes	20 minutes	339 calories | 22g fat (of which 4g saturates) 22g carbohydrate | 1.9g salt

300g (11oz) skinless boneless chicken thighs

50g (2oz) fresh breadcrumbs

50g (2oz) plain flour

2 tsp dried chilli flakes

grated zest of 1 lime

1 medium egg, beaten

2 tbsp sunflower oil

salt and ground black pepper

lime wedges to serve

For the dip

6 tbsp natural yogurt

6 tbsp mayonnaise

¼ cucumber, halved, seeded and finely diced

25g (1oz) freshly chopped coriander

juice of 1 lime

1. Put all the dip ingredients into a bowl. Season to taste with salt and pepper and mix well, then chill.

2. Cut the chicken into strips. Put the breadcrumbs into a bowl with the flour, chilli flakes, lime zest and 1 tsp salt. Mix well. Pour the egg on to a plate. Dip the chicken in egg, then coat in the breadcrumbs.

3. Heat the oil in a frying pan over a medium heat. Fry the chicken in batches for 7–10 minutes until golden and cooked through. Keep each batch warm while cooking the remainder. Transfer to a serving plate, sprinkle with a little salt, then serve with the dip and lime wedges.

Cook's Tip

For a lower-fat version, bake the goujons in the oven. Preheat the oven to 200°C (180°C fan oven) mark 6. Put the goujons on a lightly oiled baking sheet, brush each with a little oil and bake for 12–15 minutes until golden and cooked through.

Chicken Stir-fry with Noodles

Serves	Preparation Time	Cooking Time	Nutritional Information (Per Serving)
4	20 minutes	20 minutes	355 calories | 10g fat (of which 1.5g saturates) 29g carbohydrate | 0.5g salt | **DF**

2 tbsp vegetable oil

2 garlic cloves, crushed

4 skinless chicken breasts, each sliced into 10 pieces

3 medium carrots, about 450g (1lb), cut into thin strips, about 5cm (2in) long

250g pack thick egg noodles

1 bunch of spring onions, sliced

200g (7oz) mangetouts, ends trimmed

155g jar sweet chilli and lemongrass sauce

Try Something Different
Use turkey or pork escalopes instead of the chicken: you will need 450g (1lb), cut into thin strips.

1. Fill a large pan with water and bring to the boil. Meanwhile, heat the oil in a wok or frying pan, then add the garlic and stir-fry for 1–2 minutes. Add the chicken pieces and stir-fry for 5 minutes, then add the carrot strips and stir-fry for a further 5 minutes.

2. Cook the noodles in the boiling water according to the packet instructions.

3. Meanwhile, add the spring onions, mangetouts and sauce to the wok. Stir-fry for 5 minutes.

4. Drain the cooked noodles well and add to the wok. Toss everything together and serve.

Chicken Falafels

Serves	Preparation Time	Cooking Time	Nutritional Information *(Per Serving)*
4	20 minutes	20 minutes	287 calories | 14g fat (of which 3g saturates) 10g carbohydrate | 1.1g salt | **DF**

450g (1lb) minced chicken

3 shallots, finely chopped

125g (4oz) canned chickpeas (about ½ can), drained and rinsed

2.5cm (1in) piece fresh root ginger, grated

½ tsp salt

20g (¾oz) freshly chopped coriander

1 medium egg

3 tbsp olive oil

400g can chopped tomatoes

1 tsp caster sugar

For the couscous salad

200g (7oz) couscous

350ml (12fl oz) hot chicken stock

grated zest and juice of ½ lemon

25g (1oz) pinenuts

seeds from ½ pomegranate

3 tbsp extra virgin olive oil

2–3 tbsp freshly chopped parsley

1. First, make the couscous salad. Put the couscous into a bowl and add the hot stock and lemon zest. Leave to soak for 20 minutes. Meanwhile, toast the pinenuts in a pan until golden. Use a fork to fluff up the couscous, then stir in the pinenuts, pomegranate seeds, lemon juice, extra virgin olive oil and parsley.

2. Put the chicken mince into a food processor. Add 1 chopped shallot, the chickpeas, grated ginger and salt and whiz to combine.

3. Add the coriander and egg and whiz again briefly. With damp hands, shape into 12 balls, each measuring 6.5cm (2½in).

4. Heat 2 tbsp olive oil in a frying pan. Fry the patties for 2–3 minutes on each side until golden brown.

5. Meanwhile, fry the remaining shallots in a pan with the remaining oil. Stir in the tomatoes and sugar. Simmer for 10 minutes or until slightly thickened. Serve the patties with the couscous salad, with the sauce on the side.

Spiced Tikka Kebabs

Serves	Preparation Time	Cooking Time	Nutritional Information (Per Serving)
4	10 minutes	20 minutes	150 calories | 5g fat (of which 1g saturates) 4g carbohydrate | 0.3g salt | **GF**

2 tbsp tikka paste

150g (5oz) natural yogurt

juice of ½ lime

4 spring onions, chopped

350g (12oz) skinless chicken, cut into bite-sized pieces

lime wedges and mixed salad (see Cook's Tip) to serve

1. Preheat the grill. Put the tikka paste, yogurt, lime juice and spring onions into a large bowl. Add the chicken and toss well. Thread the chicken on to metal skewers.

2. Grill for 8–10 minutes on each side or until cooked through, turning and basting with the paste. Serve with lime wedges to squeeze over the kebabs and mixed salad.

Cook's Tip
Mixed Salad
Put 75g (3oz) green salad leaves into a large bowl. Add ¼ chopped avocado, a handful of halved cherry tomatoes, ½ chopped cucumber and the juice of 1 lime. Season to taste with salt and pepper and mix together.

Chicken Chow Mein

Serves	Preparation Time	Cooking Time	Nutritional Information *(Per Serving)*
4	10 minutes	10 minutes	451 calories | 11g fat (of which 2g saturates) 59g carbohydrate | 1.3g salt | DF

250g (9oz) medium egg noodles

1 tbsp toasted sesame oil

2 skinless chicken breasts, about 125g (4oz) each, cut into thin strips

1 bunch of spring onions, thinly sliced diagonally

150g (5oz) mangetouts, ends trimmed and thickly sliced diagonally

125g (4oz) bean sprouts

100g (3½oz) cooked ham, finely shredded

120g sachet chow mein sauce

salt and ground black pepper

light soy sauce to serve

1. Cook the noodles in boiling water for 4 minutes or according to the packet instructions. Drain, rinse thoroughly in cold water, drain again and set aside.

2. Meanwhile, heat a wok or large frying pan until hot, then add the oil. Add the chicken and stir-fry over a high heat for 3–4 minutes until browned all over. Add the spring onions and mangetouts, stir-fry for 2 minutes, then stir in the bean sprouts and ham. Cook for a further 2 minutes.

3. Add the drained noodles, then pour the chow mein sauce over and toss together to coat evenly. Stir-fry for 2 minutes or until piping hot. Season to taste with salt and pepper and serve immediately with light soy sauce to drizzle over.

Thrifty Tip
Use leftover cooked chicken instead. Roughly shred and add along with the ham.

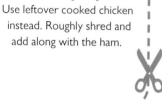

Easy Chicken and Ham Pie

Serves	Preparation Time	Cooking Time	Nutritional Information *(Per Serving)*
6	15 minutes	30–35 minutes	402 calories | 28g fat (of which 9g saturates) 17g carbohydrate | 1.2g salt

4 ready-roasted chicken breasts, about 125g (4oz) each, shredded

100g (3½oz) cooked smoked ham, cubed

150ml (¼ pint) double cream

75ml (2½fl oz) chicken gravy

2 tbsp finely chopped fresh tarragon

1 tsp cornflour

½ tsp ready-made English mustard

250g (9oz) ready-rolled puff pastry

1 medium egg, beaten

ground black pepper

seasonal vegetables to serve

Try Something Different
Replace the chicken with 450g (1lb) cooked turkey and replace the tarragon with chopped thyme leaves.

1. Preheat the oven to 200°C (180°C fan oven) mark 6. Put the chicken into a large bowl with the ham, cream, gravy, tarragon, cornflour and mustard. Season with pepper and mix well.

2. Spoon into a shallow 1 litre (1¾ pint) baking dish. Unroll the puff pastry and position over the top of the dish to cover. Trim to fit the dish, then press the edges down lightly around the rim. Brush the egg over the pastry. Cook for 30–35 minutes until the pastry is golden and puffed up. Serve hot, with vegetables.

Chicken Pot Pies

Serves	Preparation Time	Cooking Time	Nutritional Information (Per Serving)
4	45 minutes	about 1 hour	610 calories | 34g fat (of which 14g saturates) 47g carbohydrate | 1.2g salt

25g (1oz) butter

25g (1oz) plain flour

400ml (14fl oz) chicken stock

2 tbsp double cream

450g cooked chicken, shredded

100g (3½oz) each frozen peas and sweetcorn

2 tbsp freshly chopped parsley

275g (10oz) ready-made shortcrust pastry

1 medium egg, beaten

1. Melt the butter in a pan over a medium heat. Stir in the flour and cook for 1 minute, then take off the heat and gradually blend in the stock. Cook over a gentle heat, stirring, until thickened. Simmer for 5 minutes, then add the cream and cook for 5 minutes.

2. Stir the chicken meat into the sauce with the peas, sweetcorn and parsley. Cool a little.

3. Preheat the oven to 200°C (180°C fan oven) mark 6. Roll out the pastry to 3mm (⅛in) thick.

Use the top of a 300ml (½ pint) ovenproof basin as a guide and cut out four circles of pastry 2cm (¾in) larger than the diameter. Set aside.

4. Divide the chicken mixture among four 300ml ((½ pint) ovenproof basins. Dampen the edges of the pastry with water and use to top the basins, folding it over the edges. Cut a slit in the pastry to let out the steam and use the trimmings to decorate the pies, if you like. Brush with the egg and bake for 30 minutes until golden on top and the filling is piping hot.

Chicken Rarebit

Serves	Preparation Time	Cooking Time	Nutritional Information (Per Serving)
4	5 minutes	25 minutes	446 calories | 24g fat (of which 14g saturates) 9g carbohydrate | 1.3g salt

4 large chicken breasts, with skin, about 150g (5oz) each

15g (½oz) butter

1 tbsp plain flour

75ml (2½fl oz) full-fat milk

175g (6oz) Gruyère cheese, grated

25g (1oz) fresh white breadcrumbs

1 tsp ready-made English mustard

2 fat garlic cloves, crushed

1 medium egg yolk

boiled new potatoes and green beans to serve

1. Preheat the oven to 200°C (180°C fan oven) mark 6. Put the chicken in a single layer into an ovenproof dish and roast for 20 minutes or until cooked through.

2. Meanwhile, melt the butter in a pan over a low heat, then add the flour and stir for 1 minute. Gradually add the milk and stir to make a smooth sauce.

3. Add the cheese, breadcrumbs, mustard and garlic to the sauce and cook for 1 minute. Cool briefly, then beat in the egg yolk. Preheat the grill to medium-high.

4. Discard the skin from the cooked chicken and beat any juices from the dish into the cheese mixture. Spread the paste evenly over each chicken breast, then grill for 2–3 minutes until golden. Serve with boiled new potatoes and green beans.

One-pan Chicken with Tomatoes

Serves	Preparation Time	Cooking Time	Nutritional Information *(Per Serving)*
4	5 minutes	20–25 minutes	238 calories | 4g fat (of which 1g saturates) 20g carbohydrate | 1g salt | DF | GF

4 chicken thighs

1 red onion, sliced

400g can chopped tomatoes with herbs

400g can mixed beans, drained and rinsed

2 tsp balsamic vinegar

freshly chopped flat-leafed parsley to garnish

1. Heat a non-stick pan and fry the chicken thighs, skin side down, until golden. Turn over and fry for 5 minutes.

2. Add the onion and fry for 5 minutes. Add the tomatoes, mixed beans and vinegar, cover and simmer for 10–12 minutes until piping hot. Garnish with parsley and serve immediately.

Try Something Different
Use flageolet beans or other canned beans instead of mixed beans, and garnish with fresh basil or oregano.

Chicken Tarragon Burgers

Serves	Preparation Time	Cooking Time	Nutritional Information (Per Serving)
4	30 minutes, plus 30 minutes chilling	12 minutes	103 calories | 2g fat (of which trace saturates) 6g carbohydrate | 0.2g salt | **DF**

450g (1lb) minced chicken

4 shallots, finely chopped

2 tbsp freshly chopped tarragon

50g (2oz) fresh breadcrumbs

2 large egg yolks

vegetable oil to grease

salt and ground black pepper

toasted burger buns, mayonnaise or Greek yogurt, salad leaves and tomato salad to serve

Try Something Different
Pork and Apricot Burgers
Replace the chicken with minced pork, use freshly chopped sage instead of tarragon, and add 100g (3½oz) chopped ready-to-eat dried apricots to the mixture before shaping.

1. Put the chicken into a bowl with the shallots, tarragon, breadcrumbs and egg yolk. Mix well, then beat in about 75ml (2½fl oz) cold water and season with salt and pepper.

2. Lightly oil a foil-lined baking sheet. Divide the chicken mixture into four portions and put on the foil. Using the back of a wet spoon, flatten each portion to a thickness of 2.5cm (1in). Cover and chill for 30 minutes.

3. Preheat the barbecue or grill. If cooking on the barbecue, lift the burgers straight on to the grill rack; if cooking under the grill, slide the baking sheet under the grill. Cook the burgers for 5–6 minutes on each side until cooked through, then serve in a toasted burger bun with a dollop of mayonnaise or Greek yogurt, a few salad leaves and tomato salad.

Garlic and Thyme Chicken

Serves	Preparation Time	Cooking Time	Nutritional Information *(Per Serving)*
4	10 minutes	10–15 minutes	135 calories | 6g fat (of which 1g saturates) trace carbohydrate | 0.2g salt | **DF** | **GF**

2 garlic cloves, crushed

2 tbsp freshly chopped thyme leaves

2 tbsp olive oil

4 chicken thighs

salt and ground black pepper

1. Preheat the barbecue or grill. Mix together the garlic, thyme and oil in a large bowl. Season to taste with salt and pepper.

2. Using a sharp knife, make two or three slits in each chicken thigh. Put the chicken into the bowl and toss to coat thoroughly. Grill for 5–7 minutes on each side until golden and cooked through.

Thrifty Tip
Use chicken thighs on the bone with skin – they're cheaper than the skinless version and the skin will keep the chicken succulent while cooking on the barbecue.

Orange and Herb Chicken

Serves	Preparation Time	Cooking Time	Nutritional Information *(Per Serving)*
4	10 minutes	20–30 minutes	180 calories | 4g fat (of which 1g saturates) 5g carbohydrate | 0.2g salt | DF | GF

125ml (4fl oz) orange juice

zest of 1 unwaxed orange

2 tbsp freshly chopped tarragon

2 tbsp freshly chopped flat-leafed parsley

1 tbsp olive oil

1 garlic clove, crushed

4 skinless chicken breasts

4 small orange wedges

salt and ground black pepper

brown rice and watercress to serve

1. Preheat the oven to 200°C (180°C fan oven) mark 6. In a large bowl, whisk together the orange juice, orange zest, herbs, oil and garlic. Season to taste with salt and pepper.

2. Slash the chicken breasts several times and put into an ovenproof dish. Pour the marinade over them and top each with an orange wedge.

3. Cook in the oven for 20–30 minutes or until cooked through. Serve with brown rice and watercress.

Peas and Bacon with Pan-fried Chicken

Serves	Preparation Time	Cooking Time	Nutritional Information *(Per Serving)*
4	5 minutes	20 minutes	314 calories | 21g fat (of which 5g saturates) 7g carbohydrate | 0.9g salt | **DF** | **GF**

4 skinless chicken breasts, about 125g (4oz) each

2 tbsp olive oil

2 shallots, finely sliced

3 unsmoked rindless streaky bacon rashers, chopped

200g (7oz) frozen peas, thawed

2 tbsp sunblush tomato pesto

salt and ground black pepper

buttered new potatoes to serve

1. Heat a griddle. Season the chicken generously with salt and pepper. Brush with 1 tbsp oil and cook on the griddle, skin side down, for 8–10 minutes. Turn over and continue to cook on the other side for 8–10 minutes until cooked through and the juices run clear when the chicken is pierced with a sharp knife.

2. Meanwhile, heat the remaining oil in a frying pan and fry the shallots and bacon until the shallots are softened and the bacon is golden. Add the peas and cook for 2 minutes.

3. Stir in the pesto. Serve with the chicken breasts and new potatoes.

Turkey and Sesame Stir-fry with Noodles

Serves	Preparation Time	Cooking Time	Nutritional Information *(Per Serving)*
4	5 minutes, plus 5 minutes marinating	10 minutes	672 calories	18g fat (of which 4g saturates) 97g carbohydrate	0.7g salt	**DF**

300g (11oz) turkey breast fillets, cut into thin strips

3 tbsp teriyaki marinade

3 tbsp clear honey

500g (1lb 2oz) medium egg noodles

about 1 tbsp sesame oil, plus extra for the noodles

300g (11oz) ready-prepared mixed stir-fry vegetables, such as carrots, broccoli, red cabbage, mangetouts, bean sprouts and purple spring onions

2 tbsp sesame seeds, lightly toasted in a dry wok or heavy-based pan

1. Put the turkey strips into a large bowl with the teriyaki marinade and honey and stir to coat. Cover and set aside for 5 minutes.

2. Cook the noodles in a large pan of boiling water for about 4 minutes or according to the packet instructions. Drain well, then toss in a little oil.

3. Heat 1 tbsp oil in a wok or large frying pan and add the turkey, reserving the marinade. Stir-fry over a very high heat for 2–3 minutes until cooked through and beginning to brown. Add a drop more oil, if needed, then add the vegetables and reserved marinade. Continue to cook over a high heat, stirring, until the vegetables have started to soften and the sauce is warmed through.

4. Serve immediately with the noodles, scattered with the sesame seeds.

Chicken with Black-eye Beans and Greens

Serves	Preparation Time	Cooking Time	Nutritional Information (Per Serving)
4	5 minutes	15 minutes	491 calories | 26g fat (of which 4g saturates) 31g carbohydrate | 1.5g salt | DF | GF

2 tsp Jamaican jerk seasoning

4 skinless chicken breasts, about 125g (4oz) each

1kg (2¼lb) spring greens or cabbage, core removed and shredded

2 x 300g cans black-eye beans, drained and rinsed

8 tbsp olive oil

juice of 1¼ lemons

salt and ground black pepper

1. Preheat the grill. Rub the jerk seasoning into the chicken breasts and sprinkle with salt. Cook under the grill for 15 minutes or until cooked through, turning from time to time.

2. Cook the spring greens or cabbage in lightly salted boiling water until just tender – bringing the water back to the boil after adding the greens is usually enough to cook them. Drain and put back into the pan.

3. Add the beans and oil to the greens and season well with salt and pepper. Heat through and add the juice of 1 lemon.

4. To serve, slice the chicken and put on the bean mixture, then drizzle over the remaining lemon juice and serve.

Chicken and Mushroom Stroganoff

Serves	Preparation Time	Cooking Time	Nutritional Information (Per Serving)
4	20 minutes	30 minutes	494 calories | 43g fat (of which 17g saturates) 4g carbohydrate | 0.3g salt

2 tbsp olive oil

1 onion, roughly chopped

2 garlic cloves, crushed

4 x 125g (4oz) chicken thighs, including skin and bones

250g (9oz) closed-cup mushrooms, roughly chopped

200g (7oz) brown rice, washed

175ml (6fl oz) hot chicken stock

150ml (¼ pint) double cream

leaves from 2 thyme sprigs, plus extra to garnish

50g (2oz) baby leaf spinach

salt and ground black pepper

1. Heat 1 tbsp oil in a pan, add the onion and garlic, cover and cook gently for 10–15 minutes until soft. Remove from the pan and set aside. Increase the heat to medium and add the remaining oil. Fry the chicken until golden. Add the mushrooms and cook for 5 minutes until most of the liquid has evaporated.

2. Put the rice into a separate pan, then pour in 450ml (¾ pint) hot water. Cover and bring to the boil, then reduce the heat and cook according to the packet instructions.

3. Return the onion mixture to the chicken pan and gradually stir in the hot stock. Use a wooden spoon to scrape all the goodness from the base of the pan, then stir in the cream and thyme leaves. Simmer for 5 minutes.

4. Remove the chicken, discard the skin and bones and pull the meat into pieces. Return it to the pan. Add the spinach and stir to wilt. Taste for seasoning.

5. To serve, divide the rice among four warmed plates and ladle the stroganoff over. Garnish with the remaining thyme.

Tangy Chops

Serves	Preparation Time	Cooking Time	Nutritional Information (Per Serving)
4	5 minutes	45 minutes	237 calories | 16g fat (of which 5g saturates) 1g carbohydrate | 0.6g salt | DF

2 tbsp vegetable oil

4 lamb chump chops

finely grated zest and juice of 1 lemon

2 tbsp freshly chopped parsley

1 tbsp freshly chopped mint

1 tsp sugar

150ml (¼ pint) beef or chicken stock

salt and ground black pepper

1. Heat the oil in a sauté pan or frying pan, add the chops and fry over a brisk heat until browned on both sides. Lower the heat and season the chops with salt and pepper to taste.

2. Mix the lemon zest and juice with the herbs and sugar and spoon this mixture over the chops. Pour in the stock, cover the pan tightly and simmer gently for 30 minutes or until the meat is tender. Serve hot, on a warmed dish, with the juices poured over.

Cook's Tip
Serve for a family supper with grilled or oven-baked tomatoes, potatoes and a seasonal green vegetable.

Lamb Chops with Crispy Garlic Potatoes

Serves	Preparation Time	Cooking Time	Nutritional Information (Per Serving)
4	10 minutes	20 minutes	835 calories | 45g fat (of which 19g saturates) 22g carbohydrate | 0.7g salt | DF | GF

2 tbsp mint sauce (use ready-made or make your own, see Cook's Tip)

8 small lamb chops

3 medium potatoes, peeled and cut into 5mm (¼in) slices

2 tbsp garlic-flavoured olive oil

1 tbsp olive oil

salt and ground black pepper

steamed green beans to serve

1. Spread the mint sauce over the lamb chops and leave to marinate while you prepare the potatoes.

2. Cook the potatoes in a pan of lightly salted boiling water for 2 minutes until just starting to soften. Drain, tip back into the pan, season and toss through the flavoured oil.

3. Meanwhile, heat the olive oil in a large frying pan and fry the chops for 4–5 minutes on each side until just cooked, adding a splash of boiling water to the pan to make a sauce. Remove the chops and sauce from the pan and keep warm.

4. Add the potatoes to the pan and fry over a medium heat for 10–12 minutes until crisp and golden. Divide the potatoes, chops and sauce among four plates and serve with green beans.

Cook's Tip
Mint Sauce
Finely chop 20g (¾oz) fresh mint and mix with 1 tbsp each olive oil and white wine vinegar.

Lamb Meatballs with Herb Sauce

Serves	Preparation Time	Cooking Time	Nutritional Information (Per Serving)
6	30 minutes	1 hour 10 minutes	609 calories | 57g fat (of which 26g saturates) 2g carbohydrate | 1.2g salt | GF

6 spring onions

175g (6oz) unsmoked rindless streaky bacon, roughly chopped

1 garlic clove

pinch of ground cinnamon

700g (1½lb) lean lamb mince

3 tbsp olive oil

450ml (¾ pint) meat stock

4 tbsp chopped parsley or dill, plus extra sprigs to garnish

300ml (½ pint) double cream

2 egg yolks

salt and ground black pepper

1. Preheat the oven to 180°C (160°C fan oven) mark 4. Put the spring onions, bacon, garlic and cinnamon into a food processor and blend until almost smooth. Add the lamb and season with plenty of salt and pepper. Process until smooth. With wet hands, shape the mixture into 30–36 even-sized balls.

2. Heat the oil in a large frying pan and brown the meatballs in batches, then transfer to a shallow ovenproof dish. Pour the stock into the frying pan and bring to the boil, scraping up any sediment from the bottom. Pour over the meatballs, cover and bake at for 1 hour.

3. Pour the cooking liquid into a pan; cover the meatballs and keep warm. Bring the liquid to the boil and boil rapidly until reduced to 300ml (½ pint). Lower the heat and stir in the chopped parsley or dill, the cream and egg yolks. Stir over a gentle heat for about 10 minutes or until slightly thickened; do not allow to boil. Taste and adjust the seasoning.

4. Put the meatballs on warmed plates and spoon the sauce over them. Garnish with herb sprigs and serve with new potatoes or buttered noodles.

Pork Chops with Fresh Ginger and Apple

Serves	Preparation Time	Cooking Time	Nutritional Information (Per Serving)
4	10 minutes	15 minutes	434 calories | 35g fat (of which 14g saturates) 15g carbohydrate | 0.3g salt | GF

4 pork chops, rind and fat scored

3 red apples, about 350g (12oz), cored and roughly diced

5cm (2in) piece fresh root ginger, peeled and grated

300ml (½ pint) pure unsweetened apple juice

25g (1oz) chilled unsalted butter, diced

salt and ground black pepper

1. Rub the chops all over – particularly the fat – with plenty of seasoning. Put the apples in a small bowl and stir in the ginger.

2. Heat a non-stick frying pan over a medium heat, then add the chops. Leave them undisturbed for 3–4 minutes, by which time some of the fat will have been released and the underside of the meat should be a deep golden brown. Press the fat down into the pan occasionally with the back of a wooden spoon while the chops are cooking – this will help them brown and improves the flavour of the finished sauce. Turn the chops over.

3. After 1–2 minutes add the apples and ginger to the pan and cook for a further 2–3 minutes until the pork is cooked through. Remove the chops (leaving the apples in the pan) and keep them warm.

4. Increase the heat to high and pour the apple juice into the pan – it should bubble immediately. Scrape the pan with a wooden spoon to loosen any crispy brown bits from the bottom, then let the juices bubble for about 5 minutes until reduced by half.

5. Swirl the butter into the pan juices to make a glossy sauce to spoon over the pork. Taste for seasoning, then serve with new potatoes and spring greens.

Egg and Bacon Tarts

Serves	Preparation Time	Cooking Time	Nutritional Information (Per Serving)
6	20 minutes, plus 10 minutes chilling	25 minutes	498 calories | 33g fat (of which 10g saturates) 39g carbohydrate | 1.5g salt

500g pack shortcrust pastry, thawed if frozen

6 rashers smoked streaky bacon

6 medium eggs

3 tbsp freshly chopped flat-leafed parsley

Try Something Different
Replace the streaky bacon with 6 long strips of smoked salmon, and the chopped parsley with dill.

1. Preheat the oven to 200°C (180°C fan oven) mark 6 and put two baking sheets into the oven to heat up.

2. Divide the pastry into six pieces, then roll out and use to line six 10cm (4in) fluted flan tins. Prick the bases with a fork. Cover with greaseproof paper, fill with baking beans and chill for 10 minutes.

3. Put the tart tins on to the preheated baking sheets and bake blind for 10 minutes. Remove the paper and beans and cook for a further 5 minutes or until the pastry is dry. Remove the cases from the oven and increase the temperature to 220°C (200°C fan oven) mark 7.

4. Put a rasher of raw bacon across the base of each tart. Crack the eggs into a cup one at a time, then add one to each tart. Season to taste with salt and pepper and cook for 10 minutes until the egg white has set. Sprinkle with parsley to serve.

Spanish Omelette

Serves	Preparation Time	Cooking Time	Nutritional Information (Per Serving)
4	5 minutes	15 minutes	466 calories | 36g fat (of which 12g saturates) 7g carbohydrate | 3.1g salt | DF | GF

225g (8oz) piece salami, chorizo or garlic sausage, sliced or roughly chopped

50g (2oz) slightly stale sourdough bread (crusts removed), roughly chopped

8 large eggs

2 spring onions, finely chopped

1 small bunch of chives, finely chopped, plus extra to garnish

ground black pepper

green salad to serve

1. Heat a large 28cm (11in), heavy-based frying pan, add the sausage pieces and fry over a low heat until the fat begins to run. Increase the heat and cook the sausage until golden and crisp. Remove from the pan (leaving the fat in the pan) and set aside. Add the bread to the pan and fry until it's also golden and crisp. Remove the pan from the heat, mix the croûtons with the cooked sausage and keep warm.

2. In a bowl, beat together the eggs, spring onions and chives, then season with black pepper. Heat the pan used for the salami and bread. When very hot, add the egg mixture, allowing the liquid to spread across the base of the pan. Cook for 2 minutes, then, using a spatula, draw the cooked edges into the centre, tilting the pan so the mixture runs into the gaps.

3. When the omelette is almost set, reduce the heat and spoon the salami and croûton mixture evenly over the top. Cook for a further 30 seconds, then cut the omelette into four wedges. Sprinkle with chives and serve with a green salad.

Garlic Pork

Serves	Preparation Time	Cooking Time	Nutritional Information (Per Serving)
4	5 minutes	20–25 minutes	181 calories | 8g fat (of which 2g saturates) 1g carbohydrate | 0.2g salt | DF | GF

1 tbsp olive oil

2 garlic cloves, crushed

5cm (2in) piece fresh root ginger, peeled and grated

4 pork chops

salt

stir-fried shredded cabbage to serve

1. Preheat the grill to high. Put the oil into a small bowl, add the garlic and ginger and a pinch of salt and stir well to mix.

2. Grill the pork chops for 7–10 minutes on each side, then remove from the grill. Brush the oil mixture all over the chops, then return to the grill and cook for a further 2 minutes on each side. Serve with stir-fried shredded cabbage and new potatoes.

Maple, Ginger and Soy-roasted Gammon

Serves	Preparation Time	Cooking Time	Nutritional Information (Per Serving)
18	10 minutes	2 hours 10 minutes	392 calories | 21g fat (of which 7g saturates) 2g carbohydrate | 6.1g salt | **DF**

2 x 2.5kg (5⅓lb) smoked boneless
gammon joints

8 tbsp vegetable oil

7.5cm (3in) piece fresh root ginger,
grated

8 tbsp maple syrup

6 tbsp dark soy sauce

12 star anise (optional)

1. If the gammon is salty (check with your butcher), soak it in cold water overnight. Alternatively, bring to the boil in a large pan of water and simmer for 10 minutes, then drain.

2. Preheat the oven to 200°C (180°C fan oven) mark 6. Put the joints into a roasting tin and pour 4 tbsp oil over them. Cover with foil and roast for 1 hour 50 minutes or 20 minutes per 450g (1lb).

3. Mix together the ginger, maple syrup, soy sauce and the remaining oil in a bowl.

4. Take the gammon out of the oven, remove the foil and allow to cool a little, then carefully peel away the skin and discard. Score the fat in a criss-cross pattern, stud with the star anise, if using, then pour the ginger sauce over the gammon. Continue to roast for another 20 minutes or until the glaze is golden brown. Slice and serve one joint warm. Cool the other, wrap in foil and chill until needed.

Cook's Tip
Home-cooked ham is great hot or cold, but cooking a large joint is often impractical. Roasting two medium joints at the same time means you can serve a hot joint and have plenty left to eat cold or freeze for packed lunches.

Savoury Pudding

Serves	Preparation Time	Cooking Time	Nutritional Information (Per Serving)
6	15 minutes, plus 15 minutes soaking	1–1¼ hours	397 calories | 27g fat (of which 15g saturates) 17g carbohydrate | 2.2g salt

150–175g (5–6oz) thickly sliced white bread (such as sourdough), crusts left on

75g (3oz) butter, softened

Dijon mustard

200g (7oz) sliced ham, very roughly chopped

150g (5oz) mature Cheddar, grated

600ml (1 pint) full-fat milk

5 large eggs, beaten

pinch of freshly grated nutmeg

2 tbsp freshly chopped herbs, such as parsley, marjoram or thyme

salt and ground black pepper

green salad to serve

Try Something Different
For a vegetarian alternative, leave out the ham and use 250g (9oz) cheese, such as Gruyère. Add three-quarters of the cheese over the first layer of bread and scatter the remaining cheese on top.

1. Spread the bread generously with butter and sparingly with mustard. Put half the slices in the base of a 2 litre (3½ pint) ovenproof dish. Top with the ham and half the cheese, then with the remaining bread, butter side up. Whisk together the milk, eggs, nutmeg and plenty of salt and pepper. Stir in the herbs, then slowly pour the mixture over the bread. Scatter the remaining cheese on top and leave to soak for 15 minutes. Meanwhile, preheat the oven to 180°C (160°C fan oven) mark 4.

2. Put the dish in a roasting tin and fill halfway up the sides with hand-hot water, then cook for 1–1¼ hours until puffed up, golden brown and just set to the centre. Serve immediately, with a green salad.

Sausages with Roasted Onions and Potatoes

Serves	Preparation Time	Cooking Time	Nutritional Information *(Per Serving)*
4	10 minutes	1 hour 20 minutes	640 calories | 40g fat (of which 12g saturates) 55g carbohydrate | 2.5g salt | DF

900g (2lb) Desiree potatoes, cut into wedges

4 tbsp olive oil

3–4 fresh rosemary sprigs (optional)

2 red onions, each cut into 8 wedges

8 sausages

salt and ground black pepper

1. Preheat the oven to 220°C (200°C fan oven) mark 7. Put the potatoes into a roasting tin – they should sit in one layer. Drizzle with the oil and season to taste with salt and pepper. Toss well to coat the potatoes in oil, then put the rosemary on top, if using, and roast in the oven for 20 minutes.

2. Remove the roasting tin from the oven and add the onion wedges. Toss again to coat the onions and turn the potatoes. Put the sausages in between the potatoes and onions and return the tin to the oven for 1 hour.

3. Divide among four plates and serve immediately.

Cook's Tip
If you can't find Desiree potatoes, use Maris Piper or King Edward instead.

Croque Monsieur

Serves	Preparation Time	Cooking Time	Nutritional Information *(Per Serving)*
4	5 minutes	8 minutes	275 calories | 18g fat (of which 11g saturates) 14g carbohydrate | 1.8g salt

8 slices white bread

softened butter to spread, plus extra for frying

Dijon mustard, to taste

150g (5oz) Gruyère cheese

8 slices ham

1. Spread each slice of bread on both sides with the butter. Then spread one side of two slices of bread with a little Dijon mustard.

2. Divide the cheese and ham between the two mustard-spread bread slices. Put the other slice of bread on top and press down.

3. Heat a griddle with a little butter until hot and fry the sandwiches for 2–3 minutes on each side until golden and crispy and the cheese starts to melt.

4. Slice in half and serve immediately.

Winter Hotpot

Serves	Preparation Time	Cooking Time	Nutritional Information (Per Serving)
8	20 minutes, plus marinating	2 hours 20 minutes	599 calories | 25g fat (of which 8g saturates) 42g carbohydrate | 1.0g salt

1.4kg (3lb) boned shoulder of pork, cut into 2.5cm (1in) cubes

6 garlic cloves, crushed

7 tbsp olive oil

2 tbsp red wine vinegar

4 tbsp soft brown sugar

2 tsp minced chilli or a few drops of chilli sauce

3 tsp dried oregano

2 tsp dried thyme

450g (1lb) onions, sliced

2 tbsp tomato purée

2 x 400g cans haricot or flageolet beans, drained and juice put to one side

2 x 400g cans chopped tomatoes

300ml (½ pint) chicken stock

4 bay leaves

25g (1oz) butter

125g (4oz) white breadcrumbs from French bread or ciabatta

125g (4oz) grated Gruyère cheese

salt and ground pepper

fresh thyme sprigs to garnish

1. Put the pork into a large bowl with the garlic, 2 tbsp oil, the vinegar, sugar, chilli, 2 tsp oregano, all the thyme and salt and pepper to taste. Combine the ingredients, cover and leave in the fridge for at least 8 hours to marinate.

2. Drain the pork, putting the marinade to one side.

3. Preheat the oven to 180°C (160°C fan oven) mark 4. Heat 3 tbsp oil in a large flameproof casserole and fry the pork in batches until well browned on all sides. Put to one side. Add the remaining oil with the onions and cook over a high heat for 10 minutes, stirring occasionally, until they are soft and caramelised. Add the tomato purée and cook for 1 minute. Return the meat to the casserole with the drained bean juice, tomatoes, stock, bay leaves and reserved marinade. Bring to the boil, stirring, then cover and cook in the oven for 2 hours or until the pork is very tender. About 20 minutes before the end of the cooking time, stir in the beans.

4. Increase the oven temperature to 200°C (180°C fan oven) mark 6. Move the pork to a lower shelf. Heat the butter in a roasting tin, add the breadcrumbs, remaining oregano and seasoning. Brown on the top shelf for 10 minutes, then sprinkle onto the hotpot with the breadcrumbs and cheese. Garnish with thyme sprigs and serve.

Freezing Tip

- **To freeze**, complete to the end of step 3. Cool quickly, cover and freeze.

- **To use**, thaw overnight at a cool room temperature. Add 150ml (¼ pint) stock and bring to the boil. Cover and reheat at 180°C (160°C fan oven) mark 4 for 25 minutes; complete the recipe.

Cook's Tip

Curly kale would make a good accompaniment to this dish. Remove the frilly leaf from the coarse stalk and drop into a large pan of lightly salted boiling water. Return to the boil and cook for 2–3 minutes, then drain, season with pepper and serve.

Braised Beef with Mustard and Capers

Serves	Preparation Time	Cooking Time	Nutritional Information (Per Serving)
4	15 minutes	2 hours 20 minutes	391 calories | 19g fat (of which 7g saturates) 10g carbohydrate | 1.5g salt

50g (2oz) can anchovy fillets in oil, drained, chopped and oil put to one side

olive oil

700g (1½lb) braising steak, cut into small strips

2 large Spanish onions, peeled and thinly sliced

2 tbsp capers

1 tsp English mustard

6 fresh thyme sprigs

20g pack fresh flat-leafed parsley, roughly chopped

salt and ground black pepper

mashed potato or a green salad and crusty bread to serve

1. Preheat the oven to 170°C (150°C fan oven) mark 3. Measure the anchovy oil into a deep flameproof casserole, then make up to 3 tbsp with the olive oil. Heat the oil and fry the meat, a few pieces at a time, until well browned, then remove from the pan. When all the meat has been browned, pour 4 tbsp water into the empty casserole and stir to loosen any bits on the bottom.

2. Return the meat to the pan and add the onions, anchovies, capers, mustard, half the thyme and all but 1 tbsp of the parsley. Stir until thoroughly mixed.

3. Tear off a sheet of greaseproof paper big enough to cover the pan. Crumple it up and wet it under the cold tap. Squeeze out most of the water, open it out and press down over the surface of the meat.

4. Cover with a tight-fitting lid and cook in the oven for 2 hours or until the beef is meltingly tender. Check the casserole after 1 hour to make sure it's still moist. If it looks dry, add a little water.

5. Adjust for seasoning, then stir in the remaining parsley and thyme. Serve with mashed potato or a green salad and crusty bread.

Healthy Burgers

Serves	Preparation Time	Cooking Time	Nutritional Information *(Per Serving)*
4	10 minutes	8–12 minutes	80 calories | 20g fat (of which 8g saturates) 2g carbohydrate | 0.3g salt | DF | GF

450g (1lb) lean minced beef

1 onion, very finely chopped

1 tbsp dried herbes de Provence

2 tsp sun-dried tomato paste

1 medium egg, beaten

ground black pepper

chilli coleslaw to serve
(see Cook's Tip)

1. In a bowl, mix together the minced beef, onion, herbs, sun-dried tomato paste and beaten egg. Season with pepper, then shape the mixture into four round burgers about 2cm (¾in) thick.

2. Preheat the grill or griddle pan. Cook the burgers for 4–6 minutes on each side and serve with chilli coleslaw.

Cook's Tip
Chilli Coleslaw
Put 3 peeled and finely shredded carrots into a large bowl. Add ½ finely shredded white cabbage, 1 finely sliced, seeded red pepper and ½ chopped cucumber. In a small bowl, mix together ½ tsp harissa, 100g (3½oz) natural yogurt and 1 tbsp white wine vinegar. Add to the vegetables and toss well.

Perfect Roast Chicken

Serves	Preparation Time	Cooking Time	Nutritional Information *(Per Serving)*
4	5 minutes	1 hour–1¼ hours, plus resting	639 calories | 46g fat (of which 13g saturates) 0g carbohydrate | 0.6g salt | **GF**

1.8kg (4lb) chicken

25g (1oz) butter, softened

2 tbsp olive oil

1 lemon, cut in half

1 small head of garlic, cut in half horizontally

salt and ground black pepper

roast potatoes and vegetables to serve

Thrifty Tip

Roast chicken is one of the most versatile roasts. Use leftover roast chicken in salads and stir-fries, curries and soups (see opposite and page 32). Use the stripped carcass to make chicken stock (see page 30).

1. Preheat the oven to 220°C (200°C fan oven) mark 7. Put the chicken into a roasting tin just large enough to hold it comfortably. Spread the butter all over the chicken, then drizzle with the oil and season with salt and pepper.

2. Squeeze the lemon juice over it, then put one lemon half inside the chicken. Put the other half and the garlic into the roasting tin.

3. Put the chicken into the oven for 15 minutes, then turn the heat down to 190°C (170°C fan oven) mark 5 and cook for a further 45 minutes–1 hour until the leg juices run clear when pierced with a skewer. Baste from time to time with the pan juices. Add a splash of water to the tin if the juices dry out.

4. Put the chicken on a warm plate, cover with foil and 'rest' for 10 minutes, so the juices settle back into the meat, making it moist and easier to slice. Mash some of the garlic into the pan juices and serve the gravy with the chicken, with potatoes and vegetables.

Ideas with leftovers

Chicken and Basil Pasta

Serves 4
Preparation Time 5 minutes
Cooking Time 15 minutes
Per Serving 415 calories | 9g fat
(of which 2g saturates) | 62g carbohydrate
0.9g salt | DF

300g (11oz) dried pasta

1 tbsp olive oil

1 garlic clove, crushed

2 x 400g cans cherry tomatoes

300g (11oz) cooked chicken, shredded

50g (2oz) pitted black olives

handful of torn basil leaves

salt and ground black pepper

1. Cook the pasta in a large pan of lightly salted boiling water or according to the packet instructions.

2. Meanwhile, heat the oil in a pan, add the garlic and cook for 1–2 minutes, then add the tomatoes and cook for 5–7 minutes.

3. Add the chicken and olives to the pan and cook for 2–3 minutes. Stir in the basil and season to taste with salt and pepper.

4. Drain the pasta, toss in the sauce and serve.

Quick Chicken and Gruyere Salad

Serves 4
Preparation Time 15 minutes, plus cooling
Per Serving 464 calories | 39g fat
(of which 8g saturates) | 4g carbohydrate
0.6g salt | GF

350g (12oz) cooked, boned chicken, skinned and cut into bite-size pieces

2 celery sticks, thinly sliced

50g (2oz) Gruyère or Emmenthal cheese, coarsely grated

1 firm red apple, halved, cored and roughly chopped

50g (2oz) seedless black grapes, halved

100ml (3½fl oz) vegetable oil

1 tbsp white wine vinegar

2 tbsp soured cream

2 tbsp mayonnaise

2 tbsp freshly chopped parsley

40g (1½oz) toasted walnuts

salt and ground black pepper

mixed green salad to serve

1. Put the chicken, celery, cheese, apple and grapes into a bowl. Add all the other ingredients and toss well. Adjust the seasoning, cover and leave to chill for at least 10–15 minutes. Serve with a green salad.

Cook's Tips
Any strongly flavoured cheese can be used for this recipe. This whole salad can be made and kept covered in the fridge the day before. Stir well before serving.

Leftover Roast Chicken Soup

Serves 4
Preparation Time 10 minutes
Cooking Time 45 minutes
Per Serving 199 calories | 12g fat
(of which 3g saturates) | 12g carbohydrate
0.1g salt | GF

3 tbsp olive oil

1 onion, chopped,

1 carrot, chopped

2 celery sticks, chopped

2 fresh thyme sprigs, chopped

1 bay leaf

a stripped roast chicken carcass

900ml (1½ pints) boiling water

150–200g (5–7oz) cooked chicken, roughly chopped

200g (7oz) mashed or roast potato

1 tbsp double cream

1. Heat the oil in a large pan. Add the onion, carrot, celery and thyme and fry gently for 20–30 minutes until soft but not brown. Add the bay leaf, chicken carcass and boiling water to the pan. Bring to the boil, then simmer for 5 minutes.

2. Remove the bay leaf and carcass and add the chopped roast chicken and cooked potato. Simmer for 5 minutes.

3. Whiz the soup in a food processor or blender until smooth, then pour back into the pan and bring to the boil. Stir in the cream and serve immediately.

Roast Rib of Beef

Serves	**Preparation Time**	**Cooking Time**	**Nutritional Information (*Per Serving*)**
8	5 minutes	2½ hours, plus resting	807 calories | 53g fat (of which 24g saturates) 2g carbohydrate | 0.5g salt

2-bone rib of beef,
about 2.5–2.7kg (5½–6lb)

1 tbsp plain flour

1 tbsp mustard powder

600ml (1 pint) beef stock

600ml (1 pint) water from
parboiled potatoes

salt and ground black pepper

Yorkshire puddings (see page 28),
roasted root vegetables
and a green vegetable to serve

1. Preheat the oven to 230°C (210°C fan oven) mark 8. Put the beef, fat-side up, into a roasting tin just large enough to hold the joint. Mix the flour and mustard together in a small bowl and season with salt and pepper, then rub the mixture over the beef. Roast in the centre of the oven for 30 minutes.

2. Move the beef to a lower shelf, near the bottom of the oven. Turn the oven down to 220°C (200°C fan oven) mark 7 and continue to roast for a further 2 hours, basting occasionally.

3. Put the beef on a carving dish, cover loosely with foil and leave to rest while you make the gravy. Skim off most of the fat from the roasting tin. Put the roasting tin on the hob, pour in the stock and boil until syrupy. Add the vegetable water and boil until syrupy. There should be about 450ml (¾ pint) gravy. Taste and adjust the seasoning.

4. Remove the rib bone and carve the beef. Serve with gravy, Yorkshire puddings and vegetables.

Chilli con Carne

Serves 6
Preparation Time 10 minutes
Cooking Time about 50 minutes
Per Serving 289 calories | 12g fat
(of which 4g saturates) | 17g carbohydrate
0.7g salt

2 tbsp sunflower oil

1 onion, roughly chopped

2 garlic cloves, crushed

1 red pepper, seeded and chopped

450g (1lb) cooked beef, roughly chopped

1 tsp chilli powder

1 tsp chilli flakes

1 tsp ground cumin

1 tsp ground coriander

300ml (½ pint) hot beef stock

1 tbsp Worcestershire sauce

400g can chopped tomatoes

400g can kidney beans, drained and rinsed

salt and ground black pepper

grated cheese to sprinkle

guacamole or soured cream, to serve

1. Heat the oil in a large frying pan, add the onion, garlic and red pepper and cook gently for 5 minutes.

2. Add the beef to the pan and cook over a high heat for 5 minutes or until well browned.

3. Stir in the chilli powder and flakes, cumin and coriander, then cook for 2 minutes. Add the hot stock and simmer for 2 minutes.

4. Stir in the Worcestershire sauce and tomatoes, and season with salt and pepper, then cook for 15 minutes. Add the kidney beans to the mixture and cook for a further 20 minutes.

5. Serve the chilli with rice, or piled on top of baked potatoes. Sprinkle with the grated cheese and serve with guacamole or soured cream.

Notes
- This chilli is fairly mild, but it can easily be made hotter by adding more chilli powder and flakes.
- The flavour is improved if the chilli con carne is prepared a day ahead.

Cottage Pie

Serves 4
Preparation Time 15 minutes
Cooking Time about 1 hour
Per Serving 683 calories | 40g fat
(of which 20g saturates) | 55g carbohydrate
0.9g salt

1 tbsp oil

450g (1lb) onions, chopped

450g (1lb) cooked beef, roughly chopped

1 tbsp tomato purée

1 tbsp plain flour

1 tbsp Worcestershire sauce

450ml (¾ pint) hot beef stock

700g (1½lb) potatoes, peeled and cut into large chunks

450g (1lb) parsnips, peeled and quartered

25g (1oz) butter

4 tbsp milk

salt and ground black pepper

1. Heat the oil in a flameproof casserole, add the onions and fry gently for 10 minutes or until softened.

2. Add the beef and cook on a higher heat, stirring, for about 5 minutes until well browned.

3. Stir in the tomato purée and cook for 30 seconds. Stir in the flour, then add the Worcestershire sauce and stock. Bring to the boil and season generously with salt and pepper, then simmer for 20 minutes. Preheat the oven to 200°C (180°C fan oven) mark 6.

4. Meanwhile, put the potatoes and parsnips into a large pan of salted water. Bring to the boil and cook for 20–25 minutes until very soft. Drain and put back into the pan over a low heat to dry off. Mash until smooth and then beat in the butter and milk. Season to taste with salt and pepper.

5. Put the beef mixture into a 1.7 litre (3 pint) dish and spoon the mash on top. Stand the dish on a baking tray and bake for 25–30 minutes or until piping hot and the topping is golden brown.

Try Something Different
To make individual pies, use four 450ml (¾ pint) shallow ovenproof dishes.

Roast Lamb with Orange

Serves	Preparation Time	Cooking Time	Nutritional Information (*Per Serving*)
4	20 minutes	1 hour 25 minutes, plus resting	581 calories | 28g fat (of which 12g saturates) 14g carbohydrate | 0.4g salt | DF

grated zest and juice of 1 orange, plus extra wedges to garnish

2 garlic cloves, sliced

3 large fresh rosemary sprigs, leaves stripped

1 tbsp olive oil

1.4kg (3lb) leg of lamb

3 tbsp orange marmalade

1 tbsp plain flour

salt and ground black pepper

roasted vegetables to serve

1. Preheat the oven to 180°C (160°C fan oven) mark 4. In a bowl, mix together the orange zest, garlic, the leaves from 2 rosemary sprigs and the oil. Season with salt and pepper. Put the lamb on a board and make several slits all over it. Stuff the mixture into the slits. Put the lamb on a rack in a roasting tin and roast for 1¼ hours, basting with the juices from time to time.

2. About 10–15 minutes before the end of the cooking time, brush the lamb with the marmalade. Insert a few rosemary leaves into each slit in the meat.

3. Remove the lamb from the oven, wrap loosely in foil and leave to rest for 10–15 minutes.

4. Put the roasting tin on the hob, skim off and discard the fat and stir in the flour. Add 150ml (¼ pint) water and the orange juice and bring to the boil, then simmer, stirring occasionally, for 8 minutes

or until thick. Season. Carve the lamb and serve with the gravy and vegetables; garnish with orange wedges.

Try Something Different
Roast Lamb with Lemon and Thyme
Use lemon zest and juice instead of orange and replace the rosemary with 3–4 large fresh thyme sprigs.

Ideas with leftovers

Moussaka

Serves 6
Preparation Time 20 minutes
Cooking Time 1 hour 20 minutes, plus standing
Per Serving 470 calories | 35g fat
(of which 14g saturates) | 7g carbohydrate
1g salt | **GF**

1kg (2¼lb) aubergines, trimmed

5 tbsp olive oil

450g (1lb) onions, finely sliced

3 garlic cloves, crushed

700g (1½lb) cooked lamb, roughly
chopped or minced

2 tbsp sun-dried tomato paste

400g can chopped tomatoes

1 cinnamon stick, slightly crushed

2 bay leaves

salt and ground black pepper

1 tbsp freshly chopped oregano,
plus extra sprigs to garnish

Topping

200g carton Greek yogurt

1 large egg

50g (2oz) freshly grated Parmesan

freshly grated nutmeg

75g (3oz) feta cheese,
roughly crumbled

1. Preheat the oven to 200°C
(180°C fan oven) mark 6. Cut the
aubergines into 5mm (¼in) thick
slices, brush both sides with a little
oil and lay on four baking sheets.
Season with salt and pepper. Roast
for 35–40 minutes, turning halfway
through.

2. Meanwhile, heat the rest of the
oil in a large pan. Add the onions
and cook over a low heat for about
10 minutes until soft. Add the garlic
and cook for 2 minutes. Tip into a
bowl and set aside while you cook
the lamb.

3. Put the lamb in the pan and
brown, stirring, over a high heat.
Return the onions and garlic to
the pan. Add the tomato paste,
chopped tomatoes, cinnamon, bay
leaves and oregano. Bring to a
simmer and add seasoning. Simmer,
half-covered, for 20 minutes.

4. To make the topping, put the
yogurt, egg and half the grated
Parmesan into a bowl and season
with salt, pepper and a little
nutmeg. Mix together, using a
balloon whisk, until combined.

5. Spoon half the lamb mixture into
a 2 litre (3½ pint) ovenproof dish.
Cover with half the aubergine
slices, overlapping them as
necessary. Season well and repeat
the layers, finishing with aubergine
slices.

6. Scatter the crumbled feta on
top, then pour the yogurt mixture
over and sprinkle with the
remaining Parmesan. Bake for
35–40 minutes until golden brown.
Leave the moussaka to stand for
10–15 minutes before serving,
garnished with oregano and
accompanied by a green salad.

Lamb and Yogurt Wraps

Serves 4
Preparation Time 15 minutes
Per Serving 497 calories | 32g fat
(of which 12g saturates) | 9g carbohydrate
0.7g salt

cooked roast lamb

4 tbsp ready-made vinaigrette (see
page 26), or juice of 1 lemon

1 red onion, cut into thin wedges

20g pack flat-leafed parsley, roughly
chopped

25g (1oz) toasted seed mix

200g (7oz) low-fat yogurt

pinch of ground cumin

2 garlic cloves, crushed

1 tbsp clear honey

mixed salad leaves

4–8 tortilla wraps or pitta bread

1. Slice the lamb very thinly with a
sharp knife. Put into a bowl, add
half the vinaigrette or lemon juice,
the onion, parsley and seeds and
toss together.

2. Whisk together the remaining
vinaigrette or lemon juice with the
yogurt, cumin, garlic and honey.

3. Wrap the lamb with the salad
leaves and dressing inside tortilla
wraps or stuff into warm pitta
pockets.

Try Something Different
Instead of the yogurt dressing, serve
the lamb with ready-made hummus or
tzatziki.

Crisp Roast Pork with Apple Sauce

Serves	Preparation Time	Cooking Time	Nutritional Information (*Per Serving*)
6	30 minutes, plus 1–2 hours standing	2 hours, plus resting	769 calories | 50g fat (of which 18g saturates) 22g carbohydrate | 0.4g salt | DF

1.6kg (3½ lb) boned rolled loin of pork

olive oil

1kg (2¼ lb) cooking apples, cored and roughly chopped

1–2 tbsp granulated sugar

1 tbsp plain flour

600ml (1 pint) chicken stock

salt and ground black pepper

1. Score the pork skin, sprinkle generously with salt and leave at room temperature for 1–2 hours.

2. Preheat the oven to 220°C (200°C fan oven) mark 7. Wipe the salt off the skin, rub with oil and sprinkle again with salt. Put half the apples in a small roasting tin, sit the pork on top and roast for 30 minutes. Turn the oven down to 190°C (170°C fan oven) mark 5 and roast for a further 1½ hours or until cooked.

3. Meanwhile, put the remaining apples in a pan with the sugar and 2 tbsp water, cover with a tight-fitting lid and cook until just soft. Set aside.

4. Remove the pork from the tin and leave to rest. Skim off most of the fat, leaving about 1 tbsp and the apples in the tin. Stir in the flour until smooth, stir in the stock and bring to the boil. Bubble gently for 2–3 minutes, skimming if necessary. Strain the sauce through a sieve into a jug, pushing through as much of the apple as possible. Slice the pork and serve with the sauce, roast potatoes and green vegetables.

Cook's Tip
Apples discolour quickly when exposed to air. Toss with lemon juice if you are not going to use the prepared fruit immediately.

Carving pork with crackling

1. It is much easier to slice pork if you first remove the crackling. Remove any string and position the carving knife just under the skin on the topmost side of the joint. Work the knife under the crackling, taking care not to cut into the meat, until you can pull it off with your fingers.

2. Slice the meat, then snap the crackling into servings.

Perfect crackling

- If possible, ask the butcher to score the skin for you.
- The pork skin needs to be dry. Remove the shop's wrapping and pat the skin dry with kitchen paper.
- Leave the joint uncovered in the refrigerator overnight to dry out the skin.
- Use a craft knife or your sharpest knife to score the skin, cutting about halfway into the fat underneath.
- Rub the scored skin with a little olive oil and salt.

Pork and Noodle Stir-fry

Serves 4
Preparation Time 10 minutes, plus marinating
Cooking Time 7–8 minutes
Per Serving 480 calories | 9g fat (of which 2g saturates) | 65g carbohydrate | 2.9g salt | DF

1tbsp sesame oil

5cm (2in) piece fresh root ginger, peeled and grated

2tbsp soy sauce

1tbsp fish sauce

½ red chilli, finely chopped

450g (1lb) cooked pork, cut into strips

2 red peppers, seeded and roughly chopped

250g (9oz) baby sweetcorn, halved lengthways

200g (7oz) sugarsnap peas, halved

300g (11oz) beansprouts

250g pack rice noodles

1. Put the oil into a large bowl. Add the ginger, soy sauce, fish sauce, chilli and pork strips. Mix well and leave to marinate for 10 minutes.

2. Heat a large wok until hot. Lift the pork out of the marinade with a slotted spoon. Stir-fry the red peppers, sweetcorn, sugarsnap peas, beansprouts and remaining marinade for 2–3 minutes over a high heat. Add the pork and stir-fry for 2 minutes until piping hot.

3. Meanwhile, cook the noodles in a large pan of boiling water for the time stated on the pack. Drain the noodles, tip into the wok and toss together, then serve immediately.

Pork Pittas with Salsa

Serves 4
Preparation Time 10 minutes
Cooking Time 10 minutes
Per Serving 518 calories | 17g fat (of which 5g saturates) | 58g carbohydrate | 1.3g salt

1 tbsp olive oil

500g (1lb 2oz) diced cooked pork

4 tbsp spicy seasoning such as fajita seasoning

4 large pittas

100g (3½ oz) Greek yogurt

For the salsa

1 red onion, chopped

1 ripe avocado, halved, stoned, peeled and chopped

4 large tomatoes, roughly chopped

a small handful of roughly chopped fresh coriander

juice of 1 lime

salt and ground black pepper

1. Heat the oil in a pan over a medium heat and reheat the pork, stirring, for 2–3 minutes. Add the spicy seasoning and stir to coat the pork, then cook for a further minute until piping hot.

2. Meanwhile, make the salsa. Put the onion in a bowl and add the avocado, tomatoes, coriander and lime juice. Mix well, season to taste with salt and pepper, and set aside.

3. Toast the pittas until lightly golden, then slit down the side and stuff with the pork, a spoonful of salsa and a dollop of Greek yogurt. Serve immediately.

Spiced Roast Turkey

Serves	Preparation Time	Cooking Time	Nutritional Information (*Per Serving*)
10	30 minutes	about 3 hours, plus resting	611 calories | 40g fat (of which 16g saturates) 12g carbohydrate | 2.0g salt

3.6–4.5kg (8–10lb)
oven-ready turkey

Pork, Spinach and Apple Stuffing
(opposite), cooled

150g (5oz) butter, softened

salt and ground black pepper

herbs to garnish

For the sausages

8 sausages

16 thin rashers streaky bacon

1. Loosen the skin at the neck end of the turkey, ease your fingers up between the skin and the breast and, using a small, sharp knife, remove the wishbone.

2. Preheat the oven to 190°C (170°C fan oven) mark 5. Season the inside of the turkey with salt and pepper, then spoon the cold stuffing into the neck end only. Neaten the shape, turn the bird over and secure the neck skin with skewers or cocktail sticks. Weigh to calculate the cooking time, allowing 30 minutes per kg (12 minutes per lb).

3. Put the turkey into a roasting tin, smear the butter over the turkey and season with salt and pepper. Cover with a tent of foil. Roast according to its weight, basting occasionally. If the legs were tied together, loosen after the first hour so that they cook more evenly.

4. Twist each sausage in half and cut to make two mini sausages. Stretch the bacon rashers by running the blunt side of a kitchen knife along each rasher (this stops them shrinking too much when they're cooked). Roll a rasher around each mini sausage. Put in a small roasting tin or around the turkey and cook for about 1 hour. Remove the foil from the turkey 45 minutes before the end of the cooking time.

5. When the turkey is cooked, tip the bird so the juices run into the tin, then put it on a warmed serving plate with the sausages. Cover loosely with foil and leave to rest for 20–30 minutes before carving. Garnish with herbs.

Try Something Different
Spiced Roast Turkey
Use 2 tsp Cajun spice seasoning and mix the spice with the butter before smearing over the turkey.

Pork, Spinach and Apple Stuffing

Serves 8
Preparation Time 20 minutes
Cooking Time 15 minutes
Per Serving 298 calories | 21g fat
(of which 7g saturates) | 20g carbohydrate
1.3g salt | DF

2 tbsp olive oil

150g (5oz) onion, finely chopped

225g (8oz) fresh spinach, torn into pieces if leaves are large

2 sharp apples, such as Granny Smith, peeled, cored and cut into chunks

400g (14oz) pork sausagemeat, coarsely grated

zest of 1 lemon

1 tbsp freshly chopped thyme,

100g (3½oz) fresh white breadcrumbs

2 large eggs, beaten

salt and ground black pepper

1. Heat the oil in a frying pan, add the onion and cook for 10 minutes or until soft. Increase the heat, add the spinach and cook until wilted.

2. Add the apples and cook, stirring, for 2–3 minutes, then set aside to cool. When the mixture is cold, add the sausagemeat, lemon zest, thyme, breadcrumbs and eggs, then season and stir until evenly mixed.

Turkey Curry

Serves 4
Preparation Time 15 minutes
Cooking Time 35 minutes
Per Serving 319 calories | 11g fat
(of which 3g saturates) | 9g carbohydrate
0.3g salt | GF

2 tbsp oil

1 large onion, peeled and chopped

2 garlic cloves, peeled and finely chopped

1 tsp ground turmeric

½ tsp chilli powder

1½ tsp ground cumin

1½ tsp ground coriander

400g can chopped tomatoes

600g (1¼lb) cooked turkey

1 tsp garam masala

150ml (¼ pint) thick yogurt

salt

1. Heat the oil in a heavy-based pan, add the onion and garlic and fry gently until softened and golden. Add the turmeric, chilli powder, cumin and coriander and cook, stirring, for 1 minute.

2. Add the tomatoes and salt to taste. Bring to the boil, cover and simmer for 20 minutes.

3. Remove any skin from the turkey, then cut into chunks. Add to the pan with the garam masala and 4 tbsp yogurt. Cover and cook gently for 10 minutes, then stir in the remaining yogurt. Serve with rice.

Try Something Different
- For a more intense flavour, fry 1 tsp black mustard seeds with the spices.
- Scatter over 2–3 tbsp freshly chopped coriander to serve.

Turkey Soup

Serves 6
Preparation Time 25 minutes
Cooking Time 30 minutes
Per Serving 194 calories | 9g fat
(of which 1g saturates) | 19g carbohydrate
0.2g salt | DF

75g (3oz) long-grain wild rice

3 tbsp vegetable oil

1 large onion, chopped

225g (8oz) leeks, thinly sliced

225g (8oz) carrots, chopped

3 sticks celery, sliced

2 tbsp tomato purée

2 litres (3 1/2 pints) turkey stock

1 bouquet garni

225g (8oz) cooked turkey, cut into strips

salt and ground black pepper

1. Put the rice into a pan of cold salted water, bring to the boil and simmer for 30 minutes or until tender. Drain.

2. Meanwhile, heat the oil in a pan and cook the onion, leeks, carrots and celery for 3–4 minutes until soft. Add the tomato purée and cook for 1 minute.

3. Add the stock and bouquet garni, season to taste with salt and pepper and bring to the boil. Simmer for 20 minutes.

4. Add the drained rice and the turkey and heat through. Discard the bouquet garni and serve.

4

FISH

Peppered Mackerel

Serves	Preparation Time	Cooking Time	Nutritional Information (Per Serving)
4	10 minutes	15 minutes	764 calories | 63g fat (of which 22g saturates) 1g carbohydrate | 0.4g salt | GF

4 tsp whole mixed peppercorns

4 fresh mackerel, gutted, about 250g (9oz) each

1 tbsp sunflower oil

200ml (7fl oz) crème fraîche

lemon wedges to garnish

asparagus and sugarsnap peas to serve

1. Lightly crush 2 tsp peppercorns using a mortar and pestle. Sprinkle one side of each mackerel with half the crushed peppercorns.

2. Heat the oil in a frying pan over a medium-high heat. Add the fish, peppered side down, and cook for 5–7 minutes. Sprinkle the mackerel with the remaining crushed peppercorns, turn the fish over and continue to fry for 5–7 minutes until cooked (see Cook's Tips). Remove and keep warm.

3. Wipe out the pan, add the crème fraîche and bring to the boil. Stir in the remaining whole peppercorns. (If the sauce becomes too thick, add some boiling water.)

4. To serve, spoon the sauce over the mackerel, garnish with lemon wedges and serve with asparagus and sugarsnap peas.

> ### Cook's Tips
> If the mackerel are large, make three shallow slashes on either side of the fish.
>
> To test whether the fish is cooked, push with the point of a knife – the flesh should be opaque and flake easily.

Kedgeree

Serves	Preparation Time	Cooking Time	Nutritional Information *(Per Serving)*
4	15 minutes	30 minutes	457 calories | 16g fat (of which 7g saturates) 42g carbohydrate | 3g salt

550g (1¼lb) undyed smoked haddock

750ml (1¼ pints) hot fish stock

40g (1½oz) butter

1 onion, finely chopped

1 tsp curry powder

½ tsp turmeric

¼ tsp cayenne pepper

200g (7oz) long-grain rice

4 medium eggs

large handful of fresh coriander, roughly chopped

1. Put the haddock into a deep frying pan so that it fits snugly. Cover with the hot stock and bring gently to a simmer. Poach for 5 minutes. Using a slotted spoon, lift the fish out and put on to a plate. Leave to cool a little, then discard the bones and skin and break the flesh into flakes. Set aside. Strain the poaching liquor into a measuring jug up to 600ml (1 pint) and set aside. Discard any remaining stock.

2. Bring a pan of water to boil for the eggs. Melt the butter in a large pan and cook the onion on a low heat for 10 minutes. Stir in the spices and cook for 1 minute. Add the rice and stir to coat with the butter. Pour in the measured poaching liquor and bring to the boil. Cover the pan, turn the heat to its lowest setting and cook the rice according to the packet instructions.

3. Meanwhile, cook the eggs for 7 minutes in the boiling water. Drain, then peel when cool enough to handle. Chop 3 eggs and cut the remaining egg into quarters. When the rice is tender, gently stir in the haddock and chopped eggs. Spoon on to plates and garnish with the remaining egg and the coriander.

Mediterranean Fish Crumble

Serves	Preparation Time	Cooking Time	Nutritional Information *(Per Serving)*
4	20 minutes	50 minutes	334 calories | 18g fat (of which 7g saturates) 22g carbohydrate | 2g salt

1 tbsp rapeseed oil

1 onion, finely chopped

2 garlic cloves, crushed

1 medium courgette, diced

1 tbsp tomato purée

400g can chopped tomatoes

75g (3oz) pitted black olives, roughly chopped

1 tbsp capers

200ml (7fl oz) fish stock

75g (3oz) fresh brown breadcrumbs

50g (2oz) freshly grated mature Cheddar

15g (½oz) pinenuts

25g (1oz) butter, melted

400g (14oz) frozen white fish fillets, thawed

small handful of basil, roughly chopped

salt and ground black pepper

1. Heat the oil in a pan and add the onion and garlic. Cover and cook gently for 10 minutes. Stir in the courgette, tomato purée, tomatoes, olives, capers and stock. Bring to the boil, then simmer for 10 minutes until reduced and thickened slightly.

2. Preheat the oven to 200°C (180°C fan oven) mark 6. Make a crumble topping by mixing together the breadcrumbs, cheese, pinenuts and butter. Season to taste with salt and pepper and set aside.

3. Add the fish and basil to the sauce and cook for a few more minutes until the fish begins to flake. Use a spoon to break it up a little more, then divide the mixture among four 200ml (7fl oz) individual ovenproof dishes. Divide the topping into four and sprinkle over each dish. Bake for 20–25 minutes until piping hot and the crumble is golden. Serve immediately.

Salmon and Bulgur Wheat Pilaf

Serves	Preparation Time	Cooking Time	Nutritional Information *(Per Serving)*
4	5 minutes	20 minutes	323 calories | 11g fat (of which 2g saturates) 30g carbohydrate | 1.5g salt | DF

1 tbsp olive oil

1 onion, chopped

175g (6oz) bulgur wheat

450ml (¾ pint) vegetable stock

400g can pink salmon, drained and flaked

125g (4oz) spinach, roughly chopped

225g (8oz) frozen peas

zest and juice of 1 lemon

salt and ground black pepper

1. Heat the oil in a large saucepan, add the onion and cook until softened. Stir in the bulgur wheat to coat in the oil, then stir in the stock and bring to the boil. Cover, reduce the heat and simmer for 10–15 minutes until the stock has been fully absorbed.

2. Stir in the salmon, spinach, peas and lemon juice and cook until the spinach has wilted and the salmon and peas are heated through. Season to taste with salt and pepper and sprinkle with lemon zest before serving.

Try Something Different
Instead of salmon use 200g (7oz) cooked peeled prawns and 200g (7oz) cherry tomatoes.

Crispy Crumbed Fish

Serves	Preparation Time	Cooking Time	Nutritional Information (Per Serving)
4	5 minutes	10–15 minutes	171 calories | 1g fat (of which trace saturates) 10g carbohydrate | 0.8g salt | DF

50g (2oz) fresh breadcrumbs

small handful of freshly chopped flat-leafed parsley

2 tbsp capers, chopped

zest of 1 lemon

4 x 150g (5oz) haddock or pollack fillets

½ tbsp Dijon mustard

juice of ½ lemon

salt and ground black pepper

new potatoes and mixed salad to serve

1. Preheat the oven to 180°C (160°C fan oven) mark 4. Put the breadcrumbs into a bowl with the parsley, capers and lemon zest. Mix well, then set aside.

2. Put the fish fillets on a baking tray. Mix the mustard and half the lemon juice in a bowl with a little salt and pepper, then spread over the top of each piece of fish. Spoon the breadcrumb mixture over the top – don't worry if some falls off.

3. Cook in the oven for 10–15 minutes until the fish is cooked and the breadcrumbs are golden. Pour the remaining lemon juice over the top and serve with new potatoes and a mixed salad.

Thrifty Tip
If freezer space is tight, make dried breadcrumbs, which can be stored in a jar for up to three months. Arrange leftover bread on a baking sheet and bake for 30 minutes at 120°C (100°C fan oven) mark ½ until golden. Whiz in a food processor or blender and store in an airtight jar.

Prawn and Vegetable Stir-fry

Serves	Preparation Time	Cooking Time	Nutritional Information (Per Serving)
4	15 minutes	15 minutes	355 calories | 13g fat (of which 2g saturates) 44g carbohydrate | 2.3g salt

2 tbsp sunflower oil

1 garlic clove, finely chopped

4cm (1½in) piece fresh root ginger, finely chopped

¼ red chilli, finely chopped

2 carrots, cut into batons

1 red pepper, seeded and thinly sliced

200ml (7fl oz) hot vegetable stock

200g (7oz) frozen raw prawns, thawed

4 tbsp soy sauce

3 tbsp sweet chilli sauce

175g (6oz) medium egg noodles

small handful of fresh coriander

25g (1oz) roasted peanuts, roughly chopped

lime wedges to serve

1. Heat the oil in a wok or large frying pan. Add the garlic, ginger and chilli and fry for 1 minute. Add the carrots and red pepper and fry for a further 1 minute. Pour in the hot stock and simmer for 5 minutes until the vegetables are nearly cooked.

2. Stir in the prawns, soy sauce and sweet chilli sauce. Heat through until the prawns have turned pink and are piping hot – about 5 minutes.

3. Meanwhile, cook the noodles in a large pan of boiling water according to the packet instructions. Drain well, then add to the prawn sauce and toss together. Divide among four bowls, top with the coriander and peanuts, then serve with the lime wedges.

> ### Cook's Tip
> The ideal way to thaw fish and shellfish is to leave it overnight in the fridge. Thawing fish in water leads to loss of texture, flavour and nutrients. You can cook fish straight from the freezer – just add a couple of extra minutes to the cooking time
>
>

Potatoes with Anchovies

Serves	Preparation Time	Cooking Time	Nutritional Information (Per Serving)
4	5 minutes	1 hour	90 calories | 1g fat (of which trace saturates) 18g carbohydrate | 0.5g salt

butter to grease

4 medium potatoes, thinly sliced

1 large onion, thinly sliced

400ml (14fl oz) hot chicken stock

8 tbsp passata

8 anchovies, chopped

salt and ground black pepper

1. Preheat the oven to 200°C (180°C fan oven) mark 6. Grease a small 15 x 25.5cm (6 x 10in) ovenproof dish with a little butter.

2. Put half the potatoes in a thin layer in the dish, sprinkle on the onion, then top with the remaining potatoes. Pour the hot stock over, season to taste with salt and pepper and cover the dish with foil. Cook in the oven for 50 minutes.

3. Mix the passata with the anchovies, then spoon over the potatoes. Re-cover with foil and cook for a further 10 minutes.

Smoked Haddock Rarebit

Serves	Preparation Time	Cooking Time	Nutritional Information (Per Serving)
4	5 minutes	10–15 minutes	481 calories | 32g fat (of which 21g saturates) 16g carbohydrate | 3.4g salt | GF

4 x 150g (5oz) smoked haddock fillets, skinned

4 slices bread

200g (7oz) spinach

2 large tomatoes

300g (11oz) low-fat crème fraîche

salt and ground black pepper

1. Preheat the grill. Season the haddock fillets with salt and pepper and put into a shallow ovenproof dish. Grill for 6–8 minutes until opaque and cooked through.

2. Toast the bread on both sides until golden.

3. Wash the spinach, squeeze out the water and put into a pan. Cover and cook for 1–2 minutes until starting to wilt. Tip into a bowl. Slice the tomatoes.

4. Top each piece of toast with a piece of fish, then add the tomato slices and spinach. Spoon the crème fraîche over and grill for 2–3 minutes to heat through. Season with pepper and serve immediately.

Cook's Tip
To store fish, remove from its original wrapping, rinse in cold water, pat dry, cover and place towards the bottom of the fridge. Most varieties of fish can be stored for a day or two. Always check the use-by dates on packaged fish or ask the fishmonger.

Cod with Cherry Tomatoes

Serves	Preparation Time	Cooking Time	Nutritional Information (Per Serving)
4	15 minutes	20–25 minutes	168 calories | 7g fat (of which 1g saturates) 8g carbohydrate | 0.2g salt | DF

4 x 100g (3½oz) cod steaks

1 tbsp plain flour

2 tbsp olive oil

1 small onion, sliced

1 large red chilli, seeded and chopped

1 garlic clove, crushed

250g (9oz) cherry tomatoes, halved

4 spring onions, chopped

2 tbsp freshly chopped coriander

salt and ground black pepper

Try Something Different
Use another white fish such as sea bass or pollack fillets instead of the cod.

1. Season the cod with salt and pepper, then lightly dust with the flour. Heat 1 tbsp oil in a large frying pan, add the onion and fry for 5–10 minutes until golden.

2. Pour the remaining oil into the pan. Add the cod and fry for 3 minutes on each side. Add the chilli, garlic, cherry tomatoes, spring onions and coriander and season with salt and pepper. Cover and continue to cook for 5–10 minutes until everything is heated through. Serve immediately.

Cod Steaks with Fennel

Serves	Preparation Time	Cooking Time	Nutritional Information (Per Serving)
4	10 minutes, plus marinating	30 minutes	212 calories | 6g fat (of which trace saturates) 6g carbohydrate | 0.8g salt | DF

1 tbsp hoisin sauce

4 tbsp light soy sauce

4 tbsp dry vermouth (optional, see Cook's Tip)

4 tbsp orange juice

½ tsp Chinese five-spice powder

½ tsp ground cumin

1 garlic clove, crushed

4 x 150g (5oz) thick cod fillets or steaks

1 tbsp vegetable oil

2 fennel bulbs, about 700g (1½lb), thinly sliced and tops put to one side

2 tsp sesame seeds

1. For the marinade, combine the hoisin sauce, soy sauce, vermouth, if using, orange juice, five-spice powder, cumin and garlic. Put the cod into a shallow dish and pour the marinade over. Cover and leave to marinate in a cool place for at least 1 hour.

2. Preheat the grill or a lightly oiled griddle. Remove the fish and put the marinade to one side. Put the fish under the hot grill or on the hot griddle and cook for 4 minutes, then turn over and cook for 3–4 minutes until cooked.

3. Heat the oil in sauté pan. Add the fennel and cook briskly for 5–7 minutes or until brown and beginning to soften. Add the marinade, bring to the boil and bubble until reduced and sticky.

4. Put the fish on a bed of fennel, spoon any pan juices around it and sprinkle with the sesame seeds. Garnish with the reserved fennel tops and serve.

> **Cook's Tip**
> Vermouth is a fortified wine, which means it has a long shelf life; it can be used instead of white wine.

Trout and Dill Fishcakes

Serves	Preparation Time	Cooking Time	Nutritional Information *(Per Serving)*
4	15 minutes	25 minutes	196 calories | 5g fat (of which 1g saturates) 27g carbohydrate | 0.1g salt | DF

4 medium potatoes, peeled and chopped

2 trout fillets

3 spring onions, finely chopped

2 dill sprigs, finely chopped

zest of 1 lemon

1 tbsp olive oil

a little plain flour

salt

watercress to serve

1. Cook the potatoes in a pan of lightly salted boiling water for 6–8 minutes until tender. Drain, return to the pan and mash.

2. Preheat the grill to high. Grill the trout fillets for 8–10 minutes until cooked through and firm to the touch. Skin the fish, flake into pieces, removing any bones, then put into the pan with the mashed potato.

3. Add the spring onions, dill and lemon zest to the pan with the oil, season with salt and mix together well.

4. Shape the mixture into eight small patties. Dust with flour and put on a non-stick baking sheet, then grill for 3 minutes on each side. Serve the fishcakes hot, with watercress.

Try Something Different

- Replace the trout with 225g (8oz) cooked salmon, haddock or smoked haddock. Skin and flake the fish and add at stage 2.
- If you can't find dill, replace with 2 tbsp freshly chopped parsley.

Poached Pollack in Red Pepper Sauce

Serves	Preparation Time	Cooking Time	Nutritional Information (Per Serving)
4	10 minutes	25 minutes	177 calories | 4g fat (of which 1g saturates) 12g carbohydrate | 0.4g salt | DF

1 tbsp olive oil

1 onion, finely sliced

1 red pepper, seeded and finely chopped

400g can chopped tomatoes

1 tbsp red wine vinegar

4 x 125g (4oz) white fish fillets, such as pollack or coley, cut into chunks

2 tbsp finely chopped fresh coriander

salt and ground black pepper

basmati and wild rice, and green beans to serve

1. Heat the oil in a large deep frying pan. Add the onion and fry over a medium heat for 5–10 minutes until softened. Add the red pepper and fry for a further 2–3 minutes.

2. Stir in the tomatoes and vinegar, bring to the boil and cook for 1–2 minutes, then add the fish and poach gently for 10 minutes, adding a splash of water if the sauce becomes too thick. Stir the coriander through, season to taste with salt and pepper and serve with basmati and wild rice and green beans.

Napolitana Pizza

Serves	Preparation Time	Cooking Time	Nutritional Information (Per Serving)
4	15 minutes	20–25 minutes	516 calories | 25g fat (of which 7g saturates) 59g carbohydrate | 2.3g salt

290g pack pizza base mix (use both sachets)

4 tbsp olive oil, plus extra to grease

400g can chopped plum tomatoes, drained

2 garlic cloves, crushed

plain flour to dust

2–3 sprigs fresh oregano or 1 tsp dried oregano

125g (4oz) mozzarella cheese, preferably buffalo, diced

50g can anchovy fillets, drained and cut in half lengthways

50g (2oz) pitted black olives

ground black pepper

1. Preheat the oven to 240°C (220°C fan oven) mark 9. Put the bread mix into the bowl of a free-standing mixer, add 1 tbsp oil and 225ml (8fl oz) hand-hot water. Mix with a dough hook until soft and sticky. Alternatively, put into a food processor and mix with a plastic blade or knead by hand for 10 minutes.

2. Meanwhile, mix the tomatoes with the garlic and season to taste with black pepper.

3. Lightly oil a large heavy-based baking sheet. Roll out the dough on a lightly floured surface to a rectangle, about 33 x 35.5cm (13 x 14in), and transfer to the baking sheet. Spread the tomatoes over the dough, sprinkle on the oregano and put the mozzarella cheese, anchovies and olives on top. Drizzle the remaining oil over the pizza.

4. Bake for 20–25 minutes or until the mozzarella is brown and bubbling and the dough is lightly browned underneath. Leave for 5 minutes, then cut into slices to serve.

Scrambled Eggs with Smoked Salmon

Serves	Preparation Time	Cooking Time	Nutritional Information *(Per Serving)*
4	10 minutes	5 minutes	457 calories | 34g fat (of which 17g saturates) 17g carbohydrate | 2.7g salt

6 large eggs

25g (1oz) butter, plus extra to spread

100g (3½oz) mascarpone

125g pack smoked salmon, sliced, or smoked salmon trimmings

6 slices sourdough or rye bread, toasted, buttered and cut into slim rectangles for soldiers

salt and ground black pepper

1. Crack the eggs into a jug and lightly beat together. Season well with salt and pepper.

2. Melt the butter in a non-stick pan over a low heat. Add the eggs and stir constantly until the mixture thickens. Add the mascarpone and season well. Cook for 1–2 minutes longer, until the mixture just becomes firm, then fold in the smoked salmon. Serve at once with toasted bread soldiers.

Smoked Haddock and Potato Pie

Serves	Preparation Time	Cooking Time	Nutritional Information *(Per Serving)*
4	15 minutes	1¼ hours–1 hour 25 minutes	374 calories | 20g fat (of which 11g saturates) 37g carbohydrate | 0.3g salt

142ml carton double cream

150ml (¼ pint) fish stock

3 medium baking potatoes, thinly sliced

300g (11oz) skinless smoked haddock fillets, roughly chopped

20g packet fresh chives, chopped

1 large onion, finely chopped

salt and ground black pepper

green salad or green beans to serve

lemon slices to garnish

1. Preheat the oven to 200°C (180°C fan oven) mark 6. Pour the cream into a large bowl. Add the stock and stir well to combine.

2. Add the potatoes, haddock, chives and onion and season with salt and pepper. Toss everything together to coat. Spoon the mixture into a shallow 2.3 litre (4 pint) ovenproof dish.

3. Cover the dish with foil, put it on a baking tray and cook for 45 minutes. Remove the foil and cook for 30–40 minutes until bubbling and the top is golden.

4. To check that the potatoes are cooked, insert a skewer or small knife – it should push in easily. If you like, you can put the dish under a hot grill to make the top layer crisp. Leave to cool slightly, then serve with a green salad or green beans, garnished with a slice of lemon.

Cook's Tips

For the lightest texture, make sure you use floury baking potatoes, as salad potatoes are too waxy.

To cook the beans, put 200g (7oz) fine green beans into a bowl, pour in enough boiling water to cover them, and put a lid on top. Leave for 10 minutes, then drain.

Chinese-style Fish

Serves	Preparation Time	Cooking Time	Nutritional Information (Per Serving)
4	5 minutes	10 minutes	150 calories | 3g fat (of which 1g saturates) 10g carbohydrate | 0.7g salt | **DF** | **GF**

2 tsp sunflower oil

1 small onion, finely chopped

1 green chilli, seeded and finely chopped

2 courgettes, thinly sliced

125g (4oz) frozen peas, thawed

350g (12oz) skinless haddock fillet, cut into bite-size pieces

2 tsp lemon juice

4 tbsp hoisin sauce

lime wedges to serve

1. Heat the oil in a large non-stick frying pan. Add the onion, chilli, courgettes and peas. Stir over a high heat for 5 minutes until the onion and courgettes begin to soften.

2. Add the fish to the pan with the lemon juice, hoisin sauce and 150ml (¼ pint) water. Bring to the boil, then simmer, uncovered, for 2–3 minutes until the fish is cooked through. Serve with lime wedges.

Try Something Different
There are plenty of alternatives to haddock: try sea bass, sea bream or gurnard.

Prawns in Yellow Bean Sauce

Serves	Preparation Time	Cooking Time	Nutritional Information (Per Serving)
4	10 minutes, plus 4 minutes standing	5 minutes	394 calories | 10g fat (of which 2g saturates) 59g carbohydrate | 0.9g salt | DF

250g pack medium egg noodles

1 tbsp stir-fry oil or sesame oil

1 garlic clove, sliced

1 tsp peeled and grated fresh root ginger

1 bunch of spring onions, trimmed and each stem cut into four, lengthways

250g (9oz) frozen raw peeled tiger prawns, thawed

200g (7oz) pak choi, leaves separated and the white base cut into thick slices

160g jar Chinese yellow bean stir-fry sauce

1. Put the noodles into a bowl, pour 2 litres (3½ pints) boiling water over them and leave to soak for 4 minutes. Drain and set aside.

2. Heat the oil in a wok over a medium heat. Add the garlic and ginger and stir-fry for 30 seconds. Add the spring onions and prawns and cook for 2 minutes.

3. Add the chopped white part of the pak choi and the yellow bean sauce. Fill the empty sauce jar with boiling water and pour this into the wok too.

4. Add the noodles to the pan and continue to cook for 1 minute, tossing every now and then to heat through. Finally, stir in the green pak choi leaves and serve immediately.

Try Something Different
Instead of prawns, use skinless chicken breast, cut into thin strips.

Quick Pad Thai

Serves	Preparation Time	Cooking Time	Nutritional Information (Per Serving)
4	12 minutes, plus 4 minutes soaking	8 minutes	451 calories | 13g fat (of which 3g saturates) 56g carbohydrate | 2.6g salt | DF

250g (9oz) wide ribbon rice noodles

3 tbsp satay and sweet chilli pesto

125g (4oz) mangetouts, thinly sliced

125g (4oz) sugarsnap peas, thinly sliced

3 medium eggs, beaten

3 tbsp chilli soy sauce, plus extra to serve

250g (9oz) cooked peeled tiger prawns

25g (1oz) dry-roasted peanuts, roughly crushed

lime wedges to serve (optional)

1. Put the noodles into a heatproof bowl, cover with boiling water and soak for 4 minutes until softened. Drain, rinse under cold water and set aside.

2. Heat a wok or large frying pan until hot, add the chilli pesto and stir-fry for 1 minute. Add the mangetouts and sugarsnap peas and cook for a further 2 minutes. Tip into a bowl. Put the pan back on the heat, add the eggs and cook, stirring, for 1 minute.

3. Add the soy sauce, prawns and noodles to the pan. Toss well and cook for 3 minutes until piping hot.

Return the vegetables to the pan, cook for a further 1 minute until heated through, then sprinkle with the peanuts. Serve with extra soy sauce and lime wedges to squeeze over, if you like.

Cook's Tip
If you can't find satay and sweet chilli pesto, substitute 2 tbsp peanut butter and 1 tbsp sweet chilli sauce. Chilli soy sauce can be replaced with 2 tbsp light soy sauce and ½ red chilli, finely chopped.

Prawn and Vegetable Pilau

Serves	Preparation Time	Cooking Time	Nutritional Information (Per Serving)
4	10 minutes	15–20 minutes	360 calories | 5g fat (of which 1g saturates) 61g carbohydrate | 1.8g salt | DF

250g (9oz) long-grain rice

1 broccoli head, broken into florets

150g (5oz) baby sweetcorn, halved

200g (7oz) sugarsnap peas

1 red pepper, seeded and sliced into thin strips

400g (14oz) cooked and peeled king prawns

For the dressing

1 tbsp sesame oil

5cm (2in) piece fresh root ginger, grated

juice of 1 lime

1–2 tbsp light soy sauce

Did You Know...?

The word 'pilau', or 'pilaf', comes from the Persian pilaw. The dish originated in the East and consists of rice flavoured with spices, to which vegetables, poultry, meat, fish or shellfish are added.

1. Put the rice into a large wide pan – it needs to be really big, as you're cooking the rice and steaming the veg on top, then tossing it all together. Add 600ml (1 pint) boiling water. Cover, bring to the boil, then reduce the heat to low and cook the rice according to the packet instructions.

2. About 10 minutes before the end of the rice cooking time, add the broccoli, corn, sugarsnaps and red pepper. Stir well, then cover and cook until the vegetables and rice are just tender.

3. Meanwhile, put the prawns into a bowl. Add the oil, ginger, lime and soy sauce. Mix the prawns and dressing into the cooked vegetables and rice and toss through well. Serve immediately.

Crusted Trout

Serves	Preparation Time	Cooking Time	Nutritional Information (Per Serving)
4	10 minutes	10–13 minutes	259 calories	15g fat (of which 3g saturates) 1g carbohydrate	0.8g salt	DF	GF

1 tbsp sesame oil

1 tbsp soy sauce

juice of 1 lime

4 x 150g (5oz) trout fillets

2 tbsp sesame seeds

lime wedges, herb salad and fennel
to serve

1. Preheat the grill. Put the oil in a bowl, add the soy sauce and lime juice and whisk together.

2. Put the trout fillets on a baking sheet, pour the sesame mixture over them and grill for 8–10 minutes. Sprinkle with the sesame seeds and grill for a further 2–3 minutes until the seeds are golden. Serve with lime wedges, a herb salad and some finely sliced fennel.

Cook's Tip
Sesame seeds are deliciously nutty and highly nutritious. They are a valuable source of protein, good omega fats and vitamin E. Lightly toasted sesame seeds, crushed with a little salt and stirred into 1–2 tbsp olive oil, make an excellent dressing for cooked green beans, broccoli and carrots.

Quick Fish and Chips

Serves	Preparation Time	Cooking Time	Nutritional Information (Per Serving)
4	30 minutes	40–50 minutes	993 calories | 67g fat (of which 9g saturates) 64g carbohydrate | 1.6g salt | DF

900g (2lb) Maris Piper or
King Edward potatoes, peeled

2–3 tbsp olive oil

sea salt flakes

sunflower oil to deep-fry

2 x 128g packs batter mix

1 tsp baking powder

¼ tsp salt

330ml bottle of lager or sparkling
water

4 plaice fillets, about 225g (8oz)
each, skin on,
trimmed and cut in half

plain flour to dust

2 garlic cloves, crushed

8 tbsp mayonnaise

1 tsp lemon juice

salt and ground black pepper

lemon wedges and chives to garnish

1. Preheat the oven to 240°C (220°C fan oven) mark 9. Cut the potatoes into chips. Put them in a pan of lightly salted water, cover and bring to the boil. Boil for 2 minutes, drain well, then drain on kitchen paper. Tip into a large non-stick roasting tin, toss with the olive oil and season with sea salt. Roast for 40–50 minutes until golden and cooked, turning from time to time.

2. Meanwhile, half-fill a deep-fat fryer with sunflower oil and heat to 190°C. Put the batter mix into a bowl with the baking powder and salt and gradually whisk in the lager or water. Season the plaice with salt and pepper and lightly dust with flour. Dip two of the fillets into the batter and deep-fry in the hot oil until golden. Keep hot in the oven while you deep-fry the remaining plaice fillets.

3. Mix the garlic, mayonnaise and lemon juice together in a bowl and season well. Serve the garlic mayonnaise with the plaice and chips, garnished with lemon wedges and chives.

Try Something Different

Simple Tartare Sauce
Mix 8 tbsp mayonnaise with 1 tbsp each chopped capers and gherkins, 1 tbsp freshly chopped tarragon or chives and 2 tsp lemon juice.

Herby Lemon Mayonnaise
Fold 2 tbsp finely chopped parsley, grated zest of ½ lemon and 2 tsp lemon juice into 8 tbsp mayonnaise.

Cod with Sweet Chilli Glaze

Serves	Preparation Time	Cooking Time	Nutritional Information (Per Serving)
4	10 minutes	20 minutes	193 calories | 1g fat (of which trace saturates) 13g carbohydrate | 0.7g salt | GF

1 red chilli, seeded and finely chopped

2 tsp dark soy sauce

grated zest and juice of 1 lime

¼ tsp ground allspice or 6 allspice berries, crushed

50g (2oz) light muscovado sugar

4 thick cod fillets, with skin, about 175g (6oz) each

finely sliced red chilli, finely sliced lime zest and lime wedges to garnish

For the saffron mash

900g (2lb) potatoes, peeled and chopped

a pinch of saffron

50g (2oz) butter

salt and ground black pepper

1. To make the saffron mash, cook the potatoes in lightly salted boiling water until tender. Meanwhile, soak the saffron in 2 tbsp boiling water. Drain the potatoes and mash with the butter, then beat in the saffron liquid. Season to taste with salt and pepper.

2. Meanwhile, preheat the grill or griddle pan until hot. Stir the chopped chilli, soy sauce, lime zest and juice, allspice and sugar together.

3. Grill the cod for about 1 minute on the flesh side. Turn skin side up and grill for 1 minute. Spoon the chilli glaze over and grill for a further 2–3 minutes until the skin is crisp and golden. Garnish with finely sliced chilli and lime zest and the lime wedges. Serve with the saffron mash.

Sardines on Toast

Serves	Preparation Time	Cooking Time	Nutritional Information (Per Serving)
4	5 minutes	8–10 minutes	240 calories | 9g fat (of which 2g saturates) 25g carbohydrate | 1.6g salt | DF | GF

4 slices thick wholemeal bread

2 large tomatoes, sliced

2 x 120g cans sardines in olive oil, drained

juice of ½ lemon

small handful of parsley, chopped

1. Preheat the grill. Toast the slices of bread on both sides.

2. Divide the tomato slices and the sardines among the toast slices, squeeze the lemon juice over them, then put back under the grill for 2–3 minutes to heat through. Scatter the parsley over the sardines and serve immediately.

Try Something Different
Instead of sardines, use a 200g can pilchards in tomato sauce.

Cheesy Tuna Melt

Serves	Preparation Time	Cooking Time	Nutritional Information (Per Serving)
1	5 minutes	5 minutes	747 calories | 36g fat (of which 18g saturates) 51g carbohydrate | 3.4g salt

2 slices cholla bread

100g can tuna in sunflower oil, drained

75g (3oz) Gruyère cheese, sliced

1 tomato, sliced

salt and ground black pepper

1. Preheat the grill to high. Put the bread on a baking sheet and toast one side.

2. Turn the bread so that it is untoasted side up, then divide the tuna between the two pieces and add the cheese and tomato.

3. Grill until the cheese is bubbling and golden. Season with salt and pepper and serve immediately.

Cook's Tip
You can use any type of bread for this recipe.

Simple Smoked Haddock

Serves	Preparation Time	Cooking Time	Nutritional Information (Per Serving)
4	10 minutes	about 10 minutes	217 calories | 9g fat (of which 4g saturates) 1g carbohydrate | 3.4g salt | GF

25g (1oz) unsalted butter

1 tbsp olive oil

1 garlic clove, thinly sliced

4 thick smoked haddock or cod fillets, about 175g (6oz) each

a small handful of freshly chopped parsley (optional)

finely grated zest of 1 small lemon, plus lemon wedges to serve

romanesco, cauliflower or broccoli to serve

1. Heat the butter, oil and garlic in a large non-stick pan over a high heat until the mixture starts to foam and sizzle. Put the fish into the pan, skin side down, and fry for 10 minutes – this will give a golden crust underneath the fish.

2. Carefully turn the fish over. Scatter the parsley, if using, and lemon zest over each fillet, then fry for a further 30 seconds. Put a cooked fillet on each of four warmed plates and spoon some of the buttery juices over. Serve with the lemon wedges and steamed romanesco, cauliflower or broccoli.

Cook's Tip
Smoked fish is quite salty, so always taste the sauce before seasoning with any extra salt.

5

PASTA AND RICE

Pasta with Leeks, Bacon and Mushrooms

Serves	Preparation Time	Cooking Time	Nutritional Information *(Per Serving)*
4	5 minutes	15–20 minutes	765 calories | 39g fat (of which 22g saturates) 86g carbohydrate | 1.5g salt

450g (1lb) dried conchiglie pasta

50g (2oz) butter

125g (4oz) streaky bacon, diced

2 medium leeks, thickly sliced

225g (8oz) chestnut or button mushrooms, sliced

1 garlic clove, crushed

150g pack soft herby cream cheese

salt and ground black pepper

basil leaves to garnish

1. Cook the pasta in a large pan of lightly salted boiling water according to the packet instructions until al dente.

2. Meanwhile, melt the butter in a pan and add the bacon, leeks, mushrooms and garlic. Cook over a medium heat for 5–10 minutes until the leeks are tender. Reduce the heat, add the cream cheese and season well with salt and pepper.

3. Drain the pasta, add to the sauce and toss well. Garnish with basil and serve.

Cannelloni with Roasted Garlic

Serves	Preparation Time	Cooking Time	Nutritional Information (Per Serving)
6	40 minutes	about 1 hour	430 calories | 20g fat (of which 9g saturates) 29g carbohydrate | 0g salt

20 garlic cloves, unpeeled

2 tbsp extra virgin olive oil

15g (½oz) dried porcini mushrooms, soaked for 20 minutes in 150ml (¼ pint) boiling water

5 shallots or button onions, finely chopped

700g (1½lb) lean minced meat

175ml (6fl oz) beef or lamb stock

2 tbsp freshly chopped thyme

about 12 lasagne sheets

142ml carton single cream mixed with 2 tbsp sun-dried tomato paste

butter to grease

75g (3oz) Gruyère cheese, finely grated

salt and ground black pepper

1. Preheat the oven to 180°C (160°C fan oven) mark 4. Put the garlic into a small roasting tin with 1 tbsp oil. Toss to coat the garlic in the oil and cook for 25 minutes or until soft. Leave to cool.

2. Meanwhile, drain the porcini mushrooms, putting the liquor to one side, then rinse to remove any grit. Chop the mushrooms finely.

3. Heat the remaining oil in a pan. Add the shallots and cook over a medium heat for 5 minutes until soft. Increase the heat and stir in the meat. Cook, stirring frequently, until browned. Add the stock, mushrooms, with their liquor, and thyme. Cook over a medium heat for 15–20 minutes until the liquid

has almost evaporated. The mixture should be quite moist. Peel the garlic cloves and mash them to a rough paste with a fork. Stir into the meat mixture, then season with salt and pepper and set aside.

4. Cook the lasagne according to the packet instructions until al dente. Drain, rinse with cold water and drain again. Lay each lasagne sheet on a clean teatowel. Spoon the meat mixture along one long edge and roll up to enclose the filling. Cut the tubes in half.

5. Season the cream and sun-dried tomato paste mixture. Preheat the oven to 200°C (180°C fan oven) mark 6. Grease a shallow baking dish. Arrange a layer of filled tubes in the base of the dish. Spoon half the tomato cream over them and sprinkle with half the cheese. Arrange the remaining tubes on top and cover with the remaining tomato cream and cheese. Cover the dish with foil and cook in the oven for 10 minutes. Uncover and cook for a further 5–10 minutes until lightly browned, then serve.

Quick and Easy Carbonara

Serves	Preparation Time	Cooking Time	Nutritional Information (Per Serving)
4	5 minutes	10 minutes	688 calories | 39g fat (of which 19g saturates) 65g carbohydrate | 1.6g salt | GF

350g (12oz) dried tagliatelle

150g (5oz) smoked bacon, chopped

1 tbsp olive oil

2 large egg yolks

150ml (¼ pint) double cream

50g (2oz) freshly grated Parmesan

2 tbsp freshly chopped parsley

1. Cook the pasta in a large pan of lightly salted boiling water according to the packet instructions.

2. Meanwhile, fry the bacon in the oil for 4–5 minutes. Add to the drained pasta and keep hot.

3. Put the egg yolks into a bowl and add the cream. Whisk together. Add to the pasta with the Parmesan and parsley. Toss well and serve.

Pappardelle with Smoked Bacon and Sage

Serves	Preparation Time	Cooking Time	Nutritional Information (Per Serving)
4	5 minutes	15 minutes	494 calories | 18g fat (of which 7g saturates) 65g carbohydrate | 1.0g salt

200g (7oz) pack smoked lardons (or smoked rindless back bacon, chopped)

350g (12oz) dried egg pappardelle

500ml carton crème fraîche

1 tbsp fresh or sun-dried sage leaves, torn

50g (2oz) freshly grated Parmesan

salt and ground black pepper

tomato salad to serve

1. Heat a non-stick frying pan and dry cook the lardons or chopped bacon for 4 minutes or until brown and crisp. Drain on kitchen paper.

2. Cook the pappardelle in a large pan of lightly salted boiling water according to the packet instructions. Drain the pasta, reserving some of the cooking water.

3. Tip the crème fraîche into the warm pan, add the sage and heat through for 3 minutes. Return the pasta to the pan and toss together with the crème fraîche, sage and crisp bacon. Season generously with salt and pepper and sprinkle with the Parmesan. Serve immediately with a tomato salad.

Cook's Tip
To reduce the calories in this dish, use half-fat crème fraîche instead of the full-fat variety.

Pasta with Chilli and Cherry Tomatoes

Serves	Preparation Time	Cooking Time	Nutritional Information (Per Serving)
4	10 minutes	13 minutes	476 calories | 17g fat (of which 4g saturates) 69g carbohydrate | 0.4g salt

350g (12oz) dried pasta, such as fusilli

4 tbsp olive oil

1 large red chilli, seeded and finely chopped

1 garlic clove, crushed

500g (1lb 2oz) cherry tomatoes

2 tbsp freshly chopped basil

50g (2oz) Parmesan shavings (see Thrifty Tip)

salt and ground black pepper

1. Cook the pasta in a large pan of lightly salted boiling water according to the packet instructions. Drain the pasta.

2. Meanwhile, heat the oil in a large frying pan, add the chilli and garlic and cook for 30 seconds. Add the tomatoes, season to taste with salt and pepper and cook over a high heat for 3 minutes or until the skins begin to split.

3. Add the basil and drained pasta and toss together. Sprinkle the Parmesan shavings over and serve.

Thrifty Tip
Parmesan shavings can be bought in the supermarket but are more expensive than making your own. Instead, use a vegetable peeler to pare off shavings from a block of Parmesan.

Baked Gnocchi

Serves	Preparation Time	Cooking Time	Nutritional Information (Per Serving)
4	5 minutes	30 minutes	993 calories | 63g fat (of which 40g saturates) 85g carbohydrate | 2.2g salt | V

2 x 500g packs fresh gnocchi

2 x 200ml cartons crème fraîche

250g (9oz) gorgonzola cheese, roughly chopped

2 tbsp freshly chopped sage, plus extra to garnish

salt and ground black pepper

1. Preheat the oven to 200°C (180°C fan oven) mark 6. Cook the gnocchi in a large pan of boiling water according to the packet instructions. Drain well and return to the pan.

2. Add the crème fraîche, gorgonzola and sage and season well with salt and pepper.

3. Pour the mixture into a gratin dish set on a baking sheet and cook in the oven for 25 minutes until bubbling and golden. Garnish with the remaining sage leaves and serve.

Cheesy Gnocchi with Kale

Serves	Preparation Time	Cooking Time	Nutritional Information (Per Serving)
4	5 minutes	10 minutes	433 calories | 20g fat (of which 12g saturates) 49g carbohydrate | 0.5g salt | V

200g (7oz) kale, shredded

500g pack fresh gnocchi

150g (5oz) frozen petit pois, thawed

6 tbsp crème fraîche

100g (3½oz) freshly grated mature Cheddar

salt and ground black pepper

1. Bring a large pan of water to the boil, add the kale and cook for 4–5 minutes. Add the gnocchi and peas to the pan for the last 2 minutes of cooking time.

2. Preheat the grill to high. Drain the gnocchi and vegetables thoroughly, then tip back into the pan. Add the crème fraîche and half the cheese and season to taste with salt and pepper. Toss everything together gently to combine.

3. Spoon the mixture into an ovenproof dish, scatter the remaining cheese over the top and grill for 4–5 minutes until the cheese is bubbling and beginning to brown. Serve.

Risotto with Bacon and Broad Beans

Serves	Preparation Time	Cooking Time	Nutritional Information (Per Serving)
4	15 minutes	35 minutes	466 calories	19g fat (of which 9g saturates) 53g carbohydrate	1.3g salt	GF

225g (8oz) podded fresh broad beans

50g (2oz) unsalted butter

1 tsp olive oil

125g (4oz) streaky bacon, chopped

1 onion, very finely chopped

about 1.1 litre (2 pints) vegetable stock

225g (8oz) arborio rice or carnaroli rice

2 tbsp freshly chopped flat-leafed parsley

1 tbsp freshly chopped tarragon

salt and ground black pepper

freshly shaved Parmesan to serve

1. Add the broad beans to a pan of lightly salted boiling water and cook for about 4 minutes until just tender. Drain and refresh under cold running water, then slip the beans out of their skins. Put the beans to one side.

2. Melt half the butter with the oil in a large pan. Add the bacon and cook until golden, then add the onion and cook gently for 5 minutes or until softened and translucent, stirring from time to time. Meanwhile, heat the stock in a separate pan.

3. Add the rice to the onion and stir well to ensure that all the grains are coated in butter.

4. Add the stock a little at a time, allowing the rice to absorb the liquid after each addition. This should take about 25 minutes and you may not need to add all the stock.

5. Remove from the heat and gently stir in the broad beans and remaining butter. Season with pepper and a little salt if needed, then stir in the parsley and tarragon. Serve immediately, topped with Parmesan.

Spiced Pork with Lemon Pasta

Serves	Preparation Time	Cooking Time	Nutritional Information (Per Serving)
6	10 minutes	12 minutes	733 calories | 44g fat (of which 28g saturates) 71g carbohydrate | 1.8g salt

8 thick pork sausages

500g (1lb 2oz) dried pasta shells or other shapes

100ml (3½fl oz) chicken stock

grated zest of 1 lemon

juice of ½ lemon

large pinch of dried chilli flakes

300ml (½ pint) half-fat crème fraîche

2 tbsp freshly chopped flat-leafed parsley

25g (1oz) freshly grated Parmesan

salt and ground black pepper

1. Remove the skin from the sausages and pinch the meat into small pieces. Heat a non-stick frying pan over a medium heat. When hot, add the sausagemeat and cook for 5 minutes, stirring occasionally, until cooked through and browned.

2. Meanwhile, cook the pasta in a large pan of lightly salted boiling water according to the packet instructions until al dente.

3. Add the stock to the sausagemeat, bring to the boil and let bubble, stirring, for 2–3 minutes until the liquid has reduced right down. Add the lemon zest and juice, chilli flakes and crème fraîche. Season well with salt and pepper. Continue to cook for 3–4 minutes until reduced and thickened slightly.

4. Drain the pasta and return to the pan. Stir the parsley into the sauce and toss with the pasta. Serve immediately, with Parmesan.

Broccoli Pasta Bake

Serves	Preparation Time	Cooking Time	Nutritional Information (Per Serving)
4	5 minutes	30 minutes	477 calories | 19g fat (of which 9g saturates) 60g carbohydrate | 0.7g salt | V

300g (11oz) broccoli florets

250g (9oz) dried fusilli pasta

25g (1oz) butter, plus extra to grease

25g (1oz) plain flour

pinch of English mustard powder

pinch of cayenne pepper

300ml (½ pint milk)

50g (2oz) freshly grated Gruyère

3 tbsp freshly grated Parmesan

1 tsp olive oil

2 tbsp crème fraîche

1 tbsp freshly chopped basil

1 tbsp toasted pinenuts

1 tbsp fresh breadcrumbs

salt

1. Preheat the oven to 200°C (180°C fan oven) mark 6. Cook the broccoli in lightly salted boiling water for 3–4 minutes until just tender. Drain well.

2. Cook the pasta in a large pan of lightly salted boiling water according to the packet instructions. Drain.

3. Melt the butter in a pan. Stir in the flour, mustard powder and cayenne and cook for 1 minute. Take the pan off the heat and gradually stir in the milk. Return the pan to the heat and stir until thickened, then simmer for 2 minutes. Remove the sauce from the heat and stir in the Gruyère and 2 tbsp Parmesan until melted.

4. Stir the drained broccoli and pasta into the sauce with the oil, crème fraîche and basil. Tip the mixture into a greased ovenproof dish. Combine the remaining Parmesan with the pinenuts and breadcrumbs and sprinkle over the pasta. Cook in the oven for 15 minutes until golden.

Ravioli with Red Pepper Sauce

Serves	Preparation Time	Cooking Time	Nutritional Information (Per Serving)
4	10 minutes	25 minutes	406 calories | 13g fat (of which 1g saturates) 59g carbohydrate | 1.1g salt | V

1 tbsp olive oil

1 onion, finely chopped

1 red pepper, seeded and finely chopped

400g can chopped tomatoes

1 tbsp red wine vinegar

1 bay leaf

50ml (2fl oz) vegetable stock

small handful of torn basil

300g (11oz) cooked ready-made ravioli

salt and ground black pepper

freshly grated Parmesan to serve

1. Heat the oil in a large deep frying pan. Add the onion and fry over a medium heat for 5–10 minutes until softened. Add the red pepper and fry for a further 2–3 minutes. Stir in the tomatoes, vinegar, bay leaf and stock, bring to the boil and cook for 1–2 minutes.

2. Season to taste with salt and pepper and stir in the basil. Pour the sauce over the cooked ravioli, sprinkle with Parmesan and serve.

Pea, Mint and Ricotta Pasta

Serves	Preparation Time	Cooking Time	Nutritional Information (Per Serving)
4	5 minutes	10 minutes	426 calories | 14g fat (of which 5g saturates) 63g carbohydrate | 0g salt | V | GF

300g (11oz) dried farfalle pasta

200g (7oz) frozen peas

175g (6oz) ricotta

3 tbsp freshly chopped mint

2 tbsp extra virgin olive oil

salt and ground black pepper

1. Cook the pasta in a large pan of lightly salted boiling water according to the packet instructions. Add the frozen peas for the last 4 minutes of cooking.

2. Drain the pasta and peas, reserving the water, then return to the pan. Stir in the ricotta and mint with a ladleful of pasta cooking water. Season well with salt and pepper, drizzle with the oil and serve at once.

Kale, Anchovy and Crispy Bread

Serves	Preparation Time	Cooking Time	Nutritional Information (Per Serving)
4	5 minutes	15 minutes	481 calories | 14g fat (of which 2g saturates) 72g carbohydrate | 3g salt

75g (3oz) fresh breadcrumbs

300g (11oz) dried orecchiette or other shaped pasta

150g (5oz) kale, shredded

2 tbsp olive oil

1 red chilli, seeded and finely chopped

100g jar anchovies, drained and chopped

25g (1oz) freshly grated Parmesan

1. Preheat the grill to medium and toast the breadcrumbs.

2. Cook the pasta in a large pan of lightly salted boiling water according to the packet instructions until al dente. Add the kale for the last 5–6 minutes of cooking time.

3. Heat 1 tbsp oil in a pan and fry the chilli and anchovies for 3–4 minutes.

4. Drain the pasta and kale, then tip back into the pan. Add the breadcrumbs, the anchovy mixture, the remaining oil and the Parmesan. Toss to mix, then serve.

Pasta with Vegetables, Pinenuts and Pesto

Serves	Preparation Time	Cooking Time	Nutritional Information (Per Serving)
4	5 minutes	10 minutes	567 calories | 29g fat (of which 5g saturates) 60g carbohydrate | 0.4g salt | V

300g (11oz) dried penne pasta

50g (2oz) pinenuts

1 tbsp olive oil

1 garlic clove, crushed

250g (9oz) closed cup mushrooms, sliced

2 courgettes, sliced

250g (9oz) cherry tomatoes

6 tbsp fresh pesto

25g (1oz) Parmesan, shaved

salt

1. Cook the pasta in a large pan of lightly salted boiling water according to the packet instructions until al dente.

2. Meanwhile, gently toast the pinenuts in a frying pan, tossing them around until golden, then remove from the pan and set aside. Add the oil to the pan with the garlic, mushrooms and courgettes. Add a splash of water, then cover and cook for 4–5 minutes.

3. Uncover and add the tomatoes, then cook for a further 1–2 minutes. Drain the pasta and return to its pan. Add the vegetables, pinenuts and pesto to the drained pasta. Toss well to combine and serve immediately, with shavings of Parmesan.

Greek Pasta Bake

Serves	Preparation Time	Cooking Time	Nutritional Information (Per Serving)
4	10 minutes	about 1½ hours	736 calories | 30g fat (of which 13g saturates) 80g carbohydrate | 0.8g salt

2 tbsp vegetable oil

1 onion, finely chopped

2 garlic cloves, crushed

450g (1lb) extra-lean minced lamb

2 tbsp tomato purée

400g can chopped tomatoes

2 bay leaves

150ml (¼ pint) hot beef stock

350g (12oz) dried macaroni

50g (2oz) Cheddar, grated

salt and ground black pepper

For the sauce

15g (½oz) butter

15g (½oz) plain flour

300ml (½ pint) milk

1 medium egg, beaten

1. Heat the oil in a large pan, add the onion and garlic and cook for 5 minutes to soften. Add the lamb and stir-fry over a high heat for 3–4 minutes until browned all over.

2. Stir in the tomato purée and cook for 1–2 minutes. Stir in the tomatoes, bay leaves and hot stock and season with salt and pepper. Bring to the boil, lower the heat and cook for 35–40 minutes.

3. Meanwhile, make the sauce. Melt the butter in a small pan, then stir in the flour and cook over a medium heat for 1–2 minutes. Gradually add the milk, stirring constantly. Turn down the heat to low and cook, stirring, for 4–5 minutes. Remove from the heat and cool slightly. Stir in the beaten egg and season well with salt and pepper. Set aside.

4. Preheat the oven to 180°C (160°C fan oven) mark 4. Cook the macaroni in a large pan of lightly salted boiling water according to the packet instructions until al dente.

5. Drain the pasta well and spoon half into a 2 litre (3½ pint) ovenproof dish. Spoon the meat mixture over it, then top with the remaining macaroni. Pour the sauce evenly over the top and scatter with the grated cheese. Bake for 25–30 minutes until golden brown.

Ribbon Pasta with Courgettes and Capers

Serves	Preparation Time	Cooking Time	Nutritional Information (Per Serving)
4	about 5 minutes	8–10 minutes	557 calories | 18g fat (of which 2g saturates) 85g carbohydrate | 2.1g salt | DF

450g (1lb) dried pappardelle pasta

2 large courgettes, coarsely grated

50g can anchovies, drained and roughly chopped

1 red chilli, seeded and finely chopped

2 tbsp salted capers, rinsed

1 garlic clove, crushed

4 tbsp pitted black Kalamata olives, roughly chopped

4 tbsp extra virgin olive oil

2 tbsp freshly chopped flat-leafed parsley

salt and ground black pepper

1. Cook the pasta in a large pan of lightly salted boiling water according to the packet instructions. About 1 minute before the end of the cooking time, add the courgettes, then simmer until the pasta is just cooked.

2. Meanwhile, put the anchovies into a small pan and add the chilli, capers, garlic, olives and oil. Stir over a low heat for 2–3 minutes.

3. Drain the pasta and put back into the pan. Pour the hot anchovy mixture on top, mix well and toss with the parsley. Season to taste with salt and pepper and serve.

> **Cook's Tip**
> If cooking for vegetarians, omit the anchovies and serve with freshly grated vegetarian Parmesan, such as Twineham Grange.

Simple Salmon Pasta

Serves	Preparation Time	Cooking Time	Nutritional Information (Per Serving)
4	2 minutes	10 minutes	630 calories | 13g fat (of which 6g saturates) 100g carbohydrate | 2.7g salt

500g (1lb 2oz) dried linguine pasta

a little olive oil

1 fat garlic clove, crushed

200ml (7fl oz) half-fat crème fraîche

225g (8oz) hot-smoked salmon, flaked

200g (7oz) peas

salt and ground black pepper

basil leaves to garnish

1. Cook the pasta in a large pan of lightly salted boiling water according to the packet instructions, then drain, reserving a couple of tablespoons of the cooking water.

2. Meanwhile, heat the oil in a large pan, add the garlic and fry gently until golden. Add the crème fraîche, salmon and peas and stir in. Cook for 1–2 minutes until warmed through, then add the reserved water from the pasta.

3. Toss the pasta into the sauce, season with salt and pepper and serve immediately, garnished with basil leaves.

Cook's Tip
Adding the reserved pasta cooking water stops the pasta absorbing too much of the crème fraîche and makes it more saucy.

Chicken, Bacon and Leek Pasta Bake

Serves	Preparation Time	Cooking Time	Nutritional Information *(Per Serving)*
4	20 minutes	about 20 minutes	966 calories | 31g fat (of which 12g saturates) 124g carbohydrate | 2.2g salt

1 tbsp olive oil

100g pack bacon lardons

450g (1lb) boneless and skinless chicken thighs, chopped

3 medium leeks, chopped

300g (11oz) macaroni pasta

350g tub ready-made cheese sauce

2 tsp Dijon mustard

2 tbsp freshly chopped flat-leafed parsley

25g (1oz) freshly grated Parmesan

1. Heat the oil in a large frying pan. Add the bacon and chicken and cook for 7–8 minutes, then add the leeks and cook for 4–5 minutes.

2. Meanwhile, cook the pasta in a large pan of lightly salted boiling water according to the packet instructions. Drain well and return to the pan.

3. Preheat the grill. Add the cheese sauce, mustard, bacon, chicken, leek and parsley to the pasta and mix. Tip into a 2.1 litre (3¾ pint) heatproof dish and sprinkle with Parmesan. Grill for 4–5 minutes until golden.

Try Something Different
For a vegetarian version, swap the bacon and chicken for 300g (11oz) sliced mixed mushrooms and 2 tbsp thyme leaves. Add 100g (3½oz) peas to the pasta and 100g (3½oz) chopped Fontina cheese to the cheese sauce.

Spicy Tomato Pasta

Serves	Preparation Time	Cooking Time	Nutritional Information *(Per Serving)*
4	5 minutes	15 minutes	481 calories | 23g fat (of which 3g saturates) 60g carbohydrate | 1.3g salt | DF

300g (11oz) dried chunky pasta, such as tortiglioni

50g jar anchovies in oil with garlic and herbs

6 tomatoes, chopped

75g (3oz) black olives, pitted and chopped

1 lemon, cut into wedges

1. Cook the pasta in a large pan of lightly salted boiling water according to the packet instructions. Drain well and return to the pan.

2. Meanwhile, drain the oil from the anchovies and put 1 tbsp into a pan. Heat gently for 1 minute. Reserve the remaining oil to use in another recipe (see Cook's Tip).

3. Add the anchovies to the hot oil and cook for 1 minute. Add the tomatoes and simmer for 10 minutes. Stir in the olives and cook for a further 1–2 minutes. Add the sauce to the drained pasta, toss and serve with lemon wedges.

Cook's Tip
Keep the oil from the drained anchovies in the fridge for up to three days and use when frying onions for added flavour.

Ham and Mushroom Pasta

Serves	Preparation Time	Cooking Time	Nutritional Information (Per Serving)
4	5 minutes	15 minutes	415 calories | 10g fat (of which 4g saturates) 67g carbohydrate | 1g salt

350g (12oz) dried penne pasta

1 tbsp olive oil

2 shallots, sliced

200g (7oz) small button mushrooms

3 tbsp crème fraîche

125g (4oz) smoked ham, roughly chopped

2 tbsp freshly chopped flat-leafed parsley

salt and ground black pepper

1. Cook the pasta in a large pan of lightly salted boiling water according to the packet instructions until al dente.

2. Meanwhile, heat the oil in a pan. Add the shallots and fry gently for 3 minutes until starting to soften. Add the mushrooms and fry for 5–6 minutes.

3. Drain the pasta, put back into the pan and add the shallots and mushrooms. Stir in the crème fraîche, ham and parsley. Toss everything together, season to taste with salt and pepper and heat through to serve.

Penne with Smoked Salmon

Serves	Preparation Time	Cooking Time	Nutritional Information (Per Serving)
4	5 minutes	10–15 minutes	432 calories,	11g fat (of which 6g saturates) 67g carbohydrate	1.7g salt

350g (12oz) dried penne or other short tubular dried pasta

200ml (7fl oz) half-fat crème fraîche

150g (5oz) smoked salmon, roughly chopped

20g (¾ oz) fresh dill, finely chopped

salt and ground black pepper

lemon wedges to serve (optional)

1. Cook the pasta in a large pan of lightly salted boiling water according to the packet instructions. Drain.

2. Meanwhile, put the crème fraîche into a large bowl. Add the smoked salmon and dill, season well with salt and pepper and mix together. Gently stir through the drained penne and serve immediately with lemon wedges, if you like, to squeeze over.

Classic Lasagne

Serves	Preparation Time	Cooking Time	Nutritional Information (Per Serving)
6	about 1 hour	45 minutes	326 calories | 13g fat (of which 6g saturates) 37g carbohydrate | 0.5g salt

1 quantity Bolognese Sauce (see page 27)

butter to grease

350g (12oz) fresh lasagne, or 225g (8oz) 'no need to pre-cook' dried lasagne (12–15 sheets) (see Cook's Tip)

3 tbsp freshly grated Parmesan

For the béchamel sauce

300ml (½ pint) semi-skimmed milk

1 onion slice

6 peppercorns

1 mace blade and 1 bay leaf

15g (½oz) butter

15g (½oz) plain flour

freshly grated nutmeg

salt and ground black pepper

1. To make the béchamel sauce, pour the milk into a pan and add the onion, peppercorns, mace and bay leaf. Bring almost to the boil, then remove from the heat, cover and leave to infuse for about 20 minutes. Strain.

2. Melt the butter in a pan, stir in the flour and cook, stirring, for 1 minute. Remove from the heat and gradually pour in the milk, whisking constantly. Season with nutmeg, salt and pepper. Return to the heat and cook, stirring constantly, until the sauce is thickened and smooth. Simmer gently for 2 minutes.

3. Preheat the oven to 180°C (160°C fan oven) mark 4. Spoon one-third of the Bolognese sauce over the base of a greased 2.3 litre (4 pint) ovenproof dish. Cover with a layer of lasagne sheets, then a layer of béchamel. Repeat these layers twice more, finishing with a layer of béchamel to cover the lasagne.

4. Sprinkle the Parmesan over the top and stand the dish on a baking sheet. Cook for 45 minutes or until well browned and bubbling

---

Cook's Tip

If using 'no need to pre-cook' dried lasagne, add a little extra stock or water to the sauce.

Pasta with Pesto and Beans

Serves	Preparation Time	Cooking Time	Nutritional Information *(Per Serving)*
4	5 minutes	15 minutes	738 calories | 38g fat (of which 10g saturates) 74g carbohydrate | 1g salt | V

350g (12oz) dried trofie or other pasta shapes

175g (6oz) fine green beans, roughly chopped

175g (6oz) small salad potatoes, such as Anya, thickly sliced

250g (9oz) fresh pesto sauce

freshly grated Parmesan to serve

1. Bring a large pan of water to the boil. Add the pasta, bring back to the boil and cook for 5 minutes.

2. Add the beans and potatoes to the pan and continue to boil for a further 7–8 minutes until the potatoes are just tender.

3. Drain the pasta, beans and potatoes in a colander, then tip everything back into the pan and stir in the pesto sauce. Serve scattered with freshly grated Parmesan.

Did You Know...?

This combination of pasta, potatoes, green beans and pesto is a speciality of Liguria on the East coast of Italy. Traditionally, it is made with the twisted pasta shape known as trofie (see photograph) – pieces of pasta are rolled on a flat surface until they form rounded lengths of pasta with tapered ends. Each length is then twisted into its final shape.

Thrifty Tip
Make your own pesto (see page 27) and freeze in batches.

Mushroom, Bacon and Leek Risotto

Serves	Preparation Time	Cooking Time	Nutritional Information *(Per Serving)*
4	10 minutes	about 30 minutes	452 calories | 13g fat (of which 5g saturates) 62g carbohydrate | 2.6g salt | **GF**

25g (1oz) dried mushrooms

250g (9oz) dry-cure smoked bacon, rind removed, chopped

3 leeks, chopped

300g (11oz) arborio rice

20g (¾oz) chives, chopped

25g (1oz) freshly grated Parmesan, plus extra to serve

1. Put the mushrooms into a large heatproof bowl and pour in 1.5 litres (2½ pints) boiling water. Leave to soak for 10 minutes.

2. Meanwhile, fry the bacon and leeks in a large pan – no need to add oil – for 7–8 minutes until soft and golden.

3. Stir in the rice, cook for 1–2 minutes, then add the mushrooms and their soaking liquor. Cook at a gentle simmer, stirring occasionally, for 15–20 minutes until the rice is cooked and most of the liquid has been absorbed.

4. Stir in the chives and grated Parmesan, then sprinkle with extra Parmesan to serve.

Cook's Tip
To enrich the flavour, add a splash of leftover dry sherry or white wine to the pan when you add the rice.

Prawn, Courgette and Leek Risotto

Serves	Preparation Time	Cooking Time	Nutritional Information (Per Serving)
6	10 minutes	30 minutes	320 calories | 7g fat (of which 3g saturates) 49g carbohydrate | 1.3g salt | GF

1 tbsp olive oil

25g (1oz) butter

1 leek, finely chopped

2 courgettes, thinly sliced

2 garlic cloves, crushed

350g (12oz) arborio rice

1.6 litres (2¾ pints) vegetable stock

200g (7oz) cooked and peeled prawns

small bunch of parsley or mint, or a mixture of both, chopped

salt and ground black pepper

1. Heat the oil and half the butter in a large shallow pan. Add the leek, courgettes and garlic and soften over a low heat. Add the rice and cook, stirring well, for 1 minute.

2. Meanwhile, heat the stock in a separate pan to a steady, low simmer. Add a ladleful of the stock to the rice and simmer, stirring, until absorbed. Continue adding the stock, a ladleful at a time.

3. When nearly all the stock has been added and the rice is al dente (just tender but with a little bite at the centre), add the prawns. Season to taste with salt and pepper and stir in the remaining stock and the rest of the butter. Stir through and take off the heat. Cover and leave to stand for a couple of minutes, then stir the chopped herbs through it. Serve immediately.

Bacon and Garden Vegetable Risotto

Serves	Preparation Time	Cooking Time	Nutritional Information (Per Serving)
4	15 minutes	about 30 minutes	550 calories	19g fat (of which 8g saturates) 69g carbohydrate	1.8g salt

15g (½oz) butter

1 onion, finely chopped

175g (6oz) bacon, diced

1 medium fennel bulb, chopped

2 medium courgettes, diced

300g (11oz) arborio rice

1 litre (1¾ pints) chicken stock

pinch of saffron strands

50g (2oz) finely grated Parmesan, plus extra to serve

2 tbsp freshly chopped basil

salt and ground black pepper

1. Melt the butter in a heavy-based sauté pan. Add the onion and bacon and cook gently for 7–8 minutes, stirring from time to time, until golden. Halfway through the cooking time add the fennel and courgettes.

2. Add the rice and cook, stirring, for 2–3 minutes until all the grains are coated with the butter and look glossy. Heat the stock in another pan over a low to medium heat, keeping it on a low steady simmer.

3. Add the saffron and a ladleful of hot stock to the rice and simmer gently, stirring until absorbed. Continue adding the stock, a ladleful at a time, until the rice is tender but still has some bite to it. This will take about 20 minutes, and you may not need to add all the stock.

4. Add the Parmesan, season to taste with salt and pepper and sprinkle with the basil. Serve immediately with extra Parmesan sprinkled on top.

Mushroom Risotto

Serves	Preparation Time	Cooking Time	Nutritional Information (Per Serving)
4	10 minutes	45 minutes	549 calories	23g fat (of which 11g saturates) 72g carbohydrate	0.3g salt

50g (2oz) butter

2 tbsp olive oil

4 shallots, finely sliced

1 garlic clove, crushed

500g (1lb 2oz) mixed mushrooms, sliced or left whole, depending on their size

3 tbsp double cream

juice of ½ lemon

1 tbsp freshly chopped parsley

350g (12oz) arborio rice

1.1 litres (2 pints) chicken stock

1. Melt half the butter with 1 tbsp oil in a pan over a gentle heat. Fry half the shallots for 5 minutes until softened, then add the garlic and cook for 1 minute.

2. Stir in the mushrooms and fry over a medium to high heat until browned and the juices have evaporated. Stir in the cream, lemon juice and parsley.

3. Heat the remaining butter and oil in another large pan. Fry the remaining shallots for 5 minutes until softened. Stir in the rice and fry for 1 minute. Meanwhile, heat the stock in another pan over a low to medium heat, keeping it on a low steady simmer.

4. Add a ladleful of hot stock to the rice and simmer gently, stirring until absorbed. Continue adding the stock, a ladleful at a time, until the rice is tender but still has some bite to it. This will take about 20 minutes, and you may not need to add all the stock.

5. When the rice is cooked, stir in the mushrooms. Heat through for 1–2 minutes, then serve.

Risotto Milanese

Serves	Preparation Time	Cooking Time	Nutritional Information (*Per Serving*)
4	15 minutes	about 30 minutes	461 calories | 15g fat (of which 9g saturates) 64g carbohydrate | 0.6g salt | GF

50g (2oz) butter

1 onion, finely chopped

300g (11oz) arborio rice

1 litre (1¾ pints) chicken stock

large pinch of saffron strands

50g (2oz) Parmesan, freshly grated, plus shavings to serve

salt and ground black pepper

1. Melt half the butter in a heavy-based pan. Add the onion and cook gently for 5 minutes to soften. Add the rice and cook, stirring, for 1 minute until the grains are coated with the butter and glossy.

2. Meanwhile, heat the stock in a separate pan to a steady, low simmer.

3. Add the saffron and a ladleful of the stock to the rice and simmer, stirring, until absorbed. Continue adding the stock, a ladleful at a time, until the rice is tender but still has some bite to it. This will take about 25 minutes, and you may not need to add all the stock.

4. Add the remaining butter and the grated Parmesan. Season with salt and pepper to taste, garnish with shavings of Parmesan and serve.

Cook's Tip
Italian risotto is made with medium-grain arborio, vialone nano or carnaroli rice, which release starch to give a rich, creamy texture.

Squash and Bacon Risotto

Serves	Preparation Time	Cooking Time	Nutritional Information (*Per Serving*)
4	10 minutes	40 minutes	390 calories | 9g fat (of which 3g saturates) 65g carbohydrate | 2g salt | DF | GF

125g (4oz) smoked bacon, chopped

1 small butternut squash, peeled and cut into small chunks

1 onion, finely chopped

300g (11oz) arborio rice

1 litre (1¾ pints) hot vegetable stock

1. Put the bacon and the butternut squash into a large deep frying pan and fry over a medium heat for 8–10 minutes.

2. When the bacon is golden and the squash has softened, add the onion to the pan and continue to fry for 5 minutes until softened.

3. Stir in the rice, cook for 1–2 minutes, then add the hot stock. Bring to the boil and simmer for 15–20 minutes, stirring occasionally to ensure the rice doesn't stick, until almost all the stock has been absorbed and the rice and squash are tender. Serve immediately.

Try Something Different
Instead of the squash, use 750g (1lb 11oz) peeled and seeded pumpkin. Instead of the onion, use a fennel bulb.

Thrifty Tip
For an even sweeter flavour, roast the butternut squash with a sprinkle of olive oil, alongside your Sunday roast for supper the next day. Add to the risotto for the last 5 minutes of cooking time to heat through. It'll taste even more special and you won't have used extra fuel.

Tomato Risotto

Serves	Preparation Time	Cooking Time	Nutritional Information (Per Serving)
6	10 minutes	25–30 minutes	264 calories | 4g fat (of which 1g saturates) 49g carbohydrate | 0.5g salt | V | GF

1 large rosemary sprig

2 tbsp olive oil

1 small onion, finely chopped

350g (12oz) arborio rice

4 tbsp dry white wine (optional)

750ml (1¼ pints) hot vegetable stock

300g (11oz) cherry tomatoes, halved

salt and ground black pepper

shavings of Parmesan and extra virgin olive oil to serve

1. Pull the leaves from the rosemary and chop roughly. Set aside.

2. Heat the oil in a flameproof casserole, add the onion and cook for about 8–10 minutes until beginning to soften. Add the rice and stir to coat in the oil and onion. Pour in the wine, if using, then the hot stock, stirring well to mix.

3. Bring to the boil, stirring, then cover and simmer for 5 minutes. Stir in the tomatoes and chopped rosemary. Simmer, covered, for a further 10–15 minutes until the rice is tender and most of the liquid has been absorbed. Season to taste with salt and pepper.

4. Serve immediately with shavings of Parmesan and extra virgin olive oil to drizzle over.

Pumpkin Risotto with Hazelnut Butter

Serves	Preparation Time	Cooking Time	Nutritional Information (Per Serving)
4	15 minutes	40 minutes	706 calories | 50g fat (of which 27g saturates) 51g carbohydrate | 1.1g salt | GF

50g (2oz) butter

175g (6oz) onion, finely chopped

900g (2lb) pumpkin, halved, peeled, seeded and cut into small cubes (see Cook's Tip)

2 garlic cloves, crushed

225g (8oz) arborio rice

600ml (1 pint) hot chicken stock

grated zest of ½ orange

40g (1½oz) freshly shaved Parmesan

salt and ground black pepper

For the hazelnut butter

50g (2oz) hazelnuts

125g (4oz) butter, softened

2 tbsp freshly chopped flat-leafed parsley

1. To make the hazelnut butter, spread the hazelnuts on a baking sheet and toast under a hot grill until golden brown, turning frequently. Put the nuts in a clean teatowel and rub off the skins, then chop finely. Put the nuts, butter and parsley on a piece of non-stick baking parchment. Season with pepper and mix together. Mould into a sausage shape, twist the baking parchment at both ends and chill.

2. To make the risotto, melt the butter in a large pan and fry the onion until soft but not coloured. Add the pumpkin and sauté over a low heat for 5–8 minutes until just beginning to soften. Add the garlic and rice and stir until well mixed. Increase the heat to medium and add the stock a little at a time, allowing the rice to absorb the liquid after each addition. This should take about 25 minutes.

3. Stir in the orange zest and Parmesan and season to taste with salt and pepper. Serve the risotto with a slice of the hazelnut butter melting on top.

Cook's Tip
If you can't find pumpkin, use butternut squash.

Simple Fried Rice

Serves	Preparation Time	Cooking Time	Nutritional Information (Per Serving)
4	5 minutes	15–20 minutes	339 calories | 11g fat (of which 2g saturates) 37g carbohydrate | 0.4g salt | DF | GF

150g (5oz) long-grain rice

2 tbsp sesame oil

3 medium eggs, lightly beaten

250g (9oz) frozen petits pois

250g (9oz) cooked peeled prawns

1. Cook the rice in boiling water for about 10 minutes or according to the packet instructions. Drain well.

2. Heat 1 tsp oil in a large non-stick frying pan. Pour in half the beaten eggs and tilt the pan around over the heat for about 1 minute until the egg is set. Tip the omelette on to a warm plate. Repeat with another 1 tsp oil and the remaining beaten egg to make another omelette. Tip on to another warm plate.

3. Add the remaining oil to the pan and stir in the rice and peas. Stir-fry for 2–3 minutes until the peas are cooked. Stir in the prawns.

4. Roll up the omelettes, roughly chop one-third of one, then slice the remainder into strips. Add the chopped omelette to the rice, peas and prawns, and cook for 1–2 minutes until heated through. Divide the fried rice among four serving bowls, top with the sliced omelette and serve immediately.

Rice and Red Pepper Stir-fry

Serves	Preparation Time	Cooking Time	Nutritional Information (*Per Serving*)
4	5 minutes	15 minutes	146 calories | 5g fat (of which 1g saturates) 21g carbohydrate | 0.4g salt | DF

300g (11oz) long-grain rice

800ml (1 pint 7fl oz) hot vegetable stock

1 tbsp vegetable oil

1 large onion, sliced

8 rashers streaky bacon

1 large red pepper, halved, seeded and cut into chunks

150g (5oz) frozen peas

a dash of Worcestershire sauce

1. Put the rice into a pan and pour in the hot stock. Cover, bring to the boil and simmer for 10 minutes until the rice is tender and the liquid has been absorbed.

2. Heat the oil in a frying pan over a medium heat. Add the onion and fry for 5 minutes, then add the bacon and red pepper. Fry for 5 minutes until the bacon is crisp. Stir in the cooked rice and the peas. Cook, stirring occasionally, for 2–3 minutes until the rice is hot and the peas are tender. Add a dash of Worcestershire sauce and serve.

Fast Macaroni Cheese

Serves	Preparation Time	Cooking Time	Nutritional Information (*Per Serving*))
4	5 minutes	15 minutes	1137 calories | 69g fat (of which 44g saturates) 96g carbohydrate | 2g salt | V

500g (1lb 2oz) dried macaroni

500ml (18fl oz) crème fraîche

200g (7oz) freshly grated Parmesan

2 tbsp ready-made English or Dijon mustard

5 tbsp freshly chopped flat-leafed parsley

ground black pepper

green salad to serve

1. Cook the macaroni in a large pan of lightly salted boiling water according to the packet instructions. Drain and set aside.

2. Preheat the grill to high. Put the crème fraîche into a pan and heat gently. Stir in 175g (6oz) Parmesan, the mustard and parsley and season well with black pepper. Stir the pasta through the sauce, spoon into four ovenproof bowls and sprinkle with the remaining cheese. Grill until golden and serve immediately with salad.

Thrifty Tip
Leftover chopped ham can be stirred in with the Parmesan for a more substantial dish.

6

VEGETARIAN

Tomato and Butter Bean Stew

Serves	Preparation Time	Cooking Time	Nutritional Information (Per Serving)
4	10 minutes	50–55 minutes	286 calories | 8g fat (of which 1g saturates) 41g carbohydrate | 1.8g salt | **V** | **DF** | **GF**

2 tbsp olive oil

1 onion, finely sliced

2 garlic cloves, finely chopped

2 large leeks, sliced

2 x 400g cans cherry tomatoes

2 x 400g cans butter beans, drained and rinsed

150ml (¼ pint) hot vegetable stock

1–2 tbsp balsamic vinegar

salt and ground black pepper

1. Preheat the oven to 180°C (160°C fan oven) mark 4. Heat the oil in a flameproof casserole over a medium heat. Add the onion and garlic and cook for 10 minutes until golden and soft. Add the leeks and cook, covered, for 5 minutes.

2. Add the tomatoes, beans and hot stock and season well with salt and pepper. Bring to the boil, then cover and cook in the oven for 35–40 minutes until the sauce has thickened. Remove from the oven, stir in the vinegar and spoon into warmed bowls.

Leek and Broccoli Bake

Serves	Preparation Time	Cooking Time	Nutritional Information (Per Serving)
4	20 minutes	45–55 minutes	245 calories | 13g fat (of which 4g saturates) 18g carbohydrate | 0.4g salt | V | GF

2 tbsp olive oil

1 large red onion, cut into wedges

1 aubergine, chopped

2 leeks, cut into chunks

1 broccoli head, cut into florets and stalks chopped

3 large flat mushrooms, chopped

2 x 400g cans cherry tomatoes

3 rosemary sprigs, chopped

50g (2oz) freshly grated Parmesan

salt and ground black pepper

Try Something Different
Use sliced courgettes instead of aubergine.

1. Preheat the oven to 200°C (180°C fan oven) mark 6. Heat the oil in a large flameproof dish, add the onion, aubergine and leeks and cook for 10–12 minutes until golden and softened.

2. Add the broccoli, mushrooms, tomatoes, half the rosemary and 300ml (½ pint) boiling water. Season to taste with salt and pepper. Stir well, then cover and cook in the oven for 30 minutes.

3. Meanwhile, put the Parmesan into a bowl. Add the remaining rosemary and season with black pepper. When the vegetables are cooked, remove the lid and sprinkle the Parmesan mixture on top. Cook, uncovered, in the oven for a further 5–10 minutes until the topping is golden.

Aubergine and Chickpea Pilaf

Serves	Preparation Time	Cooking Time	Nutritional Information (Per Serving)
4	10 minutes	20 minutes, plus 5 minutes standing	462 calories | 20g fat (of which 5g saturates) 58g carbohydrate | 0.9g salt | V | GF

4–6 tbsp olive oil

275g (10oz) aubergine, roughly chopped

225g (8oz) onions, finely chopped

25g (1oz) butter

½ tsp cumin seeds

175g (6oz) long-grain rice

600ml (1 pint) vegetable or stock

400g can chickpeas, drained and rinsed

225g (8oz) baby spinach leaves

salt and ground black pepper

1. Heat half the oil in a large pan or flameproof casserole over a medium heat. Fry the aubergine for 4–5 minutes, in batches, until deep golden brown. Remove from the pan with a slotted spoon and set aside. Add the remaining oil to the pan and cook the onions for 5 minutes or until golden and soft.

2. Add the butter, then stir in the cumin seeds and rice. Fry for 1–2 minutes, pour in the stock, season to taste with salt and pepper and bring to the boil. Reduce the heat, then simmer, uncovered, for 10–12 minutes until most of the liquid has evaporated and the rice is tender.

3. Remove the pan from the heat. Stir in the chickpeas, spinach and reserved aubergine. Cover with a tight-fitting lid and leave to stand for 5 minutes until the spinach has wilted and the chickpeas are heated through. Adjust the seasoning to taste. Fork through the rice grains to separate and make them fluffy before serving.

Get Ahead

- **To prepare ahead**, prepare ahead, fry the aubergine and onion as in step 1. Cover and keep in a cool place for 1½ hours.
- **To use**, complete the recipe.

Tomato and Herb Quiche

Serves	Preparation Time	Cooking Time	Nutritional Information (Per Serving)
6	10 minutes	45 minutes, plus standing	389 calories | 28g fat (of which 14g saturates) 21g carbohydrate | 1g salt | V

225g (8oz) pack frozen shortcrust pastry, thawed

plain flour to dust

350g (12oz) ripe tomatoes

3 medium eggs

175g (6oz) Caerphilly cheese, grated

150ml (¼ pint) single cream

1 tbsp freshly chopped herbs, such as sage and thyme, or 2 tsp dried mixed herbs

salt and ground black pepper

1. Preheat the oven to 200°C (180°C fan oven) mark 6. Roll out the pastry on a lightly floured surface and use to line a 23cm (9in) flan tin or dish placed on a baking sheet. Prick the base with a fork, line with baking parchment and baking beans and bake blind for 15 minutes. Remove parchment and beans from the pastry case and return to the oven for 5 minutes.

2. Put the tomatoes into a heatproof bowl, pour boiling water over them and leave to stand for 2–3 minutes. Drain and plunge them into ice-cold water, then peel the skin off each one with your fingers.

3. Break the eggs into a bowl and beat lightly. Add the cheese, cream, herbs and salt and pepper to taste and beat lightly again to mix.

4. Remove the pastry case from the oven. Slice the tomatoes and arrange half of them in the bottom of the pastry case. Slowly pour the egg and cheese mixture over the tomatoes, then arrange the remaining tomatoes on top.

5. Bake in the oven for 20–25 minutes until the filling is just set. Remove and leave to stand for 15 minutes before serving.

Vegetable and Gruyère Bake

Serves	Preparation Time	Cooking Time	Nutritional Information (Per Serving)
4	20 minutes	about 50 minutes	243 calories | 11g fat (of which 5g saturates) 26g carbohydrate | 0.9g salt | V

2 large potatoes, thinly sliced

1 tbsp olive oil

250ml (9fl oz) hot vegetable stock

1 each red and yellow pepper, seeded and sliced

2 small courgettes, sliced

250g (9oz) vine-ripened tomatoes, sliced

25g (1oz) capers, chopped

25g (1oz) pitted black olives, chopped

1 tbsp freshly chopped thyme leaves

75g (3oz) freshly grated Gruyère or Parmesan

salt and ground black pepper

1. Preheat the oven to 200°C (180°C fan oven) mark 6. Arrange the potato slices, overlapping them slightly, over the base of a 2.6 litre (4½ pint) shallow ovenproof dish.

2. Drizzle with 1 tsp oil and pour 125ml (4fl oz) hot stock over them. Cook in the oven for 20 minutes until tender.

3. Remove from the oven and top with layers of sliced pepper, courgette and tomato. Scatter the capers, olives and thyme over and season to taste with salt and pepper. Drizzle on the remaining oil and stock and sprinkle the cheese on top. Return to the oven for 30 minutes or until the vegetables are tender.

> **Cook's Tip**
> Serve with a large green salad with a little vinaigrette and crusty bread.

Poached Eggs with Mushrooms

Serves	Preparation Time	Cooking Time	Nutritional Information (Per Serving)
4	15 minutes	20 minutes	276 calories | 23g fat (of which 9g saturates) 1g carbohydrate | 0.7g salt | V | GF

8 medium-sized flat or Portobello mushrooms

40g (1½oz) butter

8 medium eggs

225g (8oz) baby spinach leaves

4 tsp fresh pesto

Try Something Different
For a more substantial meal, serve on wheat-free bread, such as 100% rye bread or German pumpernickel.

1. Preheat the oven to 200°C (180°C fan oven) mark 6. Arrange the mushrooms in a single layer in a small roasting tin and dot with the butter. Roast for 15 minutes until golden brown and soft.

2. Meanwhile, bring a wide shallow pan of water to the boil. When the mushrooms are half-cooked and the water is bubbling furiously, break the eggs into the pan, spaced well apart, then take the pan off the heat. The eggs will take about 6 minutes to cook.

3. When the mushrooms are tender, put them on a warmed plate, cover and return to the turned-off oven to keep warm.

4. Put the roasting tin over a medium heat on the hob and add the spinach. Cook, stirring, for about 30 seconds until the spinach has just started to wilt.

5. The eggs should be set by now, so divide the mushrooms among four plates and top each with a little spinach, a poached egg and a teaspoonful of pesto.

Butternut Squash and Spinach Lasagne

Serves	Preparation Time	Cooking Time	Nutritional Information *(Per Serving)*
6	30 minutes	about 1 hour	273 calories	17g fat (of which 7g saturates) 18g carbohydrate	0.6g salt	**V**

1 butternut squash, peeled, halved, seeded and cut into 3cm (1¼in) cubes

2 tbsp olive oil

1 onion, sliced

25g (1oz) butter

25g (1oz) plain flour

600ml (1 pint) milk

250g (9oz) ricotta cheese

1 tsp freshly grated nutmeg

225g bag baby leaf spinach

6 'no need to pre-cook' lasagne sheets

50g (2oz) freshly grated pecorino cheese or Parmesan

salt and ground black pepper

1. Preheat the oven to 200°C (180°C fan oven) mark 6. Put the squash into a roasting tin with the oil, onion and 1 tbsp water. Mix well and season to taste with salt and pepper. Roast for 25 minutes, tossing halfway through.

2. To make the sauce, melt the butter in a pan, then stir in the flour and cook over a medium heat for 1–2 minutes. Gradually add the milk, stirring constantly. Reduce the heat to a simmer and cook, stirring, for 5 minutes or until the sauce has thickened. Crumble the ricotta into the sauce and add the nutmeg. Mix together thoroughly and season with salt and pepper.

3. Heat 1 tbsp water in a pan. Add the spinach, cover and cook until just wilted. Season generously.

4. Spoon the squash mixture into a 1.7 litre (3 pint) ovenproof dish. Layer the spinach on top, then cover with a third of the sauce, then the lasagne. Spoon the remaining sauce on top, season with salt and pepper and sprinkle with the grated cheese. Cook for 30–35 minutes until the cheese topping is golden and the pasta is cooked.

Stuffed Peppers

Serves	Preparation Time	Cooking Time	Nutritional Information (Per Serving)
4	15 minutes	55 minutes	208 calories | 5g fat (of which 1g saturates) 39g carbohydrate | 0g salt | **V** | **DF** | **GF**

225g (8oz) brown basmati rice

1 tbsp olive oil

2 onions, chopped

400g can cherry tomatoes

3 tbsp freshly chopped coriander, plus extra sprigs to garnish

4 red peppers, halved and seeded, leaving stalks intact

150ml (¼ pint) hot vegetable stock

Try Something Different
Add 25g (1oz) pinenuts or chopped cashew nuts to the cooked rice and coriander at step 2.

1. Preheat the oven to 200°C (180°C fan oven) mark 6. Cook the rice according to the packet instructions, then drain.

2. Meanwhile, heat the oil in a pan, add the onions and fry for 15 minutes. Add the tomatoes and leave to simmer for 10 minutes. Stir in the cooked rice and coriander, then spoon the mixture into the halved peppers.

3. Put the peppers into a roasting tin and pour the stock around them. Cook in the oven for 30 minutes until tender. Serve sprinkled with coriander sprigs.

Couscous-stuffed Mushrooms

Serves	Preparation Time	Cooking Time	Nutritional Information (Per Serving)
4	3 minutes	about 12 minutes	422 calories | 30g fat (of which 11g saturates) 27g carbohydrate | 0.6g salt | V

125g (4oz) couscous

200ml (7fl oz) boiling water

20g pack fresh flat-leafed parsley, roughly chopped

280g jar mixed antipasti in oil, drained and oil put to one side

8 large flat Portabellini mushrooms

25g (1oz) butter

25g (1oz) plain flour

300ml (½ pint) skimmed milk

75g (3oz) mature Cheddar, grated, plus extra to sprinkle

green salad to serve

1. Preheat the oven to 220°C (200°C fan oven) mark 7. Put the couscous in a bowl with the boiling water, parsley, antipasti and 1 tbsp of the reserved oil. Stir well.

2. Put the mushrooms on to a non-stick baking tray and spoon a little of the couscous mixture into the centre of each. Cook in the oven while you make the sauce.

3. Whisk together the butter, flour and milk in a small pan over a high heat until the mixture comes to the boil. Reduce the heat as soon as it starts to thicken and whisk constantly until smooth. Take the pan off the heat and stir in the cheese.

4. Spoon the sauce over the mushrooms and sprinkle with the remaining cheese. Put back into the oven for a further 7–10 minutes until golden. Serve with a green salad.

Thrifty Tip
Use mature Cheddar as it has a stronger flavour – you don't have to use as much and it goes a long way.

Spiced Bean and Vegetable Stew

Serves	Preparation Time	Cooking Time	Nutritional Information (Per Serving)
6	20 minutes	3 minutes	252 calories | 7g fat (of which 1g saturates) 43g carbohydrate | 0.6g salt | V

3 tbsp olive oil

2 small onions, sliced

2 garlic cloves, crushed

1 tbsp sweet paprika

1 small dried red chilli, seeded and finely chopped

700g (1½lb) sweet potatoes, peeled and cubed

700g (1½lb) pumpkin, peeled and cut into chunks

125g (4oz) green beans, trimmed

500g jar passata

400g can haricot or cannellini beans, drained

salt and ground black pepper

seeded wholemeal bread to serve

1. Heat the oil in a large heavy-based pan, add the onions and garlic and cook over a very gentle heat for 5 minutes. Stir in the paprika and chilli and cook for 2 minutes.

2. Add the sweet potatoes, pumpkin, beans, passata and 900ml (1½ pints) water. Season generously with salt and pepper.

3. Cover the pan, bring to the boil, then reduce the heat and simmer for 20 minutes, until the vegetables are tender. Add the drained beans and cook for 3 minutes to warm through. Serve with warm seeded wholemeal bread.

Chickpea and Vegetable Stew

Serves	Preparation Time	Cooking Time	Nutritional Information (Per Serving)
4	20 minutes	30 minutes	491 calories | 10g fat (of which 1g saturates) 87g carbohydrate | 1.9g salt

1 tbsp rapeseed oil

1 red onion, finely sliced

½ red chilli, finely chopped

½ tsp smoked paprika

½ tsp ground ginger

½ tsp ground turmeric

1 yellow pepper, seeded and thinly sliced

1 medium sweet potato, peeled and roughly diced

2 x 400g cans chickpeas, drained and rinsed

400g can chopped tomatoes

4 wholemeal pitta breads

100ml (3½fl oz) crème fraîche (optional)

salt and ground black pepper

1. Heat the oil in a large pan and cook the onion on a low heat for 10 minutes until softened. Stir in the chilli, spices and ½ tsp salt, then cook for 1 minute. Add the sliced pepper and sweet potato and cook for 5 minutes until the vegetables are beginning to caramelise around the edges.

2. Stir in the chickpeas and tomatoes. Cover the pan and simmer for 10 minutes until the sweet potato is cooked.

3. Toast the pitta breads and slice in half. Stir the crème fraîche, if using, into the stew, then heat through and taste for seasoning. Ladle into warmed bowls and serve with the hot pitta.

New Potato, Pea and Mint Frittatas

Serves	Preparation Time	Cooking Time	Nutritional Information *(Per Serving)*
6	15 minutes, plus cooling	about 40 minutes	315 calories | 23g fat (of which 8g saturates) 13g carbohydrate | 0.6g salt | **V** | **GF**

3 tbsp olive oil, plus extra to grease

50g (2oz) Parmesan, finely grated

150g (5oz) baby new potatoes, roughly chopped

125g (4oz) freshly shelled peas – you'll need about 350g (12oz) peas in their pods

2 red onions, cut into thin wedges

1 tbsp freshly chopped mint

8 large eggs

142ml carton single cream

salt and ground black pepper

cherry tomato and leaf salad to serve

1. Preheat the oven to 180°C (160°C fan oven) mark 4. Lightly oil a deep 12-hole non-stick muffin tin. Sprinkle a pinch of Parmesan into each hole.

2. Cook the potatoes in lightly salted boiling water for about 5 minutes or until just tender. Add the peas to the potatoes for the last 3 minutes of cooking time. Drain well.

3. Heat the oil in a large non-stick frying pan and fry the onions for 7–10 minutes until soft and golden. Add the drained vegetables and the mint. Cook, stirring, for 1 minute. Set aside to cool.

4. Beat the eggs in a large bowl with the cream and half the remaining Parmesan. Season well with salt and pepper.

5. Divide the vegetables equally among the holes in the muffin tin, then pour in the egg mixture. Sprinkle with the remaining cheese. Cook for 20–25 minutes or until just set and golden. Cool in the tin for 20 minutes, then run a knife around the edge of each frittata and turn out on to a board. Leave to cool, then chill. The frittatas will keep for up to two days. Serve with a cherry tomato and leaf salad.

Freezing Tip
- **To freeze:** complete the recipe, put the cooled frittatas in an airtight container and freeze. They will keep for up to 1 month.
- **To use:** thaw overnight in the fridge, taking them out about 1 hour before you're ready to serve.

Baked Eggs

Serves	Preparation Time	Cooking Time	Nutritional Information (Per Serving)
4	10 minutes	15 minutes	119 calories | 11g fat (of which 3g saturates) 1g carbohydrate | 0.3g salt | V | GF

3 tbsp olive oil

250g (9oz) mushrooms, chopped

450g (1lb) fresh spinach

4 medium eggs

4 tbsp single cream

salt and ground black pepper

1. Preheat the oven to 200°C (180°C fan oven) mark 6. Heat the oil in a large frying pan, add the mushrooms and stir-fry for 30 seconds. Add the spinach and stir-fry until wilted. Season to taste with salt and pepper, then divide the mixture between two shallow ovenproof dishes.

2. Carefully break an egg into the centre of each dish, then spoon 1 tbsp single cream over each.

3. Cook in the oven for about 12 minutes until just set – the eggs will continue to cook a little once they're out of the oven. Grind a little more pepper over the top, if liked, and serve.

Potato and Broccoli Curry

Serves	Preparation Time	Cooking Time	Nutritional Information *(Per Serving)*
4	20 minutes	about 40 minutes	302 calories | 10g fat (of which 1g saturates) 46g carbohydrate | 0.5g salt | V

For the spice mix

2 tsp cumin seeds

2 tsp paprika

1 tsp ground coriander

finely grated zest of ½ orange

For the curry

600g (1lb 5oz) new potatoes, cut into two-bite cubes

2 tbsp sunflower oil

2 onions, sliced

400g can chickpeas, drained and rinsed

250ml (9fl oz) hot vegetable stock

150g (5oz) chopped broccoli

salt and ground black pepper

2 tbsp each mango chutney and Greek yogurt, mixed together, and naan bread to serve

1. Cook the potatoes in a pan of lightly salted boiling water for 5 minutes, then drain.

2. Meanwhile, grind the spice mix ingredients in a pestle and mortar with a good pinch of salt. Dry-fry the spice mix for 2–3 minutes in a large frying pan, then add the oil and onions and fry for 7–8 minutes until soft and golden.

3. Add the potatoes, chickpeas and hot stock. Season to taste with salt and pepper, then cook for 15–20 minutes, adding the broccoli for the last 4–5 minutes of cooking time. Serve with the mango chutney sauce and naan bread.

Leek and Potato Cold-night Pie

Serves	Preparation Time	Cooking Time	Nutritional Information *(Per Serving)*
4	5 minutes	20–25 minutes	162 calories | 9g fat (of which 6g saturates) 18g carbohydrate | 0.6g salt | V | GF

4 medium potatoes, chopped

4 tbsp butter

2 large leeks, chopped into chunks

50g (2oz) freshly grated Cheddar

salt and ground black pepper

1. Put the potatoes into a pan of lightly salted water, cover and bring to the boil. Simmer for 10–15 minutes until tender.

2. Meanwhile, melt 1 tbsp butter in a frying pan, add the leek and fry for 10–15 minutes until soft and golden. Preheat the grill.

3. Drain the potatoes and tip back into the pan. Season to taste with salt and pepper, then mash with the remaining butter. Put the leek into a small ovenproof dish and cover with the mash. Top with the grated cheese and grill for 10 minutes or until hot and golden.

Black-eye Bean Chilli

Serves	Preparation Time	Cooking Time	Nutritional Information (Per Serving)
4	10 minutes	20 minutes	245 calories | 5g fat (of which 1g saturates) 39g carbohydrate | 1.8g salt | V

1 tbsp olive oil

1 onion, chopped

3 celery sticks, finely chopped

2 x 400g cans black-eye beans, drained and rinsed

2 x 400g cans chopped tomatoes

2 or 3 splashes of Tabasco sauce

3 tbsp freshly chopped coriander

warm tortillas and soured cream to serve

1. Heat the oil in a heavy-based frying pan over a low heat. Add the onion and celery and fry for 10 minutes until softened.

2. Add the black-eye beans to the pan with the tomatoes and Tabasco sauce. Bring to the boil, then simmer for 10 minutes.

3. Just before serving, stir in the coriander. Spoon the chilli on to warm tortillas and serve with soured cream.

Try Something Different
Replace half the black-eye beans with red kidney beans.

Chilli Bean Cake

Serves	Preparation Time	Cooking Time	Nutritional Information *(Per Serving)*
4	10 minutes	20 minutes	265 calories | 6g fat (of which 1g saturates) 41g carbohydrate | 2.1g salt | V

3 tbsp olive oil

75g (3oz) wholemeal breadcrumbs

1 bunch of spring onions, finely chopped

1 orange pepper, seeded and chopped

1 small green chilli, seeded and finely chopped

1 garlic clove, crushed

1 tsp ground turmeric (optional)

400g can mixed beans, drained

3 tbsp mayonnaise

small handful of fresh basil, chopped

salt and ground black pepper

soured cream, freshly chopped coriander and lime wedges to serve (optional)

1. Heat 2 tbsp oil in a non-stick frying pan over a medium heat and fry the breadcrumbs until golden and beginning to crisp. Remove and set aside.

2. Using the same pan, add the remaining oil and fry the spring onions until soft and golden. Add the orange pepper, chilli, garlic and turmeric, if using. Cook, stirring, for 5 minutes.

3. Tip in the beans, mayonnaise, two-thirds of the breadcrumbs and the basil. Season to taste with salt and pepper, mash roughly with a fork, then press the mixture down to flatten. Sprinkle with the remaining breadcrumbs.

4. Fry the bean cake over a medium heat for 4–5 minutes until the base is golden. Remove from the heat, cut into wedges and serve with soured cream, coriander and lime wedges, if you like.

Glamorgan Sausages

Serves	Preparation Time	Cooking Time	Nutritional Information *(Per Serving)*
4	25 minutes	15 minutes	403 calories | 20g fat (of which 9g saturates) 39g carbohydrate | 1.7g salt | V

150g (5oz) Caerphilly cheese, grated

200g (7oz) fresh white breadcrumbs

3 spring onions, finely chopped

1 tbsp freshly chopped flat-leafed parsley

leaves from 4 thyme sprigs

3 large eggs, 1 separated

vegetable oil for frying

salt and ground black pepper

green salad and chutney to serve

1. Preheat the oven to 140°C (120°C fan oven) mark 1. Mix the cheese with 150g (5oz) breadcrumbs, the spring onions and herbs in a large bowl. Season well with salt and pepper.

2. Add the 2 whole eggs plus the extra yolk and mix well to combine. Cover and chill for 5 minutes.

3. Lightly beat the egg white in a shallow bowl. Tip the rest of the breadcrumbs on to a large plate.

4. Take 2 tbsp of the cheese mixture and shape into a small sausage, about 4cm (1½in) long. Roll first in the egg white, then in the breadcrumbs to coat. Repeat to make 12 sausages in total.

5. Heat 2 tsp oil in a large heavy-based pan until hot and fry the sausages in two batches for 6–8 minutes, turning until golden all over. Keep warm in the oven while cooking the rest. Serve with salad and chutney.

Vegetable Galette

Serves	Preparation Time	Cooking Time	Nutritional Information (Per Serving)
6	10 minutes, plus chilling	35 minutes	323 calories | 21g fat (of which 1g saturates) 29g carbohydrate | 1.2g salt | V

375g pack puff pastry

100g (3½oz) waxy salad potatoes, thinly sliced

2 tbsp olive oil

2 leeks, thinly sliced

4 tbsp basil pesto

150g (5oz) cherry tomatoes, halved

75g (3oz) pitted black olives

1 tbsp capers

salt and ground black pepper

basil leaves to garnish

1. Roll out the puff pastry to a square roughly 30.5 x 30.5cm (12 x 12in). Round off the edges to make a circle. Put the pastry on a non-stick baking sheet and lightly score a circle 2.5cm (1in) in from the edge. Prick the base of the pastry inside the border all over with a fork, Cover and chill for 20 minutes.

2. Preheat the oven to 200°C (180°C fan oven) mark 6. Bake the pastry base for 25–30 minutes until golden and cooked through – if the centre of the pastry rises, push it down gently with the back of a spoon.

3. Meanwhile, parboil the potatoes until just tender. Drain and drizzle with 1 tbsp oil and season to taste with salt and pepper. Heat the remaining oil and cook the leeks gently, covered, for 10 minutes or until softened.

4. Spread 2 tbsp pesto over the base of the pastry, inside the border. Cover with potatoes and leeks, then top with the tomatoes, olives and capers. Return to the oven for 5 minutes to heat through. Serve the galette immediately, garnished with the remaining pesto and the basil leaves.

Onion, Thyme and Goat's Cheese Tart

Serves	Preparation Time	Cooking Time	Nutritional Information (Per Serving)
6	40 minutes, plus chilling	1¼ hours	507 calories | 36g fat (of which 21g saturates) 41g carbohydrate | 0.7g salt | V

225g (8oz) plain flour, plus extra to dust

75g (3oz) chilled unsalted butter, cubed

For the filling

40g (1½oz) butter

4 large onions, finely sliced

leaves from 5 thyme sprigs, plus extra sprigs to garnish

100g (3½oz) soft goat's cheese

2 medium eggs mixed with 150ml carton double cream

salt and ground black pepper

1. Whiz the flour and unsalted butter in a food processor until they look like breadcrumbs. Pour in 3–4 tbsp cold water and pulse until the mixture comes together. Tip out and lightly bring together. Wrap in clingfilm and chill for 30 minutes.

2. Melt the butter in a pan. Add the onions, cover and cook gently for 40 minutes until softened. Uncover and turn up the heat slightly. Add the thyme leaves and cook for 10 minutes, stirring occasionally.

3. Roll out the pastry on a lightly floured surface to fit a 23cm (9in) diameter fluted tart case. Use to line the tart case, then prick the base. Cover and chill for 30 minutes. Preheat the oven to 200°C (180°C fan oven) mark 6. Line the tart case with greaseproof paper and fill with baking beans. Bake for 12–15 minutes, then remove the beans and paper and cook for 10 minutes until dry. Lower the oven to 170°C (150°C fan oven) mark 3. Spoon the onions into the tart case and dot with the goat's cheese. Season the egg and cream with salt and pepper and pour into the tart. Top with thyme sprigs. Bake for 25 minutes or until the filling is set. Cool in the tin for 5 minutes, then transfer to a wire rack and leave to cool.

Courgette and Parmesan Frittata

Serves	Preparation Time	Cooking Time	Nutritional Information (Per Serving)
4	10 minutes	15 minutes	457 calories | 38g fat (of which 18g saturates) 5g carbohydrate | 1.2g salt | **V** | **GF**

40g (1½oz) butter

1 small onion, finely sliced

225g (8oz) courgettes, finely sliced

6 medium eggs, beaten

25g (1oz) freshly grated Parmesan, plus shavings to garnish

salt and ground black pepper

crusty bread to serve

1. Melt 25g (1oz) butter in an 18cm (7in) non-stick frying pan, and cook the onion until soft. Add the courgettes and fry gently for 5 minutes or until they begin to soften.

2. Preheat the grill. Add the remaining butter to the frying pan. Season the eggs with salt and pepper and pour into the pan. Cook for 2–3 minutes until golden underneath and cooked around the edges.

3. Scatter the grated cheese over the frittata and put under the preheated grill for 1–2 minutes or until just set. Garnish with Parmesan shavings, cut the frittata into quarters and serve with crusty bread.

Try Something Different
Instead of courgettes, use leftover boiled potatoes, cut into small cubes.

Curried Tofu Burgers

Serves	Preparation Time	Cooking Time	Nutritional Information (Per Serving)
4	20 minutes	6–8 minutes	253 calories | 18g fat (of which 3g saturates) 15g carbohydrate | 0.2g salt | V | DF

1 tbsp sunflower oil, plus extra to fry

1 large carrot, finely grated

1 large onion, finely grated

2 tsp coriander seeds, finely crushed (optional)

1 garlic clove, crushed

1 tsp curry paste

1 tsp tomato purée

225g pack tofu

25g (1oz) fresh wholemeal breadcrumbs

25g (1oz) mixed nuts, finely chopped

plain flour to dust

salt and ground black pepper

rice and green vegetables to serve

1. Heat the oil in a large frying pan. Add the carrot and onion and fry for 3–4 minutes until the vegetables are softened, stirring all the time. Add the coriander seeds, if using, the garlic, curry paste and tomato purée. Increase the heat and cook for 2 minutes, stirring all the time.

2. Mash the tofu with a potato masher, then stir in the vegetables, breadcrumbs and nuts. Season with salt and pepper and beat thoroughly until the mixture starts to stick together. With floured hands, shape the mixture into eight burgers.

3. Heat some oil in a frying pan and fry the burgers for 3–4 minutes on each side until golden brown. Alternatively, brush lightly with oil and cook under a hot grill for about 3 minutes on each side or until golden brown. Drain on kitchen paper and serve hot, with rice and green vegetables.

Cheese and Vegetable Bake

Serves	Preparation Time	Cooking Time	Nutritional Information *(Per Serving)*
4	15 minutes	15 minutes	471 calories | 13g fat (of which 7g saturates) 67g carbohydrate | 0.8g salt | V

250g (9oz) macaroni

1 cauliflower, cut into florets

2 leeks, finely chopped

100g (3½oz) frozen peas

crusty bread to serve

For the cheese sauce

15g (½oz) butter

15g (½oz) plain flour

200ml (7fl oz) skimmed milk

75g (3oz) freshly grated Parmesan

2 tsp Dijon mustard

25g (1oz) wholemeal breadcrumbs

salt and ground black pepper

1. Cook the macaroni in a large pan of boiling water for 6 minutes, adding the cauliflower and leeks for the last 4 minutes, and the peas for the last 2 minutes.

2. Meanwhile, make the cheese sauce. Melt the butter in a pan and add the flour. Cook for 1–2 minutes, then take off the heat and gradually stir in the milk. Bring to the boil slowly, stirring until the sauce thickens. Stir in 50g (2oz) Parmesan and the mustard. Season to taste with salt and pepper.

3. Preheat the grill to medium. Drain the pasta and the vegetables, and put back in the pan. Add the cheese sauce and mix well. Spoon into a large shallow 2 litre (3½ pint) ovenproof dish and scatter the remaining Parmesan and the breadcrumbs over. Grill for 5 minutes or until golden and crisp. Serve hot with bread.

Cook's Tip
Make the cheese sauce in the microwave: put the butter, flour and milk into a large microwave-proof bowl and whisk together. Cook in a 900W microwave on full power for 4 minutes, whisking every minute, until the sauce has thickened. Stir in the cheese until it melts. Stir in the mustard and season to taste.

Tart with a Twist

Serves	Preparation Time	Cooking Time	Nutritional Information (Per Serving)
10	20 minutes	50 minutes	332 calories | 24g fat (of which 14g saturates) 21g carbohydrate | 0.9g salt | V

250g (9oz) plain flour, sifted, plus extra to dust

150g (5oz) chilled butter, diced

1 tbsp milk powder

½ tsp salt

4 large eggs

300g (11oz) frozen spinach

15g (½oz) butter

pinch of freshly grated nutmeg

6 tbsp double cream

250g (9oz) cottage cheese

50g (2oz) freshly grated Parmesan

1. Whiz the flour, chilled butter, milk powder and salt together in a food processor until they look like fine breadcrumbs. Mix 1 egg with a scant tbsp cold water. With the food processor running, add enough of the egg to bind the pastry into a firm dough. Knead it briefly on a clean surface to bring the mixture together. Wrap in clingfilm and chill for 30 minutes. Roll out the pastry on a lightly floured surface into a 25.5cm (10in) circle and use to line a 23cm (9in) loose-bottomed fluted flan tin. Chill again for 30 minutes.

2. Preheat the oven to 200°C (180°C fan oven) mark 6. Fill the pastry case with parchment paper and baking beans. Bake blind for 15–20 minutes. Remove the beans and paper. Bake for 5 minutes until the pastry feels dry. Remove from the oven and set aside to cool. Reduce the oven temperature to 170°C (150°C fan oven) mark 3.

3. Put the spinach into a pan with the butter and nutmeg and cook until thawed. Drain, cool and finely chop. Mix with the remaining eggs, the cream and cottage cheese. Sprinkle the pastry base with the Parmesan and pour in the spinach mixture. Bake for 25–30 minutes. Serve hot or cold.

Mushroom and Thyme Omelette

Serves	Preparation Time	Cooking Time	Nutritional Information (Per Serving)
1	10 minutes	5 minutes	353 calories | 35g fat (of which 14g saturates) 2g carbohydrate | 1.7g salt | V

1 tbsp vegetable oil

75g (3oz) chopped mushrooms

1 tbsp freshly chopped thyme

¼ tsp freshly grated nutmeg

2 tsp crème fraîche

1 tsp wholegrain mustard

2 medium eggs, at room temperature

15g (½oz) butter

salt and ground black pepper

1. Heat the oil in a non-stick frying pan and fry the mushrooms for 5 minutes until softened. Stir in the thyme and nutmeg and cook for a further 2 minutes. Stir through the crème fraîche and mustard, then season to taste with salt and pepper.

2. Break the eggs into a bowl and season with plenty of black pepper and a pinch of salt. Whisk together with a balloon whisk, if you have one, or a fork.

3. Put the butter into an omelette pan or small frying pan over a low to medium heat. Allow the butter to melt completely, then continue to heat until it starts to foam. Pour in the beaten eggs and tilt the pan so that it covers the base. Using a wooden spoon, pull the cooked egg into the middle and allow the remaining raw egg to flow into the empty spaces. Continue to cook until the omelette is almost set – it shouldn't be too solid – then add the mushroom mixture and flip the outside edge of the omelette over the filling. Slide on to a warm plate and serve.

Chickpea Patties

Serves	Preparation Time	Cooking Time	Nutritional Information *(Per Serving)*
4	20 minutes, plus chilling	about 15 minutes	344 calories | 17g fat (of which 2g saturates) 37g carbohydrate | 1g salt | **V** | **DF**

2 x 400g cans chickpeas, drained and rinsed

4 garlic cloves, crushed

1 tsp ground cumin

1 small red onion, chopped

20g pack fresh coriander

2 tbsp plain flour, plus extra to dust

olive oil for frying

mixed salad and lemon wedges to serve

Freezing Tip

- **To freeze:** make the patties, then cool, put in a freezerproof container and freeze. They will keep for up to one month.
- **To use:** thaw overnight at a cool room temperature, then reheat in the oven at 180°C (160°C fan oven) mark 4 for 20 minutes.

1. Pat the chickpeas dry with kitchen paper then put them into a food processor with the garlic, cumin, onion and coriander. Blend until smooth, then stir in the flour.

2. With floured hands, shape the chickpea mixture into 12 small round patties and chill in the fridge for 20 minutes.

3. Heat a little oil in a non-stick frying pan over a medium heat and fry the patties in batches for about 2 minutes on each side or until heated through and golden. Serve warm with mixed salad and lemon wedges.

White Nut Roast

Serves	Preparation Time	Cooking Time	Nutritional Information (Per Serving)
8	20 minutes	about 1 hour	371 calories | 28g fat (of which 9g saturates) 20g carbohydrate | 0.8g salt | V

40g (1½oz) butter, plus extra to grease

1 onion, finely chopped

1 garlic clove, crushed

225g (8oz) mixed white nuts, such as brazils, macadamias, pinenuts and whole almonds, ground in a food processor

125g (4oz) fresh white breadcrumbs

grated zest and juice of ½ lemon

75g (3oz) sage Derby cheese or vegetarian Parmesan, grated

125g (4oz) cooked, peeled (or vacuum-packed) chestnuts, roughly chopped

½ x 400g can artichoke hearts, roughly chopped

1 medium egg, lightly beaten

2 tsp each freshly chopped parsley, sage and thyme, plus extra sprigs

salt and ground black pepper

Freezing Tip

- **To freeze:** complete the recipe to step 3, cool, cover and freeze for up to one month.
- **To use:** cook from frozen for 45 minutes, then unwrap the foil slightly and cook for a further 15 minutes until turning golden.

1. Preheat the oven to 200°C (180°C fan oven) mark 6. Melt the butter in a pan and cook the onion and garlic for 5 minutes or until soft. Put into a large bowl and set aside to cool.

2. Add the nuts, breadcrumbs, lemon zest and juice, cheese, chestnuts and artichokes. Season well with salt and pepper and bind together with the egg. Stir in the herbs.

3. Put the mixture on to a large piece of buttered foil and shape into a fat sausage, packing tightly. Scatter with the extra herb sprigs and wrap in the foil.

4. Cook on a baking sheet in the oven for 35 minutes, then unwrap the foil slightly and cook for a further 15 minutes until turning golden.

Asparagus, Mushroom and Tomato Pizza

Serves	Preparation Time	Cooking Time	Nutritional Information *(Per Serving)*
4	15 minutes	18–20 minutes, plus standing	386 calories | 17g fat (of which 6g saturates) 46g carbohydrate | 0.9g salt | V

- 25.5cm (10in) thin pizza base
- 2 tbsp olive oil
- 225g (8oz) firm tomatoes, thickly sliced
- 150g (5oz) asparagus tips, blanched
- 100g (3½oz) large flat mushrooms, roughly chopped
- 1 tbsp freshly chopped tarragon
- 150g pack mozzarella cheese, sliced
- salt and ground black pepper

1. Preheat the oven to 200°C (180°C fan oven) mark 6. Put the pizza base on a baking sheet and brush with 1 tbsp oil. Scatter on the tomatoes, asparagus, mushrooms and tarragon, then season to taste with salt and pepper.

2. Arrange the cheese slices on top, season with black pepper and drizzle with the remaining oil. Leave to stand for 5 minutes. Bake for 18–20 minutes or until the cheese is lightly brown.

Try Something Different
- Use courgettes, trimmed and cut into batons, in place of the asparagus.
- See page 45 for making pizza dough from scratch.

Mozzarella, Tomato and Basil Pizza

Serves	Preparation Time	Cooking Time	Nutritional Information *(Per Serving)*
4	15 minutes	25 minutes, plus standing	529 calories | 23g fat (of which 12g saturates) 59g carbohydrate | 1.1g salt | V

- 290g pack pizza base mix (use both sachets – see Cook's Tip)
- 1 tbsp olive oil, plus extra to drizzle
- plain flour to dust
- 6 tbsp tomato pasta sauce
- 2 x 125g packs mozzarella cheese, chopped
- 50g (2oz) freshly grated Parmesan
- 10 small basil leaves (optional)
- salt and ground black pepper

1. Preheat the oven to 230°C (210°C fan oven) mark 8. Put a pizza stone or baking sheet in the oven to heat up.

2. Put the pizza mix into the bowl of a free-standing mixer, add the oil and 225ml (8fl oz) hand-hot water. Mix with a dough hook until the dough is soft and sticky. Alternatively, put in a food processor and mix with a plastic blade.

3. Put the dough on a lightly floured surface and punch down with your fists to knock out the air. Roll into a 30cm (12in) round and put on the hot pizza stone or baking sheet. Spoon the tomato sauce over the dough, scatter on the cheeses and basil, if using. Season well with salt and pepper and drizzle with a little oil. Leave to stand for 5 minutes.

4. Bake for 25 minutes or until the pizza is golden and the cheeses have melted. Slice into wedges and serve.

> **Cook's Tip**
> If you use a pizza base mix you can make your base as thin and crispy or soft and doughy as you want. This recipe is a doughy base; if you prefer a thinner crust, use just one sachet of mix.

Garlic Cheese Pizza

Serves	Preparation Time	Cooking Time	Nutritional Information (Per Serving)
4	20 minutes	30 minutes	536 calories | 30g fat (of which 9g saturates) 54g carbohydrate | 0.6g salt | V

280g pack pizza base mix

flour to dust

2 x 150g packs garlic and herb cheese

12 whole sun-dried tomatoes, drained of oil and cut into rough pieces

40g (1½ oz) pinenuts

12 fresh basil leaves

3 tbsp olive oil

green salad to serve

1. Put a pizza stone or large baking sheet in the oven and preheat to 220°C (200°C fan oven) mark 7.

2. Mix the pizza base dough according to the packet instructions. On a lightly floured worksurface, knead for a few minutes or until smooth. Roll out to a 33cm (13in) round. Transfer the dough to the preheated pizza stone or baking sheet. Pinch a lip around the edge.

3. Crumble the cheese over the dough and flatten with a palette knife, then sprinkle on the sun-dried tomatoes, pinenuts and basil leaves.

4. Drizzle with the oil and bake for 20–30 minutes until pale golden and cooked to the centre. Serve with a green salad.

Try Something Different
Use goat's cheese instead of the garlic and herb cheese.

Lentil Casserole

Serves	Preparation Time	Cooking Time	Nutritional Information (Per Serving)
6	20 minutes	1 hour	239 calories | 6g fat (of which 1g saturates) 36g carbohydrate | 0.4g salt | V | DF | GF

2 tbsp olive oil

2 onions, sliced

4 carrots, sliced

3 leeks, sliced

450g (1lb) button mushrooms

2 garlic cloves, crushed

2.5cm (1in) piece fresh root ginger, grated

1 tbsp ground coriander

225g (8oz) split red lentils

750ml (1¼ pints) hot vegetable stock

4 tbsp freshly chopped coriander

salt and ground black pepper

1. Preheat the oven to 180°C (160°C fan oven) mark 4. Heat the oil in a flameproof ovenproof casserole, add the onions, carrots and leeks and fry, stirring, for 5 minutes. Add the mushrooms, garlic, ginger and ground coriander, and fry for 2–3 minutes.

2. Rinse and drain the lentils, then stir into the casserole with the hot stock. Season to taste with salt and pepper and return to the boil. Cover and cook in the oven for 45–50 minutes until the vegetables and lentils are tender. Stir in the chopped coriander before serving.

Lentil Chilli

Serves	Preparation Time	Cooking Time	Nutritional Information (Per Serving)
6	10 minutes	30 minutes	195 calories | 2g fat (of which trace saturates) 32g carbohydrate | 0.1g salt | V | DF | GF

oil-water spray (see Cook's Tip)

2 red onions, chopped

1½ tsp each ground coriander and ground cumin

½ tsp ground paprika

2 garlic cloves, crushed

2 sun-dried tomatoes, chopped

¼ tsp crushed dried chilli flakes

325ml (11fl oz) vegetable stock

2 x 400g cans brown or green lentils, drained and rinsed

2 x 400g cans chopped tomatoes

sugar to taste

salt and ground black pepper

natural low-fat yogurt and rice to serve

1. Spray a saucepan with the oil-water spray and cook the onions for 5 minutes until softened. Add the coriander, cumin and paprika. Combine the garlic, sun-dried tomatoes, chilli and stock and add to the pan. Cover and simmer for 5–7 minutes. Uncover and simmer until the onions are very tender and the liquid has almost gone.

2. Stir in the lentils and tomatoes and season to taste with salt and pepper. Simmer, uncovered, for 15 minutes until thick. Stir in sugar to taste. Remove from the heat.

3. Ladle out a quarter of the mixture and blend in a food processor or blender. Combine the puréed and unpuréed portions. Serve with yogurt and rice.

Cook's Tip
Oil-water spray is far lower in calories than oil alone and, as it sprays on thinly and evenly, you'll use less. Fill one-eighth of a travel-sized spray bottle with oil such as sunflower, light olive or vegetable (rapeseed) oil, then top up with water. To use, shake well before spraying. Store in the fridge.

Piperade

2 tbsp olive oil

1 onion, finely chopped

1 garlic clove, finely chopped

1 red pepper, seeded and chopped

375g (13oz) tomatoes, peeled, seeded and chopped

pinch of cayenne pepper

8 large eggs

salt and ground black pepper

freshly chopped flat-leafed parsley to garnish

fresh bread to serve (optional)

1. Heat the oil in a heavy-based frying pan. Add the onion and garlic and cook gently for 5 minutes. Add the red pepper and cook for 10 minutes or until softened.

2. Add the tomatoes, increase the heat and cook until they are reduced to a thick pulp. Season well with cayenne pepper, salt and pepper.

3. Lightly whisk the eggs and add to the frying pan. Using a wooden spoon, stir gently until they've just begun to set but are still creamy. Garnish with parsley and serve with bread, if you like.

Creamy Baked Eggs

Serves	Preparation Time	Cooking Time	Nutritional Information (Per Serving)
4	5 minutes	15–18 minutes	153 calories | 14g fat (of which 7g saturates) 1g carbohydrate | 0.2g salt | V | GF

butter to grease

4 sun-dried tomatoes

4 medium eggs

4 tbsp double cream

salt and ground black pepper

Granary bread to serve (optional)

1. Preheat the oven to 180°C (160°C fan oven) mark 4. Grease four individual ramekins.

2. Put 1 tomato in each ramekin and season to taste with salt and pepper. Carefully break an egg on top of each, then drizzle 1 tbsp cream over each egg.

3. Bake for 15–18 minutes – the eggs will continue to cook once they have been taken out of the oven.

4. Leave to stand for 2 minutes before serving. Serve with Granary bread, if you like.

Classic French Omelette

Serves	Preparation Time	Cooking Time	Nutritional Information (Per Serving)
1	5 minutes	5 minutes	449 calories | 40g fat (of which 19g saturates) 1g carbohydrate | 1g salt | **V** | **GF**

2–3 medium eggs

1 tbsp milk or water

25g (1oz) unsalted butter

salt and ground black pepper

sliced or grilled tomatoes and freshly chopped flat-leafed parsley to serve

1. Whisk the eggs in a bowl, just enough to break them down – overbeating spoils the texture of the omelette. Season with salt and pepper and add the milk or water.

2. Heat the butter in an 18cm (7in) omelette pan or non-stick frying pan until it is foaming, but not brown. Add the eggs and stir gently with a fork or wooden spatula, drawing the mixture from the sides to the centre as it sets and letting the liquid egg in the centre run to the sides. When set, stop stirring and cook for 30 seconds or until the omelette is golden brown underneath and still creamy on top; don't overcook. If you are making a filled omelette (see above), add the filling at this point.

3. Tilt the pan away from you slightly and use a palette knife to fold over one-third of the omelette to the centre, then fold over the opposite third. Slide the omelette out on to a warmed plate, letting it flip over so that the folded sides are underneath. Serve immediately, with tomatoes, sprinkled with parsley.

Try Something Different

- Blend 25g (1oz) mild goat's cheese with 1 tbsp crème fraîche; put in the centre of the omelette before folding.
- Toss 25g (1oz) chopped smoked salmon or cooked smoked haddock with a little chopped dill and 1 tbsp crème fraîche; scatter over the omelette before folding.

Mixed Mushroom Frittata

Serves	Preparation Time	Cooking Time	Nutritional Information (Per Serving)
4	15 minutes	15–20 minutes	148 calories | 12g fat (of which 3g saturates) 0g carbohydrate | 0.3g salt | V | DF | GF

1 tbsp olive oil

300g (11oz) mixed mushrooms, sliced

2 tbsp freshly chopped thyme

zest and juice of ½ lemon

50g (2oz) watercress, chopped

6 medium eggs, beaten

salt and ground black pepper

stoneground wholegrain bread (optional) and a crisp green salad to serve

1. Heat the oil in a large deep frying pan over a medium heat. Add the mushrooms and thyme and stir-fry for 4–5 minutes until starting to soften and brown. Stir in the lemon zest and juice, then bubble for 1 minute. Lower the heat.

2. Preheat the grill. Add the watercress to the beaten eggs, season with salt and pepper and pour into the pan. Cook on the hob for 7–8 minutes until the sides and base are firm but the centre is still a little soft.

3. Transfer to the grill and cook for 4–5 minutes until just set. Cut into wedges and serve with chunks of bread, if you like, and a salad.

Spicy Beans with Jazzed-up Potatoes

Serves	Preparation Time	Cooking Time	Nutritional Information *(Per Serving)*
4	12 minutes	about 1½ hours	298 calories | 4g fat (of which 1g saturates) 56g carbohydrate | 0.8g salt | V | GF

4 baking potatoes

1 tbsp olive oil, plus extra to rub

1 tsp smoked paprika, plus a pinch

2 shallots, finely chopped

1 tbsp freshly chopped rosemary

400g can cannellini beans, drained and rinsed

400g can chopped tomatoes

1 tbsp light muscovado sugar

1 tsp Worcestershire sauce

150ml (¼ pint) hot vegetable stock

small handful of freshly chopped flat-leafed parsley

grated mature Cheddar to sprinkle

salt and ground black pepper

Try Something Different
The spicy beans are just as good served with toast for a quick meal that takes less than 25 minutes.

1. Preheat the oven to 200°C (180°C fan oven) mark 6. Rub the baking potatoes with a little oil and put them on a baking tray. Scatter some sea salt over and a pinch of smoked paprika. Bake for 1–1½ hours.

2. Meanwhile, heat 1 tbsp oil in a large pan, then fry the shallots over a low heat for 1–2 minutes until they start to soften.

3. Add the rosemary and 1 tsp paprika and fry for 1–2 minutes, then add the beans, tomatoes, sugar, Worcestershire sauce and hot stock. Season to taste with salt and pepper, then bring to the boil and simmer, uncovered, for 10–15 minutes.

4. Serve with the baked potatoes, scattered with parsley and grated cheese.

Beans on Toast

Serves	Preparation Time	Cooking Time	Nutritional Information (Per Serving)
4	5 minutes	10 minutes	364 calories | 9g fat (of which 2g saturates) 55g carbohydrate | 2.1g salt | V

1 tbsp olive oil

2 garlic cloves, finely sliced

400g can borlotti or cannellini beans, drained and rinsed

400g can chickpeas

400g can chopped tomatoes

leaves from 2 fresh rosemary sprigs

4 thick slices Granary bread

25g (1oz) Parmesan

chopped fresh parsley to serve

1. Heat the oil in a pan over a low heat, add the garlic and cook for 1 minute, stirring gently.

2. Add the beans and chickpeas to the pan with the tomatoes and bring to the boil. Chop the rosemary leaves finely and add to the pan. Reduce the heat and simmer for 8–10 minutes until thickened.

3. Meanwhile, toast the bread and put on to plates. Grate the Parmesan into the bean mixture, stir once, then spoon over the bread. Serve immediately, scattered with parsley.

Try Something Different
This will be just as good with toasted soda bread or seeded bread, mixed beans instead of borlotti or cannellini, and grated Gruyère or Cheddar instead of Parmesan.

Rösti Potatoes with Fried Eggs

Serves	Preparation Time	Cooking Time	Nutritional Information (Per Serving)
4	20 minutes, plus 15 minutes cooling	20–25 minutes	324 calories | 16g fat (of which 7g saturates) 36g carbohydrate | 0.4g salt | V | GF

900g (2lb) red potatoes, scrubbed and left whole

40g (1½oz) butter

4 large eggs

salt and ground black pepper

sprigs of flat-leafed parsley to garnish

1. Put the potatoes into a pan of cold water. Cover, bring to the boil and parboil for 5–8 minutes. Drain and leave to cool for 15 minutes.

2. Preheat the oven to 150°C (130°C fan oven) mark 2. Put a baking tray inside to warm. Peel the potatoes and coarsely grate them lengthways into long strands. Divide into eight portions and shape into mounds.

3. Melt half the butter in a large non-stick frying pan. When it is beginning to brown, add four of the potato mounds, spacing them well apart, and flatten them a little. Fry slowly for 6–7 minutes until golden brown, then turn them and brown the second side for 6–7 minutes. Transfer to a warmed baking tray and keep warm in the oven while you fry the rest.

4. Just before serving, carefully break the eggs into the hot pan and fry for about 2 minutes until the white is set and the yolk is still soft. Season to taste with salt and pepper and serve at once, with the rösti. Garnish with sprigs of parsley.

Mushroom and Bean Hotpot

Serves	Preparation Time	Cooking Time	Nutritional Information (Per Serving)
6	15 minutes	30 minutes	280 calories | 10g fat (of which 1g saturates) 34g carbohydrate | 1.3g salt | V | DF

3 tbsp olive oil

700g (1½lb) chestnut mushrooms, roughly chopped

1 large onion, finely chopped

2 tbsp plain flour

2 tbsp mild curry paste

150ml (¼ pint) hot vegetable stock

400g can chopped tomatoes

2 tbsp sun-dried tomato paste

2 x 400g cans mixed beans, drained and rinsed

3 tbsp mango chutney

3 tbsp roughly chopped fresh coriander and mint

1. Heat the oil in a large pan over a low heat and fry the mushrooms and onion until the onion is soft and dark golden. Stir in the flour and curry paste and cook for 1–2 minutes, then add the hot stock, tomatoes, sun-dried tomato paste and beans.

2. Bring to the boil, then simmer gently for 30 minutes or until most of the liquid has reduced. Stir in the chutney and herbs before serving.

Thrifty Tip

Canned beans save time but dried beans are even cheaper: 100g (3½oz) dried beans equal the cooked drained weight of a 400g can.

Chickpea and Chilli Stir-fry

Serves	Preparation Time	Cooking Time	Nutritional Information *(Per Serving)*
4	10 minutes	15–20 minutes	258 calories | 11g fat (of which 1g saturates) 30g carbohydrate | 1g salt | **V | DF | GF**

2 tbsp olive oil

1 tsp ground cumin

1 red onion, sliced

2 garlic cloves, finely chopped

1 red chilli, seeded and finely chopped

2 x 400g cans chickpeas, drained and rinsed

400g (14oz) cherry tomatoes

125g (4oz) baby spinach leaves

brown rice or pasta to serve

1. Heat the oil in a wok. Add the ground cumin and fry for 1–2 minutes. Add the onion and stir-fry for 5–7 minutes.

2. Add the garlic and chilli and stir-fry for 2 minutes.

3. Add the chickpeas to the wok with the tomatoes. Reduce the heat and simmer until the chickpeas are hot. Add the spinach and stir to wilt. Serve with brown rice or pasta.

Cook's Tips

Chillies vary enormously in strength, from quite mild to blisteringly hot, depending on the type of chilli and its ripeness. Taste a small piece first to check it's not too hot for you.

Be extremely careful when handling chillies not to touch or rub your eyes with your fingers, as they will sting.

Wash knives immediately after handling chillies for the same reason. As a precaution, use rubber gloves when preparing them if you like.

7

Tarte Tatin

Serves	Preparation Time	Cooking Time	Nutritional Information (*Per Serving*)
8	30 minutes, plus 30 minutes chilling	about 1 hour, plus cooling	545 calories | 29g fat (of which 18g saturates) 71g carbohydrate | 0.5g salt | V

Sweet Shortcrust Pastry (see page 38), made with 225g (8oz) plain flour, ¼ tsp salt, 150g (5oz) unsalted butter, 50g (2oz) golden icing sugar, 1 medium egg and 2–3 drops vanilla extract

flour to dust

For the topping

200g (7oz) golden caster sugar

125g (4oz) chilled unsalted butter

1.4–1.6kg (3–3½lb) crisp dessert apples, peeled and cored

juice of ½ lemon

1. To make the topping, sprinkle the caster sugar over the base of a 20.5cm (8in) tarte tatin tin or ovenproof frying pan. Cut the butter into slivers and arrange on the sugar. Halve the apples and pack them tightly, cut side up, on top of the butter.

2. Put the tin or pan on the hob and cook over a medium heat for 30 minutes (making sure it doesn't bubble over or catch on the bottom) until the butter and sugar turn a dark golden brown (see Cook's Tip). Sprinkle with the lemon juice, then allow to cool for 15 minutes. Meanwhile, preheat the oven to 220°C (200°C fan oven) mark 7.

3. Lightly flour a large sheet of baking parchment and put the pastry on top. Roll out the pastry to make a round 2.5cm (1in) larger than the tin or pan. Prick several times with a fork. Lay the pastry over the apples, tucking the edges down the side of the tin. Remove the paper. Bake for 25–30 minutes until golden brown. Leave in the tin for 10 minutes, then carefully upturn on to a serving plate. Serve warm.

Cook's Tip
When caramelising the apples in step 2, be patient. Allow the sauce to turn a dark golden brown – any paler and it will be too sickly. Don't let it burn, though, as this will make the caramel taste bitter.

Summer Pudding

Serves	Preparation Time	Cooking Time	Nutritional Information *(Per Serving)*
8	10 minutes, plus overnight chilling	10 minutes	173 calories | 1g fat (of which trace saturates) 38g carbohydrate | 0.4g salt | **V** | **DF**

800g (1lb 12oz) mixed summer berries, such as 250g (9oz) each redcurrants and blackcurrants and 300g (11oz) raspberries

125g (4oz) golden caster sugar

3 tbsp crème de cassis (optional)

9 thick slices slightly stale white bread, crusts removed

crème fraîche or clotted cream to serve

1. Put the redcurrants and blackcurrants into a medium pan. Add the sugar and cassis, if using. Bring to a simmer and cook for 3–5 minutes until the sugar has dissolved. Add the raspberries and cook for 2 minutes. Once the fruit is cooked, taste it – there should be a good balance between tart and sweet.

2. Meanwhile, line a 1 litre (1¾ pint) bowl with clingfilm. Put the base of the bowl on one piece of bread and cut around it. Put the circle of bread in the base of the bowl.

3. Line the inside of the bowl with more slices of bread, slightly overlapping to avoid any gaps. Spoon in the fruit, making sure the juice soaks into the bread. Keep back a few spoonfuls of juice in case the bread is unevenly soaked when you turn out the pudding.

4. Cut the remaining bread to fit the top of the pudding neatly, using a sharp knife to trim any excess bread from around the edges. Wrap in clingfilm, weigh down with a saucer and a tin can and chill overnight.

5. To serve, unwrap the outer clingfilm, upturn the pudding on to a plate and remove the inner clingfilm. Drizzle the reserved juice over the pudding and serve with crème fraîche or clotted cream.

Rice Pudding

Serves	Preparation Time	Cooking Time	Nutritional Information *(Per Serving)*
6	5 minutes	1½ hours	235 calories | 7g fat (of which 5g saturates) 35g carbohydrate | 0.2g salt | **V** | **GF**

butter to grease

125g (4oz) short-grain pudding rice

1.1 litres (2 pints) full-fat milk

4 tbsp golden caster sugar

grated zest of 1 small orange

2 tsp vanilla extract

whole nutmeg to grate

1. Preheat the oven to 180°C (160°C fan oven) mark 4. Lightly butter a 900ml (1½ pint) ovenproof dish. Add the rice, milk, sugar, orange zest and vanilla extract and stir everything together. Grate a little nutmeg all over the top of the mixture.

2. Bake the pudding in the oven for 1½ hours or until the top is golden brown, then serve.

Thrifty Tip
There's no need to buy a packet of pudding rice – if you have risotto rice in the cupboard, you can use it with similar results.

Saucy Hot Lemon Puddings

Serves	**Preparation Time**	**Cooking Time**	**Nutritional Information (Per Serving)**
4	15–20 minutes	35–40 minutes	323 calories | 16g fat (of which 9g saturates) 40g carbohydrate | 0.4g salt | V

50g (2oz) butter, plus extra to grease

125g (4oz) golden caster sugar

finely grated zest and juice of 2 lemons

2 medium eggs, separated

50g (2oz) self-raising flour, sifted

300ml (½ pint) semi-skimmed milk

Try Something Different
Replace 1 lemon with a large lime for an added citrus twist.

1. Preheat the oven to 190°C (170°C fan oven) mark 5. Lightly grease four 200ml (7fl oz) ovenproof cups or glasses.

2. In a bowl, cream the butter, sugar and lemon zest together until pale and fluffy. Beat in the egg yolks, then the flour, until combined. Stir in the milk and lemon juice – the mixture will curdle, but don't panic.

3. In a clean grease-free bowl, whisk the egg whites until soft peaks form, then fold into the lemon mixture. (The mixture will still look curdled – don't worry.) Divide among the four cups and stand them in a roasting tin.

4. Add enough boiling water to the tin to come halfway up the sides of the cups and bake the puddings for 35–40 minutes until spongy and light golden. If you like softer tops, cover the entire tin with foil. When cooked, the puddings will have separated into a tangy lemon custard layer on the bottom, with a light sponge on top. Serve immediately.

Express Apple Tart

Serves	Preparation Time	Cooking Time	Nutritional Information (Per Serving)
8	10 minutes	20 minutes	197 calories | 12g fat (of which 0g saturates) 23g carbohydrate | 0.4g salt | V

375g pack ready-rolled puff pastry

500g (1lb 2oz) dessert apples, such as Cox's, cored and thinly sliced, then tossed in the juice of 1 lemon

golden icing sugar to dust

Try Something Different
Swap the apples for the same amount of firm pears.

1. Preheat the oven to 200°C (180°C fan oven) mark 6. Put the pastry on to a 28 x 38cm (11 x 15in) baking sheet and lightly roll over it with a rolling pin to smooth down the pastry. Score lightly around the edge, leaving a 3cm (1¼in) border.

2. Put the apple slices on top of the pastry within the border. Turn the edge of the pastry halfway over to reach the edge of the apples, press down and use your fingers to crimp the edge.

3. Dust heavily with icing sugar. Bake for 20 minutes or until the pastry is cooked and the sugar has caramelised. Serve warm, dusted with more icing sugar.

Pear and Blackberry Crumble

Makes	Preparation Time	Cooking Time	Nutritional Information (Per Crumble)
2 crumbles	20 minutes	35–40 minutes	1571 calories | 64g fat (of which 29g saturates) 242g carbohydrate | 1g salt | V

900g (2lb) blackberries

900g (2lb) pears

juice of 2 lemons

450g (1lb) golden caster sugar

2 tsp ground mixed spice

200g (7oz) chilled butter, cut into cubes, plus extra to grease

450g (1lb) plain flour

150g (5oz) ground almonds

custard or vanilla ice cream to serve

1. Fill the sink with cold water. Put the blackberries into a colander and carefully lower into the water. Toss to wash thoroughly. Lift the colander out and leave to drain.

2. Peel the pears, then halve and core. Slice each half into pieces, put into a bowl, add the lemon juice and toss well. Add 200g (7oz) sugar and the spice to the pears with the blackberries and toss well to coat.

3. Preheat the oven to 200°C (180°C fan oven) mark 6. Grease two 1.8 litre (3¼ pint) shallow dishes with a little butter. Tip the fruit into the prepared dishes.

4. Put the butter, flour, ground almonds and remaining sugar into a food processor and whiz until the mixture looks like breadcrumbs. Tip into a bowl and bring parts of it together with your hands to make lumps.

5. Spoon the crumble topping over the fruit, dividing equally between the two dishes, and bake for 35–45 minutes until the fruit is tender and the whole pie is bubbling hot. Serve with custard or vanilla ice cream.

Bread and Butter Pudding

Serves	Preparation Time	Cooking Time	Nutritional Information (Per Serving)
4	10 minutes, plus 10 minutes soaking	30–40 minutes	450 calories | 13g fat (of which 5g saturates) 70g carbohydrate | 1.1g salt | V

50g (2oz) butter, softened, plus extra to grease

275g (10oz) white farmhouse bread, cut into 1cm (½in) slices, crusts removed

50g (2oz) raisins or sultanas

3 medium eggs

450ml (¾ pint) milk

3 tbsp golden icing sugar, plus extra to dust

1. Lightly butter four 300ml (½ pint) gratin dishes or one 1.1 litre (2 pint) ovenproof dish. Butter the bread, then cut into quarters to make triangles. Arrange the bread in the dish(es) and sprinkle with the raisins or sultanas.

2. Beat the eggs, milk and sugar in a bowl. Pour the mixture over the bread and leave to soak for 10 minutes. Preheat the oven to 180°C (160°C fan oven) mark 4.

3. Put the pudding(s) in the oven and bake for 30–40 minutes. Dust with icing sugar to serve.

Lemon Meringue Pie

Serves	Preparation Time	Cooking Time	Nutritional Information (*Per Serving*)
8	30 minutes, plus 1 hour chilling	about 1 hour, plus standing	692 calories | 36g fat (of which 21g saturates) 83g carbohydrate | 0.6g salt | V

Sweet Shortcrust Pastry (see page 38), made with 225g (8oz) plain flour, a pinch of salt, 2 tbsp caster sugar, 150g (5oz) butter, cut into pieces, 1 egg yolk and 3 tbsp cold water

flour to dust

a little beaten egg

For the filling and topping

7 medium eggs, 4 separated, at room temperature

finely grated zest of 3 lemons

175ml (6fl oz) freshly squeezed lemon juice (about 4 lemons), strained

400g can condensed milk

150ml (¼ pint) double cream

225g (8oz) golden icing sugar

1. Roll out the pastry on a lightly floured surface and use to line a 23cm (9in), 4cm (1½in) deep, loose-based fluted tart tin. Prick the base with a fork. Chill for 30 minutes. Meanwhile, preheat the oven to 190°C (170°C fan oven) mark 5.

2. Line the pastry case with greaseproof paper and baking beans and bake blind for 10 minutes. Remove the beans and paper and bake for a further 10 minutes or until golden and cooked. Brush the inside with beaten egg and put back in the oven for 1 minute to seal. Increase the oven temperature to 180°C (160°C fan oven) mark 4.

3. To make the filling, put 4 egg yolks in a bowl with the 3 whole eggs. Add the lemon zest and juice and whisk lightly. Mix in the condensed milk and cream.

4. Pour the filling into the pastry case and bake for 30 minutes or until just set in the centre. Set aside to cool while you prepare the meringue. Increase the oven temperature to 200°C (180°C fan oven) mark 6.

5. For the meringue, whisk the egg whites and icing sugar together in a heatproof bowl set over a pan of gently simmering water, using a hand-held electric whisk, for 10 minutes or until shiny and thick. Take off the heat and continue to whisk at low speed for 5–10 minutes until the bowl is cool. Pile the meringue on to the filling and swirl to form peaks. Bake for 5–10 minutes until the meringue is tinged brown. Leave to stand for about 1 hour, then serve.

Steamed Syrup Sponge Puddings

Serves	Preparation Time	Cooking Time	Nutritional Information *(Per Serving)*
4	20 minutes	35 minutes or 1½ hours	580 calories, 29g fat (of which 17g saturates) 76g carbohydrate | 0.7g salt | V

125g (4oz) butter, softened, plus extra to grease

3 tbsp golden syrup

125g (4oz) golden caster sugar

few drops of vanilla extract

2 medium eggs, beaten

175g (6oz) self-raising flour, sifted

about 3 tbsp milk

custard or cream to serve

4. Cover with greased and pleated greaseproof paper and foil and secure with string. Steam for 35 minutes for individual puddings or 1½ hours for one large pudding, checking the water level from time to time and topping up with boiling water as necessary. Turn out on to warmed plates and serve with custard or cream.

Try Something Different

- **Steamed Jam Sponge Puddings**
  Put 4 tbsp raspberry or blackberry jam into the bottom of the basins instead of the syrup.
- **Steamed Chocolate Sponge Puddings**
  Omit the golden syrup. Blend 4 tbsp cocoa powder with 2 tbsp hot water, then gradually beat into the creamed mixture before adding the eggs.

1. Half-fill a steamer or large pan with water and put it on to boil. Grease four 300ml (½ pint) basins or a 900ml (1½ pint) pudding basin and spoon the golden syrup into the bottom.

2. In a bowl, cream the butter and sugar together until pale and fluffy. Stir in the vanilla extract. Add the eggs, a little at a time, beating well after each addition.

3. Using a metal spoon, fold in half the flour, then fold in the rest with enough milk to give a dropping consistency. Spoon the mixture into the prepared pudding basin(s).

Quick Gooey Chocolate Puddings

Serves	Preparation Time	Cooking Time	Nutritional Information *(Per Serving)*
4	15 minutes	12–15 minutes	468 calories | 31g fat (of which 19g saturates) 46g carbohydrate | 0.6g salt | V

100g (3½oz) butter, plus extra to grease

100g (3½oz) golden caster sugar, plus extra to dust

100g (3½oz) plain chocolate (at least 70% cocoa solids), broken into pieces

2 large eggs

20g (¾oz) plain flour

icing sugar to dust

1. Preheat the oven to 200°C (180°C fan oven) mark 6. Butter four 200ml (7fl oz) ramekins and dust with sugar. Melt the chocolate and butter in a heatproof bowl over a pan of gently simmering water. Take the bowl off the pan and leave to cool for 5 minutes.

2. Whisk the eggs, caster sugar and flour together in a bowl until smooth. Fold in the chocolate mixture and pour into the ramekins.

3. Stand the dishes on a baking tray and bake for 12–15 minutes until the puddings are puffed and set on the outside, but still runny inside. Turn out, dust with icing sugar and serve immediately.

Baked Apples

Serves	Preparation Time	Cooking Time	Nutritional Information (Per Serving)
6	5 minutes, plus 10 minutes soaking	15–20 minutes	280 calories | 13g fat (of which 1g saturates) 36g carbohydrate | 0g salt | V | DF | GF

125g (4oz) hazelnuts

125g (4oz) sultanas

2 tbsp brandy

6 large Bramley apples, cored

4 tbsp soft brown sugar

100ml (3½fl oz) apple juice

thick cream to serve

1. Preheat the oven to 190°C (170°C fan oven) mark 5. Spread the hazelnuts over a baking sheet and toast under a hot grill until golden brown, turning them frequently. Put the hazelnuts in a clean teatowel and rub off the skins, then chop the nuts. Set aside.

2. Soak the sultanas in the brandy and set aside for 10 minutes. Using a small sharp knife, score around the middle of the apples to stop them from bursting, then stuff each apple with equal amounts of brandy-soaked sultanas. Put the apples in a roasting tin and sprinkle with the sugar and apple juice. Bake in the oven for 15–20 minutes until soft.

3. Serve the apples with the toasted hazelnuts and a dollop of thick cream.

Thrifty Tip
Soak the sultanas in apple juice instead of brandy.

Easy Pear and Toffee Tarte Tatin

Serves	Preparation Time	Cooking Time	Nutritional Information (Per Serving)
6	15 minutes	25–30 minutes	294 calories | 12g fat (of which 2g saturates) 46g carbohydrate | 0.5g salt | V

4 small rosy pears, quartered and cored – no need to peel them

8 tbsp dulce de leche toffee sauce

225g (8oz) ready-rolled puff pastry

flour to dust

cream or vanilla ice cream to serve

1. Preheat the oven to 200°C (180°C fan oven) mark 6. Put the pears and toffee sauce into a large non-stick frying pan. Cook over a medium heat for 5 minutes or until the pears are well coated and the sauce has turned a slightly darker shade of golden brown.

2. Tip the pears and sauce into a 20.5cm (8in) non-stick sandwich or tart tin. Arrange the pears, skin side down, in a circle and leave to cool for 10 minutes.

3. If necessary, roll out the puff pastry on a lightly floured surface until it is wide enough to cover the tin. Lay it over the pears and press down on to the edge of the tin. Trim off any excess pastry. Prick the pastry all over, then bake for 20–25 minutes until well risen and golden.

4. Leave to cool for 5 minutes. To turn out, hold a large serving plate or baking sheet over the tart, turn over and give a quick shake to loosen. Lift off the tin. Serve the tart immediately, cut into wedges, with cream or ice cream.

Try Something Different
Replace the pears with 3–4 bananas, thickly sliced on the diagonal. Cook the dulce de leche for 5 minutes in step 1, stir in the bananas to coat, then arrange in the tin in an overlapping circle. Complete the recipe.

Cherry and Tangerine Sticky Puddings

Serves	Preparation Time	Cooking Time	Nutritional Information (Per Serving)
8	20 minutes, plus soaking	25 minutes	738 calories | 39g fat (of which 22g saturates) 96g carbohydrate | 1.2g salt | V

about 25g (1oz) white vegetable fat, melted

200g (7oz) dried cherries

150ml (¼ pint) boiling water

2 tbsp orange-flavoured liqueur

¾ tsp bicarbonate of soda

75g (3oz) unsalted butter, softened

150g (5oz) golden caster sugar

2 medium eggs, beaten

175g (6oz) self-raising flour

For the sauce

175g (6oz) light muscovado sugar

125g (4oz) unsalted butter

6 tbsp double cream

25g (1oz) pecan nuts, chopped

juice of 1 tangerine

1. Preheat the oven to 180°C (160°C fan oven) mark 4. Using the melted fat, lightly oil eight 175ml (6fl oz) metal pudding basins or ramekins, then put a circle of non-stick baking parchment into the base of each.

2. Put 175g (6oz) dried cherries into a bowl and pour the boiling water over them. Stir in the liqueur and bicarbonate of soda, then leave to soak for 1 hour.

3. Whisk the butter and caster sugar in a large bowl until pale and fluffy, then beat in the eggs, a little at a time. Fold in the cherry mixture.

4. Add the flour and fold in with a large metal spoon. Divide the mixture equally among the basins, then bake on a baking sheet for about 25 minutes or until well risen and firm.

5. Meanwhile, make the sauce. Put the muscovado sugar, butter, cream, pecans and remaining cherries in a pan. Heat gently until the sugar has dissolved, then stir in the tangerine juice.

6. Leave the puddings to cool for 5 minutes, then turn out. Serve topped with the sauce.

Cheat's Chocolate Pots

Serves	Preparation Time	Cooking Time	Nutritional Information (Per Serving)
4	5 minutes, plus chilling	5 minutes	385 calories | 17g fat (of which 9g saturates) 53g carbohydrate | 0.1g salt | V

500g carton fresh custard

200g (7oz) plain chocolate (at least 50 per cent cocoa solids), broken into pieces

Try Something Different
Serve the mixture warm as a sauce for vanilla ice cream.

1. Put the custard in a small pan with the chocolate. Heat gently, stirring all the time, until the chocolate has melted.

2. Pour the mixture into four small coffee cups and chill in the fridge for 30 minutes to 1 hour before serving.

Strawberry Brûlée

Serves	Preparation Time	Cooking Time	Nutritional Information (Per Serving)
4	15 minutes, plus chilling	5 minutes	240 calories | 10g fat (of which 5g saturates) 35g carbohydrate | 0.2g salt | V | GF

250g (9oz) strawberries, hulled and sliced

2 tsp golden icing sugar

1 vanilla pod

400g (14oz) Greek yogurt

100g (3½oz) golden caster sugar

1. Divide the strawberries among four ramekins and sprinkle with icing sugar.

2. Scrape the seeds from the vanilla pod and stir into the yogurt, then spread the mixture evenly over the fruit.

3. Preheat the grill to high. Sprinkle the sugar evenly over the yogurt until it's well covered.

4. Put the ramekins on a baking sheet or into the grill pan and grill until the sugar turns dark brown and caramelises. Leave for 15 minutes or until the caramel is cool enough to eat, or chill for up to 2 hours before serving.

Try Something Different
Use raspberries or blueberries instead of strawberries.

Rustic Blackberry and Apple Pie

Serves	Preparation Time	Cooking Time	Nutritional Information (Per Serving)
6	25 minutes, plus minimum 15 minutes chilling	40 minutes	372 calories | 19g fat (of which 11g saturates) 49g carbohydrate | 0.4g salt | V

200g (7oz) plain flour, plus extra to dust

125g (4oz) chilled unsalted butter, diced

1 medium egg, beaten

75g (3oz) golden caster sugar, plus 3 tbsp

pinch of salt

500g (1lb 2oz) eating apples, quartered, cored and cut into chunky wedges

300g (11oz) blackberries

¼ tsp ground cinnamon

juice of 1 small lemon

1. Pulse the flour and butter in a food processor until it resembles coarse crumbs. (Alternatively, rub the butter into the flour by hand or using a pastry cutter.) Add the egg, 2 tbsp sugar and the salt and pulse again to combine, or stir in. Wrap in clingfilm and chill for at least 15 minutes. Meanwhile, preheat the oven to 200°C (180°C fan oven) mark 6.

2. Put the apples, blackberries, 75g (3oz) sugar, the cinnamon and lemon juice in a bowl and toss together, making sure the sugar dissolves in the juice.

3. Grease a 25.5cm (10in) enamel or metal pie dish. Using a lightly floured rolling pin, roll out the pastry on a large sheet of baking parchment to a 30.5cm (12in) circle. Lift up the paper, upturn the pastry on to the pie dish and peel away the paper.

4. Put the prepared fruit in the centre of the pie dish and fold the pastry edges up and over the fruit a little. Sprinkle with the remaining sugar and bake for 40 minutes or until the fruit is tender and the pastry golden.

Mocha Chocolate Soufflés

Serves	Preparation Time	Cooking Time	Nutritional Information *(Per Serving)*
6	20 minutes	20 minutes	134 calories | 4g fat (of which 2g saturates) 22g carbohydrate | 0.1g salt | **V** | **GF**

50g (2oz) plain chocolate
(at least 70% cocoa solids), broken
into pieces

2 tbsp cornflour

1 tbsp cocoa powder

1 tsp instant coffee granules

4 tbsp golden caster sugar

150ml (¼ pint) skimmed milk

2 medium eggs, separated,
plus 1 egg white

Try Something Different
Use flavoured plain chocolate for an
unusual twist, such as ginger, mint or
even chilli.

1. Preheat the oven to 190°C
(170°C fan oven) mark 5 and put a
baking sheet inside to heat up. Put
the chocolate into a pan with the
cornflour, cocoa powder, coffee,
1 tbsp caster sugar and the milk.
Warm gently to melt the
chocolate. Increase the heat and
stir until the mixture thickens.
Allow to cool a little, then stir in
the egg yolks. Cover with damp
greaseproof paper.

2. Whisk the egg whites in a clean
grease-free bowl until soft peaks
form. Gradually whisk in the
remaining caster sugar until the
mixture is stiff.

3. Stir one-third of the egg whites
into the chocolate mixture. Fold in
the remaining whites and divide
among six 150ml (¼ pint) ramekins.
Put the ramekins on the baking
sheet and bake for 12 minutes or
until well risen. Serve immediately.

American-style Plum Cobbler

Serves	Preparation Time	Cooking Time	Nutritional Information *(Per Serving)*
6	25 minutes	40 minutes	451 calories | 15g fat (of which 9g saturates) 76g carbohydrate | 0.3g salt | V

900g (2lb) plums, halved and stoned

150g (5oz) golden caster sugar, plus 3 tbsp

1 tbsp cornflour

250g (9oz) self-raising flour

100g (3½oz) chilled unsalted butter, diced

175ml (6fl oz) buttermilk or whole natural yogurt

Try Something Different
Toss the plums with the grated zest of ½ orange before baking and add the grated zest of the remaining ½ orange to the cobbler mixture along with the buttermilk.

1. Preheat the oven to 200°C (180°C fan oven) mark 6. Cut the plums into chunky wedges. Tip into an ovenproof dish measuring 25.5 x 18 x 7.5cm (10 x 7 x 3in) and toss together with 3 tbsp sugar and the cornflour.

2. Whiz the flour, butter and 100g (3½oz) sugar in a food processor until the mixture forms fine crumbs. (Alternatively, rub the fat into the flour by hand or using a pastry cutter, then stir in the sugar.) Add the buttermilk or yogurt and blend for a few seconds until just combined.

3. Scatter clumps of the dough over the plums, leaving some of the fruit exposed. Sprinkle the cobbler with the remaining sugar and bake for 40 minutes or until the fruit is tender and the topping is pale golden.

Cinnamon Pancakes

Serves	Preparation Time	Cooking Time	Nutritional Information *(Per Serving)*
6	5 minutes	20 minutes	141 calories | 5g fat (of which 1g saturates) 20g carbohydrate | 0.1g salt | V

150g (5oz) plain flour

½ tsp ground cinnamon

1 medium egg

300ml (½ pint) skimmed milk

olive oil to fry

fruit compote or sugar and Greek yogurt to serve

Try Something Different
Serve with sliced bananas and vanilla ice cream instead of the fruit compote and yogurt.

1. In a large bowl, whisk together the flour, cinnamon, egg and milk to make a smooth batter. Leave to stand for 20 minutes.

2. Heat a heavy-based frying pan over a medium heat. When the pan is really hot, add 1 tsp oil, pour in a ladleful of batter and tilt the pan to coat the base with an even layer. Cook for 1 minute or until golden. Flip over and cook for 1 minute. Repeat with the remaining batter, adding more oil if necessary, to make six pancakes.

3. Serve with a fruit compote or a sprinkling of sugar, and a dollop of yogurt.

Toffee Cheesecake

Serves	Preparation Time	Cooking Time	Nutritional Information *(Per Serving)*
10	15 minutes, plus chilling	55 minutes–1 hour	439 calories | 32g fat (of which 19g saturates) 29g carbohydrate | 1.2g salt | V

300g (11oz) digestive biscuits, broken

125g (4oz) butter, melted

For the filling

450g (1lb) curd cheese

150ml (¼ pint) double cream

juice of ½ lemon

3 medium eggs, beaten

50g (2oz) golden caster sugar

6 tbsp dulce de leche toffee sauce, plus extra to drizzle

1. Preheat the oven to 200°C (180°C fan oven) mark 6. To make the crust, put the biscuits into a food processor and grind until fine. (Alternatively, put them in a plastic bag and crush with a rolling pin. Transfer to a bowl.) Add the butter and blend briefly, or stir in, to combine. Press the mixture evenly into the base and up the sides of a 20.5cm (8in) springform cake tin. Chill in the refrigerator.

2. To make the filling, put the curd cheese and cream in a food processor or blender and blend until smooth. Add the lemon juice, eggs, sugar and toffee sauce, then blend again until smooth. Pour into the chilled biscuit case and bake for 10 minutes. Reduce the oven temperature to 180°C (160°C fan oven) mark 4, then bake for 45 minutes or until set and golden brown.

3. Turn off the oven, leave the door ajar and let the cheesecake cool. When completely cool, chill to firm up the crust.

4. Remove the cheesecake from the tin by running a knife around the edge. Open the tin carefully, then use a palette knife to ease the cheesecake out. Cut into wedges, put on a serving plate, then drizzle with toffee sauce.

Cook's Tip
To slice the cheesecake easily, use a sharp knife dipped into a jug of boiling water and then wiped dry.

Treacle Tart

Serves	Preparation Time	Cooking Time	Nutritional Information (Per Serving)
6	25 minutes, plus 30 minutes chilling	45–50 minutes, plus cooling	486 calories | 15g fat (of which 8g saturates) 88g carbohydrate | 1.1g salt | V

Sweet Shortcrust Pastry (see page 38), made with 225g (8oz) plain flour, 150g (5oz) unsalted butter, 15g (½oz) golden caster sugar and 1 medium egg yolk

flour to dust

For the filling

700g (1½lb) golden syrup

175g (6oz) fresh white breadcrumbs

grated zest of 3 lemons

2 medium eggs, lightly beaten

Try Something Different
For the pastry, replace half the plain flour with wholemeal flour. For the filling, use fresh wholemeal breadcrumbs instead of white.

1. Preheat the oven to 180°C (160°C fan oven) mark 4. Roll out the pastry on a lightly floured surface and use to line a 25.5cm (10in), 4cm (1½in) deep, loose-based fluted tart tin. Prick the base with a fork.

2. To make the filling, heat the golden syrup in a pan over a low heat until thinned in consistency. Remove from the heat and mix in the breadcrumbs and lemon zest. Stir in the beaten eggs.

3. Pour the filling into the pastry case and bake for 45–50 minutes until the filling is lightly set and golden. Allow to cool slightly. Serve warm.

Lemon and Passion Fruit Fool

Serves	Preparation Time	Nutritional Information (Per Serving)
6	20 minutes	210 calories	17g fat (of which 10g saturates)	14g carbohydrate	0.1g salt	V	GF

6 tbsp lemon curd

4 ripe passion fruits

150ml (¼ pint) double cream

1 tbsp icing sugar

200g (7oz) Greek yogurt

toasted flaked almonds to decorate

1. Put the lemon curd into a small bowl. Halve the passion fruits and spoon the pulp into a sieve resting over a bowl. Stir to separate the seeds from the juice. Add 1 tbsp of the passion fruit juice to the lemon curd and mix well.

2. In a large bowl, whip the cream with the icing sugar until soft peaks form. Stir in the yogurt.

3. Put a dollop of yogurt cream into each of six small glasses. Layer with a spoonful of lemon curd mixture and 1 tsp passion fruit juice. Repeat to use up all the ingredients. Scatter over some toasted flaked almonds and serve immediately.

Cook's Tips
Choose wrinkly passion fruits – these are the ripest and juiciest.

To hasten ripening, put into a paper bag with a banana.

Banoffee Pie

Serves	Preparation Time	Cooking Time	Nutritional Information *(Per Serving)*
14	15 minutes, plus chilling	2–3 minutes	262 calories | 22g fat (of which 13g saturates) 17g carbohydrate | 0.5g salt | V

100g (3½oz) butter, melted, plus extra to grease

200g (7oz) digestive biscuits, roughly broken

2 small bananas

8 tbsp dulce de leche

284ml carton double cream

1 tbsp cocoa powder to dust

1. Grease the base and sides of a 23cm (9in) loose-based tart tin. Whiz the biscuits in a food processor until they resemble breadcrumbs. Pour in the melted butter and whiz briefly to combine. Press the mixture into the prepared tart tin and leave to chill for 2 hours.

2. Peel and slice the bananas and arrange the banana slices evenly over the biscuit base, then spoon the dulce de leche on top. Whip the cream until thick and spread it over the top. Dust with a sprinkling of cocoa powder and serve.

Try Something Different
- Top with a handful of toasted flaked almonds instead of the cocoa powder.
- Whiz 25g (1oz) chopped pecan nuts into the biscuits with the butter.
- Scatter grated plain dark chocolate over the cream.

Pecan Pie

Serves	Preparation Time	Cooking Time	Nutritional Information (Per Serving)
8	25 minutes, plus 50 minutes chilling	1 hour 10 minutes, plus cooling	549 calories | 40g fat (of which 16g saturates) 45g carbohydrate | 0.4g salt | V

Sweet Shortcrust Pastry (see page 38) made with 175g (6oz) plain flour, 75g (3oz) chilled butter, 50g (2oz) icing sugar and 1 medium egg

ice cream to serve

For the filling

125g (4oz) butter

4 tbsp clear honey

25g (1oz) caster sugar

75g (3oz) dark soft brown sugar

3 tbsp double cream

grated zest of 1 small lemon

1 tsp vanilla extract

175g (6oz) pecan nuts

1. Roll the pastry into a 30.5cm (12in) diameter circle and use to line a 20.5cm (8in) diameter, 2.5cm (1in) deep, loose-based fluted tart tin. Put the tin on a baking sheet and chill for 20 minutes. Meanwhile, preheat the oven to 200°C (180°C fan oven) mark 6.

2. Line the pastry case with greaseproof paper and baking beans and bake for 15 minutes. Remove the paper and beans, then return the pastry case to the oven for a further 10 minutes. Reduce the oven temperature to 150°C (130°C fan oven) mark 2.

3. To make the filling, melt the butter with the honey and sugars over a low heat, bring to the boil without stirring and bubble for 2–3 minutes. Remove from the heat, stir in the cream, lemon zest, vanilla extract and nuts and leave to cool for 15 minutes.

4. Pour the pecan mixture into the pastry case. Bake for 40 minutes or until the mixture begins to bubble in the middle (cover with foil if it gets too dark). Serve warm with ice cream.

Get Ahead

- **To prepare ahead**, complete the recipe, then cool and store in an airtight container for up to two days.
- **To use**, heat the pie at 180°C (160°C fan oven) mark 4 for 15–20 minutes.
- **To freeze**, complete the recipe, then cool, wrap and freeze the pie in its tin.
- **To use**, reheat from frozen at 180°C (160°C fan oven) mark 4 for 25 minutes or until warm. Cover with foil if it gets too dark.

8

BASIC BAKES

Bran and Apple Muffins

Makes	Preparation Time	Cooking Time	Nutritional Information (Per Serving)
10	20 minutes	30 minutes	137 calories | 1g fat (of which trace saturates) 31g carbohydrate | 0.3g salt | V

250ml (9fl oz) semi-skimmed milk

2 tbsp orange juice

50g (2oz) All Bran

9 ready-to-eat prunes

100g (3½oz) light muscovado sugar

2 medium egg whites

1 tbsp golden syrup

150g (5oz) plain flour, sifted

1 tsp baking powder

1 tsp ground cinnamon

1 eating apple, peeled and grated

demerara sugar to sprinkle

1. Preheat the oven to 190°C (170°C fan oven) mark 5. Line a bun tin or muffin pan with ten paper muffin cases.

2. In a bowl, mix the milk and orange juice with the All Bran. Set aside for 10 minutes.

3. Put the prunes in a food processor or blender with 100ml (3½fl oz) water and whiz for 2–3 minutes to make a purée, then add the muscovado sugar and whiz briefly to mix.

4. In a grease-free bowl, whisk the egg whites until they form soft peaks. Add the whites to the milk mixture with the golden syrup, flour, baking powder, cinnamon, grated apple and prune mixture. Fold all the ingredients together gently.

5. Spoon the mixture into the muffin cases and bake for 30 minutes or until well risen and golden brown. Sprinkle with demerara sugar just before serving.

Chocolate Banana Muffins

Makes	Preparation Time	Cooking Time	Nutritional Information (Per Serving)
12	15 minutes	20 minutes, plus cooling	228 calories | 7g fat (of which 4g saturates) 40g carbohydrate | 0.5g salt | V

275g (10oz) self-raising flour

1 tsp bicarbonate of soda

½ tsp salt

3 large bananas, about 450g (1lb)

125g (4oz) golden caster sugar

1 large egg, beaten

50ml (2fl oz) semi-skimmed milk

75g (3oz) unsalted butter, melted and cooled

50g (2oz) plain chocolate, chopped

1. Preheat the oven to 180°C (160°C fan oven) mark 4. Line a bun tin or muffin pan with 12 paper muffin cases. Sift the flour, bicarbonate of soda and salt together into a large mixing bowl and set aside.

2. Peel the bananas and mash with a fork in a bowl. Add the sugar, egg, milk and melted butter and mix until well combined.

3. Add this to the flour mixture, with the chopped chocolate. Stir gently, using only a few strokes, until the flour is only just incorporated – do not over-mix. The mixture should be lumpy.

4. Spoon the mixture into the muffin cases, half-filling them. Bake in the oven for 20 minutes or until the muffins are well risen and golden. Transfer to a wire rack to cool. Serve warm or cold.

Freezing Tip

- **To freeze:** complete the recipe up to the end of step 4. Once the muffins are cold, pack, seal, label and freeze for up to one month.
- **To use:** thaw at a cool room temperature or individually in the microwave, allowing 30 seconds on full power.

Wholemeal Banana Muffins

Makes	Preparation Time	Cooking Time	Nutritional Information (Per Serving)
6	15 minutes, plus 1 hour soaking	20–25 minutes	341 calories | 13g fat (of which 2g saturates) 51g carbohydrate | 0.6g salt | V

butter to grease (optional)

50g (2oz) raisins

finely grated zest and juice of 1 orange

125g (4oz) wholemeal flour

25g (1oz) wheatgerm

3 tbsp caster sugar

2 tsp baking powder

a pinch of salt

1 medium egg, beaten

50ml (2fl oz) milk

50ml (2fl oz) sunflower oil

2 medium-sized ripe bananas, about 225g (8oz) when peeled, roughly mashed

For the topping

5 tbsp orange marmalade

50g (2oz) banana chips, roughly chopped

50g (2oz) walnuts, roughly chopped

1. Preheat the oven to 200°C (180°C fan oven) mark 6. Line a bun tin or muffin pan with six paper muffin cases or grease the tin or pan. Put the raisins in a bowl, pour the orange juice over and leave to soak for 1 hour.

2. Put the orange zest in a bowl with the flour, wheatgerm, sugar, baking powder and salt and mix together. Make a well in the centre.

3. In a separate bowl, mix the egg, milk and oil, then pour into the flour mixture and stir until just blended. Drain the raisins, reserving 1 tbsp juice, and stir into the mixture with the bananas. Don't overmix. Fill each muffin case two-thirds full. Bake for 20–25 minutes until a skewer inserted into the centre comes out clean. Transfer to a wire rack to cool slightly.

4. For the topping, gently heat the marmalade with the reserved orange juice until melted. Simmer for 1 minute, then add the banana chips and walnuts. Spoon on top of the muffins. Serve while still warm.

Blueberry Muffins

Makes	Preparation Time	Cooking Time	Nutritional Information (*Per Serving*)
12	15 minutes	15 minutes	228 calories | 8g fat (of which 3g saturates) 36g carbohydrate | 0.1g salt | V

250g (9oz) plain flour

2 tsp baking powder

1 tsp bicarbonate of soda

125g (4oz) golden caster sugar

75g (3oz) ground almonds

finely grated zest of 1 lemon

125g (4oz) dried blueberries

1 medium egg

1 tsp vanilla extract

250ml (9fl oz) skimmed milk

50g (2oz) unsalted butter, melted

Try Something Different
Use chopped dried apricots, dried sour cherries or dried cranberries instead of the blueberries.

1. Preheat the oven to 200°C (180°C fan oven) mark 6. Line a muffin tin with 12 paper muffin cases.

2. Put the flour, baking powder and bicarbonate of soda into a bowl, then stir in the sugar, ground almonds, lemon zest and blueberries.

3. Put the egg, vanilla extract, milk and butter into a jug and mix together with a fork. Pour this liquid into the dry ingredients and lightly fold together.

4. Spoon the mixture into the muffin cases to three-quarters fill them and bake in the oven for 15 minutes or until the muffins are risen, pale golden and just firm.

5. Transfer the muffins to a wire rack and leave to cool slightly before serving.

Orange Syrup Cake

Makes	Preparation Time	Cooking Time	Nutritional Information (Per Serving)
10 slices	20 minutes, plus soaking	30–40 minutes	380 calories | 20g fat (of which 11g saturates 57g carbohydrate | 0.5g salt | V

175g (6oz) butter, plus extra to grease

225g (8oz) caster sugar

2 medium eggs, beaten

200g (7oz) rice flour

2 tsp baking powder

75g (3oz) ground almonds

grated zest and juice of 1 large orange

250ml carton orange juice

2 tbsp lemon juice

2 large oranges, peeled and thickly sliced

blueberries to serve

1. Preheat the oven to 190°C (170°C fan oven) mark 5. Grease and baseline a shallow 20cm (8in) round tin.

2. Cream the butter and 75g (3oz) sugar, then beat in the eggs gradually. Fold in the flour, baking powder and ground almonds. Stir in the zest and juice of the orange and 8 tbsp orange juice. The mixture should be of a soft dropping consistency.

3. Bake in the oven for 40 minutes or until firm. Leave to cool in the tin for 10 minutes, then turn out on to a wire rack.

4. Just before serving, combine the remaining sugar and orange juice plus the lemon juice in a small pan. Add the orange slices, bring to the boil and cook for 1–2 minutes.

Take the pan off the heat and leave to cool for 5 minutes. Remove the orange slices from the syrup and set aside.

5. Put the cake on a serving plate and, with a cocktail stick, prick the cake in a number of places. Drizzle with the syrup and leave to soak for 30 minutes. Serve with the orange slices and blueberries.

Freezing Tip

- **To freeze:** complete the recipe to the end of step 3, then cool, wrap and freeze.
- **To use:** thaw at a cool room temperature for 2–3 hours. Complete the recipe.

Chocolate Victoria Sandwich

Makes	Preparation Time	Cooking Time	Nutritional Information *(Per Serving)*
8 slices	20 minutes	20 minutes, plus cooling	520 calories | 30g fat (of which 19g saturates) 62g carbohydrate | 1g salt | V

175g (6oz) unsalted butter, softened, plus extra to grease

3 tbsp cocoa powder

175g (6oz) golden caster sugar

3 medium eggs, beaten

160g (5½oz) self-raising flour, sifted

golden caster sugar to dredge

For the chocolate buttercream

1 tbsp cocoa powder

75g (3oz) unsalted butter, softened

175g (6oz) icing sugar, sifted

a few drops of vanilla extract

1–2 tbsp milk or water

1. Preheat the oven to 190°C (170°C fan oven) mark 5. Grease two 18cm (7in) sandwich tins and line the base of each with a round of baking parchment. Blend the cocoa powder with 3 tbsp hot water to a smooth paste and allow to cool.

2. Cream the butter and sugar together, using a free-standing mixer or electric whisk, until pale and fluffy. Add the cooled cocoa mixture and beat until evenly blended.

3. Add the beaten eggs, a little at a time, beating well after each addition. Fold in half the flour, using a metal spoon or large spatula, then carefully fold in the rest.

4. Divide the mixture evenly between the tins and level the surface with a palette knife. Bake both cakes on the middle shelf of the oven for about 20 minutes or until well risen, springy to the touch and beginning to shrink away from the sides of the tins. Leave in the tins for 5 minutes, then turn out and cool on a wire rack.

5. To make the chocolate buttercream, blend the cocoa powder with 3 tbsp boiling water and set aside to cool. Put the butter into a bowl and beat with a wooden spoon until light and fluffy.

Gradually stir in the icing sugar. Add the blended cocoa, vanilla extract and milk or water and beat well until light and smooth.

6. When the cakes are cool, sandwich them together with the chocolate buttercream and sprinkle the top with caster sugar.

Get Ahead
This cake will keep well for up to one week if stored in an airtight tin in a cool place.

Chocolate Cup Cakes

Makes	Preparation Time	Cooking Time	Nutritional Information (Per Serving)
18	15 minutes	20 minutes, plus cooling and setting	203 calories | 14g fat (of which 8g saturates) 19g carbohydrate | 0.2g salt | V

125g (4oz) unsalted butter, softened

125g (4oz) light muscovado sugar

2 medium eggs, beaten

15g (½oz) cocoa powder

100g (3½oz) self-raising flour

100g (3½oz) plain chocolate (at least 70% cocoa solids), roughly chopped

For the topping

150ml (¼ pint) double cream

100g (3½oz) plain chocolate (at least 70% cocoa solids), broken up

1. Preheat the oven to 190°C (170°C fan oven) mark 5. Line bun tins or muffin pans with 18 paper muffin cases.

2. Beat together the butter and sugar until light and fluffy. Gradually beat in the eggs. Sift the cocoa powder with the flour and fold into the creamed mixture with the chopped chocolate.

3. Divide the mixture among the paper cases and lightly flatten the surface with the back of a spoon. Bake for 20 minutes. Cool in the cases.

4. For the topping, put the cream and chocolate into a heavy-based pan over a low heat and heat until melted, then allow to cool and thicken slightly. Spoon on to the cooled cakes and leave to set for 30 minutes.

Quick Chocolate Slices

Makes	Preparation Time	Cooking Time	Nutritional Information *(Per Serving)*
40	10 minutes	2 minutes	137 calories | 9g fat (of which 6g saturates) 13g carbohydrate | 0.3g salt | V

225g (8oz) butter or olive oil spread

50g (2oz) cocoa, sifted

3 tbsp golden syrup

300g pack digestive biscuits, crushed

400g (14oz) plain chocolate (at least 70 per cent cocoa solids), broken into pieces

1. Put the butter or olive oil spread into a heatproof bowl, add the cocoa and golden syrup and melt over a pan of gently simmering water. Mix everything together.

2. Remove from the heat and stir in the biscuits. Mix well until thoroughly coated in chocolate, crushing down any large pieces of biscuit. Turn into a greased 25.5 x 16.5cm (10 x 6½in) tin. Cool, cover and chill for 20 minutes.

3. Melt the chocolate in a heatproof bowl in a 900W microwave on full power for 1 minute 40 seconds, stirring twice. Alternatively, melt over a pan of gently simmering water. Stir once more and pour over the chocolate biscuit base, then chill for 20 minutes.

4. Cut in half lengthways. Cut each half into 20 rectangular fingers.

Thrifty Tip
Buy chocolate from the baking aisle – it's often cheaper than the well-known brands.

Chocolate Fudge Shortbread

Makes	Preparation Time	Cooking Time	Nutritional Information *(Per Serving)*
20 squares	30 minutes	20 minutes, plus cooling	369 calories | 19g fat (of which 12g saturates) 48g carbohydrate | 0.4g salt | V

175g (6oz) butter, at room temperature, diced, plus extra to grease

250g (9oz) plain flour, plus extra to dust

75g (3oz) golden caster sugar

For the topping

2 x 397g cans sweetened condensed milk

100g (3½oz) light muscovado sugar

100g (3½oz) butter

250g (9oz) plain chocolate (at least 70% cocoa solids), broken into pieces

1. Preheat the oven to 180°C (160°C fan oven) mark 4. Grease and line a 33 x 23cm (13 x 9in) Swiss roll tin with baking parchment. Put the flour, caster sugar and butter in a food processor and blend until the mixture forms crumbs, then pulse a little more until it forms a ball. (Alternatively, use a food mixer.) Turn out on to a lightly floured surface and knead lightly to combine.

2. Press the mixture into the prepared tin and bake for 20 minutes or until firm to the touch and very pale brown.

3. To make the topping, put the condensed milk, muscovado sugar and butter into a non-stick pan and cook over a medium heat, stirring continuously. (Alternatively, put into a large bowl and microwave on full power for 12 minutes or until the mixture is thick and fudgey, beating with a balloon whisk every 2–3 minutes.) Spoon the caramel on to the shortbread, smooth over and allow to cool.

4. To finish, melt the chocolate in a heatproof bowl over a pan of gently simmering water, then pour over the caramel layer. Leave to set at room temperature, then cut into squares to serve.

Hazelnut and Chocolate Flapjacks

Makes	Preparation Time	Cooking Time	Nutritional Information (*Per Serving*)
12	10 minutes	30 minutes, plus cooling	229 calories | 14g fat (of which 6g saturates) 26g carbohydrate | 0.2g salt | V

125g (4oz) unsalted butter, plus extra to grease

125g (4oz) light muscovado sugar

1 tbsp golden syrup

50g (2oz) hazelnuts, roughly chopped

175g (6oz) jumbo or porridge oats

50g (2oz) plain chocolate, roughly chopped

1. Preheat the oven to 180°C (160°C fan oven) mark 4. Lightly grease a shallow 28 x 18cm (11 x 7in) baking tin.

2. Put the butter, sugar and golden syrup in a pan and melt together over a low heat. Stir in the hazelnuts and oats. Leave the mixture to cool slightly, then stir in the chocolate.

3. Spoon the mixture into the prepared tin and bake for about 30 minutes or until golden and firm.

4. Leave to cool in the tin for a few minutes, then cut into 12 pieces. Turn out on to a wire rack and leave to cool completely. Store in an airtight container for up to one week.

Try Something Different

- **Tropical Fruit and Coconut Flapjacks**
  Replace the hazelnuts and chocolate with chopped, dried mixed tropical fruit. Replace 50g (2oz) of the oats with desiccated coconut.

- **Apricot and Mixed Seed Flapjacks**
  Replace the hazelnuts with 50g (2oz) mixed seeds (such as pumpkin, sunflower, linseed and sesame). Reduce the oats to 125g (4oz) and replace the chocolate with 100g (3½oz) chopped dried apricots.

Peanut and Raisin Cookies

Makes	Preparation Time	Cooking Time	Nutritional Information (Per Serving)
30	10 minutes	15 minutes, plus cooling	111 calories | 6g fat (of which 3g saturates) 14g carbohydrate | 0.2g salt | V

125g (4oz) unsalted butter, softened, plus extra to grease

150g (5oz) caster sugar

1 medium egg

150g (5oz) plain flour, sifted

½ tsp baking powder

½ tsp salt

125g (4oz) crunchy peanut butter

175g (6oz) raisins

1. Preheat the oven to 190°C (170°C fan oven) mark 5 and grease two baking sheets. Beat together all the ingredients except the raisins, until well blended. Stir in the raisins.

2. Spoon large teaspoonfuls of the mixture on to the baking sheets, leaving room for the mixture to spread. Bake for about 15 minutes or until golden brown around the edges.

3. Leave to cool slightly, then transfer to a wire rack to cool completely.

Try Something Different

- **Chocolate Nut Cookies**
  Omit the peanut butter and raisins and add 1 tsp vanilla extract. Stir in 175g (6oz) roughly chopped chocolate and 75g (3oz) roughly chopped walnuts.
- **Coconut and Cherry Cookies**
  Omit the peanut butter and raisins, reduce the sugar to 75g (3oz) and stir in 50g (2oz) desiccated coconut and 125g (4oz) rinsed, roughly chopped glacé cherries.
- **Oat and Cinnamon Cookies**
  Omit the peanut butter and raisins and add 1 tsp vanilla extract. Stir in 1 tsp ground cinnamon and 75g (3oz) rolled oats.

Apricot and Hazelnut Bread

Makes	Preparation Time	Cooking Time	Nutritional Information (Per Serving)
2 loaves	25 minutes, plus rising	30–35 minutes, plus cooling	94 calories | 3g fat (of which 1g saturates) 14g carbohydrate | 0g salt | V

75g (3oz) hazelnuts

450g (1lb) strong Granary bread flour, plus extra to dust

1 tsp salt

25g (1oz) butter, diced, plus extra to grease

75g (3oz) ready-to-eat dried apricots, chopped

2 tsp fast-action (easy-blend) dried yeast

2 tbsp molasses

milk to glaze

1. Spread the hazelnuts over a baking sheet. Toast under a hot grill until golden brown, turning frequently. Put the hazelnuts in a clean teatowel and rub off the skins. Cool, then chop them.

2. Put the flour into a large bowl. Add the salt, then rub in the butter. Stir in the hazelnuts, apricots and yeast.

3. Make a well in the middle and gradually work in the molasses and about 225ml (8fl oz) hand-hot water to form a soft dough, adding a little more water if the dough feels dry.

4. Knead for 8–10 minutes until smooth, then transfer the dough to a greased bowl. Cover and leave to rise in a warm place for 1–1¼ hours until doubled in size.

5. Preheat a large baking sheet on the top shelf of the oven at 220°C (200°C fan oven) mark 7. Punch the dough to knock back, then divide in half. Shape each portion into a small, flattish round and put on a well-floured baking sheet. Cover loosely and leave to rise for a further 30 minutes.

6. Using a sharp knife, cut several slashes on each round, brush with a little milk and transfer to the heated baking sheet. Bake for 15 minutes, then lower the oven temperature to 190°C (170°C fan oven) mark 5 and bake for a further 15–20 minutes until the bread is risen and sounds hollow when tapped underneath. Cool on a wire rack.

Try Something Different
Replace the hazelnuts with walnuts or pecan nuts and use sultanas instead of apricots.

Index

Special thanks to Alison Walker at
Good Housekeeping magazine for all
her help with this book.

Temperature

°C	Fan oven	Gas mark	°C	Fan oven	Gas mark
110	90	¼	190	170	5
130	110	½	200	180	6
140	120	1	220	200	7
150	130	2	230	210	8
170	150	3	240	220	9
180	160	4			

Liquids

Metric	Imperial	Metric	Imperial
5ml	1tsp	200ml	7fl oz
15ml	1tbsp	250ml	9fl oz
25ml	1fl oz	300ml	½ pint
50ml	2fl oz	500ml	18fl oz
100ml	3½ fl oz	600ml	1 pint
125ml	4fl oz	900ml	1½ pints
150ml	5fl oz/¼ pint	1 litre	1¾ pints
175ml	6fl oz		

Measures

Metric	Imperial	Metric	Imperial
5mm	¼in	10cm	4in
1cm	½in	15cm	6in
2cm	¾in	18cm	7in
2.5cm	1in	20.5cm	8in
3cm	1¼in	23cm	9in
4cm	1½in	25.5cm	10in
5cm	2in	28cm	11in
7.5cm	3in	30.5cm	12in

Weights

Metric	Imperial	Metric	Imperial
15g	½oz	275g	10oz
25g	1oz	300g	11oz
40g	1½oz	350g	12oz
50g	2oz	375g	13oz
75g	3oz	400g	14oz
100g	3½oz	425g	15oz
125g	4oz	450g	1lb
150g	5oz	550g	1¼lb
175g	6oz	700g	1½lb
200g	7oz	900g	2lb
225g	8oz	1.1kg	2½lb
250g	9oz		

Always remember...

- Ovens and grills must be preheated to the specified temperature.
- For fan ovens the temperature should be set to 20°C less.
- Use one set of measurements; do not mix metric and imperial.
- All spoon measures are level.

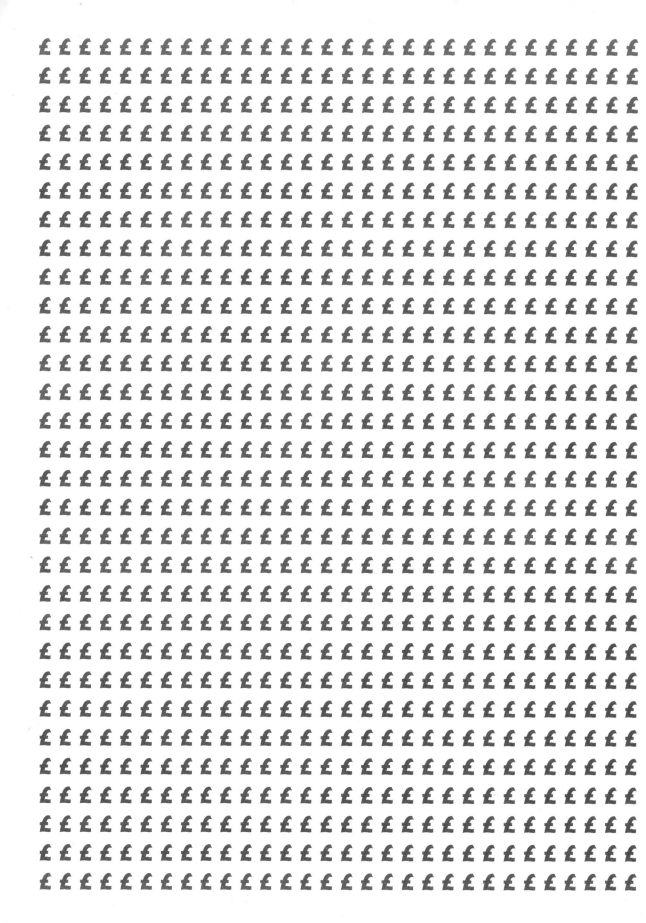